ADVANCE PRAISE

"This book has profound implications for teaching. Ariel Sacks shows us how to humanize this test-driven profession with courage, wisdom, and the gorgeous, clear writing of an accomplished storyteller. It is not just the progression of assignments from most accessible to most complex, but the articulate defense of imaginative work that is inspiring, rigorous, and necessary for the overall well-being of us all. You simply must study this book with your colleagues."

—**Penny Kittle**, cofounder of the Book Love Foundation

"Ariel Sacks provides a comprehensive playbook for English Language Arts teachers on why and how to engage students in fiction writing. The book shares stories and practical tips for making imaginative writing accessible for all students, using a framework that promotes equity and literacy. I highly recommend it for any teacher of writing."

—**Starr Sackstein**, chief operations officer of Mastery Portfolio and author of *Hacking Assessment*

"Ariel Sacks is one of the more thoughtful and expansive thinkers around literacy that I've come across over the course of my career. From the outset of *Who Gets to Write Fiction?*, the reader recognizes the sense of the urgency with which Sacks treats literacy in her former and present students. Here's to hoping that, with this book, more of us can incorporate fiction as imaginative dreaming in our work with students!"

—**José Vilson**, educator, executive director of EduColor, and author of *This Is Not A Test: A New Narrative on Race, Class, and Education*

"As someone who has taught fiction writing *and* written fiction about teaching, I found so much to love about this book. It's a thorough and useful guide that addresses the *why* and the *how* of writing fiction with students. Teaching students to read like writers will help them communicate better throughout their lives—and better enjoy the fiction they read. This book will help teachers do these things and so much more."

—**Roxanna Elden**, educator and author of *Adequate Yearly Progress: A Novel*

"*Who Gets to Write Fiction?* is a clarion call to return fiction writing to the curriculum. Sacks persuasively argues that inspiring students to write stories promotes agency, encourages risk-taking, moves writers away from dull, formulaic writing, and lends voice to students who are often marginalized. The cultivation of creativity in schools should not be a luxury, and this book provides a valuable roadmap on how to bring fiction writing back to its rightful place—your classroom. Highly recommended."

—**Kelly Gallagher**, author of *Write Like This* and *Teaching Adolescent Writers*

"This is a book I wish my own teachers had had! Ariel Sacks empowers literacy educators to give serious space to imaginative writing in a way that awakens academic and social–emotional learning. With concrete examples, Sacks also shows how this work can shift power dynamics between and among teachers and students. I suspect *Who Gets to Write Fiction?* will call many English teachers back to the heart of their choice to teach."

—**Elena Aguilar**, author of *The Art of Coaching* and *Onward*

Who Gets to Write Fiction?

Who Gets to Write Fiction?

Opening Doors to Imaginative Writing for All Students

Ariel Sacks

Norton Professional Books

An Imprint of W. W. Norton & Company
Celebrating a Century of Independent Publishing

Who Gets to Write Fiction is intended as a general information resource for professionals practicing in the field of education. It is not a substitute for appropriate training. No technique or recommendation is guaranteed to be effective in all circumstances, and neither the publisher nor the author can guarantee the complete accuracy, efficacy, or appropriateness of any recommendation in every respect.

The names and potentially identifying characteristics of certain individuals and organizations have been changed and some characters and organizations are composites. Also, some dialogue and scenarios have been reconstructed and some are composites.

Any URLs displayed in this book link or refer to websites that existed as of press time. The publisher is not responsible for, and should not be deemed to endorse or recommend, any website, app, or other content that it did not create. The author, also, is not responsible for any third-party material.

For information about permission to reproduce selections from this book, write to Permissions, W. W. Norton & Company, Inc., 500 Fifth Avenue, New York, NY 10110

For information about special discounts for bulk purchases, please contact W. W. Norton Special Sales at specialsales@wwnorton.com or 800-233-4830

Manufacturing by Versa Press
Production manager: Gwen Cullen

ISBN: 978-1-324-05248-7 (pbk)

W. W. Norton & Company, Inc., 500 Fifth Avenue, New York, NY 10110
www.wwnorton.com

W. W. Norton & Company Ltd., 15 Carlisle Street, London W1D 3BS

1 2 3 4 5 6 7 8 9 0

*Dedicated to the memory of
my Baba, Lillian Sacks*

Contents

Acknowledgments   xi

CHAPTER 1: Unleashing Imaginative Writing   1

CHAPTER 2: Harnessing Imaginative Writing for Academic Development   26

CHAPTER 3: Empowering Students' Social–Emotional Development   60

CHAPTER 4: Utilizing Imaginative Writing as a Tool For Equity
and Community   90

CHAPTER 5: Designing Assignments That Teach Through Experience   129

CHAPTER 6: Deciding What to Teach Directly: Style and Mechanics   166

CHAPTER 7: Organizing and Assessing Imaginative Writing Instruction in a
Standards-Based ELA Classroom   198

References   223

Index   227

Acknowledgments

Writing a book is mostly a startlingly solo endeavor; and yet, as I write these acknowledgments, I realize how many people have touched this work. Without them, this book simply would not be.

First, I acknowledge my family for believing in me and supporting me through the process: my husband, Samuel, my mother, and my father, each in their own ways.

I thank Madeleine Ray, my mentor at Bank Street College, for teaching me many of the practices that set me on a path toward understanding fiction writing as the missing piece in literature study for young people, and Nancy Toes Tangle, a thought partner around these practices. We continue the quest.

I'm grateful to W. W. Norton who worked with me to make this book real, public, and beautiful: Carol Collins, my editor, who believed in the book and my ability to write it; Jamie Vincent, Mariah Eppes, Renata Mitchell, Olivia Guarnieri, and the rest of the team who ushered it into print and publication.

Thank you to Rachel Beerman, Meredith Byers, Barney Brawer, and Ruth Sacks for being early readers, offering feedback and encouragement.

Thank you to the school leaders and my colleagues at The Renaissance Charter School for cocreating a space that allows for creative teaching and celebrates the creative productions of students.

Finally, I'm grateful to my students, present and past. Not only are you some of the coolest, most creative people I know, but you've taught me how to see what matters most in teaching, and how to teach better. Your sparks have informed this book from start to finish.

Who Gets to Write Fiction?

1

Unleashing Imaginative Writing

IT WAS 1994, and my eighth-grade English teacher, Mr. Z., surprised us when he announced that we would do something different for the final quarter of the year. It was called "writing workshop," and it meant that we would spend English periods writing whatever we wanted, every single day. Mr. Z. was a tall, suit-wearing teacher, who was close to retiring. His tone, as usual, was unemotional; it was hard to discern what he actually thought about this initiative. In my vague recollection, he simply gave us each a folder and told us to start writing.

The fact that Mr. Z. proceeded to run the laxest writing workshop you can imagine, mostly from his desk, is not my point, though. I'm recounting this memory because of what it revealed about us, his students, when the usual agenda of English class fell away.

Despite the disorienting feeling of walking into class with little to no directions, I appreciated time to write freely during class. On the other hand, I never received feedback on my pieces, save for one comment on a poem that I still recall: "Nice use of ellipsis marks," it read. Were my pieces lousy? Did he not have time for more substantial response? Did he read them at all? I'll never know. I was self-driven, so my teacher's silence neither helped nor hurt me.

The most memorable aspect of that unusual school experience was Corey. Corey was a girl I assumed I knew, but didn't. In an affluent suburb of Boston, she was from "the projects," a small row of houses in a poorer part of town. Like almost everyone else in the town, she was white. She was not a member of the so-called popular clique, nor did she meet the silently agreed upon middle school standards of fashion or beauty. She wore unfortunate, very thick glasses, which made her eyes look large and blurry. I'm ashamed to admit that I also assumed she was "not smart." Maybe that was because she wasn't nerdy in a stereotypical sense; maybe it was because she wasn't a star participator in class; and maybe, it was due to an unspoken perception that the "smart" kids didn't live where she lived.

I wish I could remember more details about how the change happened. What I know is that one day, in the middle of class, Corey started reading a story she had written out loud to the rest of us. Our teacher seemed to be on board with this, though I don't know whose idea it was.

We all looked up and listened. Corey wasn't a timid person, but we definitely weren't used to hearing her speak in class. The story seemed to be about a group of friends hanging out after school, playing around and getting into some mild trouble with a neighbor. It was funny with realistic characters and dialogue. It sounded "like a real book!" someone remarked. She assured us the characters were made-up, but the story still gave me a vivid picture of a neighborhood and reality I didn't know— but Corey did.

"That's all I got so far," Corey said when she came to the end of her writing.

"Nooo!" whined a chorus of classmates. "Keep going!"

"Don't worry," she said, beaming. "I can write more."

This was toward the end of the school year. After that day, Corey kept writing, and her readings became a regular way of closing out class on those non-air-conditioned, June afternoons. We would ask to hear whatever she had been working on that period.

I recall, at some point, a twist of genre from humorous to scary, and students asking, "Was that real?!" She would laugh and sometimes give us a hint, but never revealed what was true or imagined.

In those moments, she was by far the most popular person in the class. She was also smart and accomplished. Her imaginative writing had disrupted an ingrained hierarchy, connected to social class, that was an unspoken reality in our school, town, and beyond.

As imperfect as this classroom scenario may be from a pedagogical standpoint, it illustrates the power of fiction writing for young people, a power that very often lies untapped where it would be most useful and transformative—in the discipline of English Language Arts and in our troubled country.

As a teacher, I've seen the dramatic power of creative writing to shift young people's behavior and thinking so many times, among so many different students in the New York City public school classrooms in which I've taught. I think back now to my own middle school experience with Corey and understand that it was no chance event. I also know that had my teacher taken some additional steps, we would have taken many more social and intellectual leaps across the borders that divided us.

After that one quarter in middle school, I recall writing just one poem for a class in high school and zero fictional stories. I wrote on my own, though, and I was thrilled to get to college, where I had the opportunity to take creative writing workshops.

During the writing of this book, I happened to learn through a Facebook page created for my 20th high school reunion that Corey had passed away years ago. I looked for more information and found that she was just twenty-three when she died. She was the mother of two daughters and a son, and her death had been sudden.

I was struck by this tragedy. I also found it a little uncanny that I learned of it when I did, having so recently written down my one vivid memory of her from middle school. I couldn't help but wonder, did she continue writing after eighth grade? Did her children have access to any of the writing she did? Did anyone other than us, her eighth-grade English classmates, know of her wild and compelling storytelling voice? Stretching a little further, would her trajectory have gone somehow differently if she'd had support to keep writing fiction, sharing and developing her talent throughout high school?

I imagine the author she might have become. I imagine a world where everyone has that chance.

EIGHT DOORS WE OPEN FOR STUDENTS WHEN WE INCLUDE IMAGINATIVE WRITING

The ability to write fiction and other imaginative forms in English Language Arts opens many doors for young people. All of them are critical to the development of our students, our education system, and our democracy. Here are the big ones. I will return to them in more practical detail later in this book.

Door 1: Capture attention.

The process of students writing and sharing their own literary work wakes up their attention and interest toward one another. We live in an "attention economy," where every device, page, and platform is designed to compete for our attention. Educators know well that a significant part of our jobs has become competing with those same attention grabbers.

Students' motivation to attend to one another and be receptive to what they hear and see is especially high in a classroom full of fiction writers for two main reasons:

- *First, young people are driven to interact with their peers.* We might even call it an obsession, especially in middle grades. When we attempt to curb this innate drive, students find covert ways to interact—"eye conversations," passing notes, meeting up in the bathroom, texting under the table, etc. Creating a peer writing community is one way to harness students' social inclination for learning.
- *Second, human beings are biologically driven to pay attention to and engage with stories.* Brain research confirms the almost magical quality of story to capture our often unfocused and overwhelmed brains. When truly interested, children don't hold back. We can plainly see this when we are in the middle of a good read-aloud: our allotted time is up, yet students beg to hear more. We see the same phenomenon in my classmates' spontaneous requests to hear more of Corey's story—and in her eagerness to share and continue creating.

If students create and share imaginative writing as an ongoing piece of their language arts education, we can marry the two primal drives of peer interaction and story in a process that has tremendous personal and academic impact.

Door 2: Shift power dynamics around definitions of intelligence.

Possibly my favorite thing about imaginative writing in the English Language Arts (ELA) classroom is that it shakes up our preconceived notions about who is "smart." We often see boosts of motivation coming from students who've been disengaged from classroom activities or have settled into underachiever identities. In fiction writing, many students' intelligence and voices come through with new excitement. Imaginative writing is different from other learning activities because every child is the authority of their own story (real or imagined). Everyone's knowledge is valuable in the creation of a story, play, or poem. All experience is equal in the literary world because we are equal in our humanity.

That's a huge shift for children, who, most of the time, are the authority of very little in their lives, having to defer to adults for so much. This power is even more profound for children who experience their culture, race, or funds of knowledge being discounted at school. In education, we often hear talk of students coming from poverty as lacking "prior knowledge." Everyone who has lived has prior knowledge—but academic environments have been biased toward certain kinds of knowledge which tend to be based in middle class, white, adult, able, cisgender experiences.

The story world is universal though. Humans from every culture and time period tell and told stories. Literature has the power to illuminate and draw forth our common humanity. In such a space, there is a golden opportunity for students who feel shut out of academic processes to engage more freely and confidently in creative writing—seeing themselves and being seen by their peers in a new way. A positive relationship with imaginative writing can then become a foothold for students to enter into other processes in English Language Arts as well.

Door 3: Give students first-hand experience with literary elements.

One of those other processes we need to invite students more fully into is analysis of literature. Do you ever feel like students learn about literary elements each year, yet still don't remember them? Literary elements are abstract concepts that are not especially interesting to kids—unless their purpose becomes clear in a compelling context.

When we involve young people in imaginative writing, they gain firsthand experience using literary elements, which are the building blocks of stories and the tools writers use to tell them. When students work to create a setting or make difficult plot decisions or think through why a character would make a particular choice . . . they are knowledgeable about and invested in that context because they dreamed it up. Teachers can then help them apply literary terms to name and discuss the choices they're making.

Later, when students see other writers using these same elements—published authors as well as their own classmates—they have personal experience (or prior knowledge) to help them identify and analyze the writers' craft. Raising students' awareness of literary elements in their own writing is a key component to the methods I'll share throughout this book. Imaginative writing experience, I believe, provides a strategic and missing link in students' critical understanding and engagement with literature.

Door 4: Create empathy and interest across differences, disrupting segregation.

We know well that reading literature expands our worldviews by allowing us to empathize with characters different from ourselves. That effect multiplies when students experience *each other's* imaginative writing, and find themselves crossing invisible boundaries. I'm talking about persistent, difficult boundaries that don't just diminish over time—race, class, religion, ethnicity, gender, sexuality, and ability. These are borders adults and children alike have been conditioned to avoid, and which manifest clearly in the social groupings of adolescents. I paid attention to Corey because of her storytelling and crossed an invisible boundary into her world quickly and voluntarily. This remains a significant memory because it was so unlikely to happen otherwise.

I've now had the opportunity to teach in four different schools in New York

City. Two are considered more homogeneous—majority Latinx in East Harlem, or majority Black in Crown Heights, Brooklyn—though there was still much diversity in those contexts. Two, including my current school, are more visibly diverse, with Black, white, Latinx, and Asian students from different linguistic, religious, and socioeconomic backgrounds. In all of these contexts, and in the mostly middle-class white suburb of Boston I grew up in, I've found that diverse groups of students going to school together is not enough to fight the forces of segregation that persist in the adult world and play out in schools. Students can usually coexist together without much trouble, but they learn to segregate themselves socially, often without much thought about it.

Consistently though, through imaginative writing—with opportunities to share and respond in class—I've seen the usual dividing lines fall away. Students pay attention to one another's stories and poetry in an open and fair way. The concepts that guide effective literary art—compelling language, intensity of emotion, risk-taking, and awareness of audience, to name a few—are what sway students. That allows for genuine interest and appreciation of one another, rather than judgment, fear, and separation. Even if the connections among students appear to be temporary, they are nonetheless powerful and informative to my students' world views and understandings of each other. The coming together of a literary community offers a crucial step for students toward shedding biases and combatting discrimination. English teachers have the amazing opportunity to set up structures to support a creative writing community and participate in the culture and connections that flow from it.

Door 5: Desegregate children's literature—create an inclusive, professional pathway.

Another place we need to break down barriers is in the literary writing world. Imaginative writing in schools can help the growing movement to diversify the literature children and teens have access to so that all students can read characters who look like them and reflect aspects of their lives. The organizations We Need Diverse Books and Disrupt Texts have called on publishing and educator communities to elevate books with characters of all races, cultures, family structures, abilities, and LGBTQ+ identities. Through their advocacy, along with the many committed teachers, librarians, and school leaders who've taken up the call, the landscape of our curriculum maps and classroom libraries is becoming more diverse and equitable.

Another necessary way to combat the cultural and racial homogeneity that has characterized children's literature is to look at the writing education of children across the country, particularly in schools that serve children of color. Which students, in fact, get to experience the powerful feeling of putting an original story onto paper? Who gets told their imaginative productions are wonderful and important?

Who gets training in the craft of creating poems and plays? Who receives only "the basics," year after year?

When creative writing is treated as inessential, schools tend to deny it to students who are deemed underperforming on the skills considered most important—disproportionately these are low-income students of color in systems where skills are defined and measured by standardized tests. This cycle exacerbates so-called achievement gaps, when we could be uplifting children from marginalized communities to tap into their own imaginative and intellectual resources.

Imaginative writing must not be a luxury of the privileged. Many more people from oppressed groups might see a pathway for themselves toward professional writing if they were given more space to explore it in school. I've seen this happen for some of my students, and I'm not alone in this. In addition to challenging biased gate-keeping practices in publishing and competitive writing programs, we can support the development of the full diversity of writers we want to see in the adult world right in our English classrooms.

Door 6: Provide an outlet for learning through play, risk-taking, and identity development.

Play is an essential tool in human development and learning. Culturally, we are more accepting of young children's need to learn from play than we are of older children—even so, though there is a raging battle to protect children's play in the youngest grades of school. For older children and adolescents, most play opportunities have been removed from school. That's a disservice to youth, because they still learn through play—and will often play during class even if that runs counter to a teacher's agenda.

The design thinking movement and the economic and cultural power of the start-ups that represent it have been a wake-up call for the education community around the value of play for all age groups. To solve problems, to create, and to compete with the automation of the twenty-first century marketplace, we must be able to play. In the English Language Arts classroom, stories and words are the tools for it.

Through the play opportunities of creative writing, students can explore ideas and issues they are working through in their real lives. The virtual world of fiction is a safe place to take risks and imagine where they might lead. Students can grapple with real conflicts through made-up characters. They are less vulnerable doing this in fiction than in memoir-type narratives. They can disguise real people into characters as much as they want and often very cleverly. Their self-expression through writing helps them make sense of the world and build their unique identities.

To utilize writing as a form of play, teachers need to emphasize process more than product. We need to give students enough decision-making power over their work and build in time for reflection. Rather than creating a pressured assessment environment that shuts down students' willingness to take risks, we can create safe conditions for risk-taking in writing, and then facilitate students to name their choices, assess their impact, and determine next steps.

Door 7:   Provide opportunities to improve mental health and process trauma.

In addition to all of the challenges inherent in growing up today, our students are dealing with overwhelming levels of trauma. We have both the acute and ongoing traumas caused or exacerbated by the COVID-19 pandemic: grief, economic instability, job loss, domestic violence, anxiety, and depression. Unrelated, we've had mass shootings across the country at an unreal frequency, an epidemic of police brutality, and PTSD rates in poor urban neighborhoods that are higher than those of Iraq war veterans, rising rates of hate crimes, and the abstract threat of climate change becoming tangible in extreme weather events.

The issues students are working through personally and existentially as they sit in our classes can't simply be ignored. Schools need to work on many levels to create truly supportive environments for learning and healing. One way we can help within the context of an English Language Arts class, is to welcome artistic production through literary forms into our curricula. A 2016 study shows that making art significantly lowers cortisol levels. All participants benefited substantially from 45 minutes of art, but those with past experience showed increased benefits, suggesting that ongoing practice of making art is more powerful than an isolated experience (Kaimal et.al., 2016).

The methods of this book are based on the idea that students benefit from writing their own imaginative pieces as a *regular* way to engage with literature in English class. Through their writing, some of my students do process their own real-life traumas. It's a door they can choose to open or not, and they keep their personal business as private as they want as they create fictional characters.

In the virtual world, and under the right classroom conditions, students can recount traumatic events to release and reflect on them. They can also right wrongs they've witnessed or experienced, and they can imagine solutions to deep personal and societal problems. Imaginative writing in a safe context has therapeutic effects for all students, and for some, it can be transformative.

Door 8:   Resist oppression and create a better world.

In art, we are commenting on the world as we know it and playing out our observations and fantasies from an aesthetic distance. When we make ELA class a place for artistic expression, as well as reading, discussion, and other forms of writing, we create space for each of us and the alternate universes we carry in our imaginations that are born of our experiences, emotions, questions, and hopes.

In her amazing book, *We Want To Do More Than Survive: Abolitionist Teaching and the Pursuit of Educational Freedom*, Dr. Bettina Love explains that art is an essential tool of resisting oppression: " . . . it is how dark children make sense of this unjust world and a way to sustain who they are as they (re)call . . . what it means to thrive." Art, she argues, is how we see the world that we want—the world we are living for, but is not yet real. She calls this "freedom dreaming," and it begins with a critique of injustice, but, she explains, "The imaginary world creates new worlds that push democracy" (Love, pp. 100–101).

I see how my students have responded to the space to imagine. I've seen a plot pattern of protagonists raging against injustice in their lives and finding their ways to better places. I've seen students ask questions through their fiction of what will happen if we allow our destruction of the planet to continue? I've seen outrageous humor from students who present as depressive. I've seen students write protagonists who come out as gay in their stories—and receive heartfelt applause from their classmates when they chose to share.

Bettina Love is right—without the space to imagine, what chance does anyone have to overcome the overwhelming obstacles to justice and personal fulfillment?

CALL TO ACTION

Every teacher of English has the opportunity to facilitate the magic of our students developing their literary imaginations. The tools are not new, really. We just need to believe that it's worthwhile and manageable to open those doors—and that doing so will not take us farther from our primary goals as teachers, but closer to them and faster.

Am I implying here that teachers don't already know about the power of imaginative writing? No, I'm certain that every teacher of English Language Arts has experienced it. However, longstanding traditions and biases as well as current curricular and organizational trends stand in the way of us maximizing the potential of creative writing in our classrooms.

I'm writing this book to challenge those traditions. I'm writing this book to call attention to the doorways between the worlds of literature, analytical writing, imaginative writing, and classroom communities, which are dying to be busted open. I want to share my maps of where the doors are located in the various threads of English Language Arts, the methods through which my students and I venture through them, and some of the surprising places they've led.

I'm hoping that my call to action and the practical approach I share will compel many more teachers to lean into the creative side and journey farther with their students into imaginative realms and the structures that define them.

For teachers who are deep into this already, I hope to create space for us to share our experiences and methods. I want for us to build out this neglected piece of our discipline and create a new era of creative practice and possibility for all student writers.

PERMISSION TO CENTER ARTISTIC PRODUCTION IN LITERACY

If creative writing is like a literary superpower, why is it so often untapped in schools? The answer is that we've been programmed not to use it. I'm kidding . . . sort of. We work in a society and education system that holds the arts as less valuable than the "core" disciplines of English, math, science, and social studies. We can see the hierarchy in scheduling requirements in schools, in how student achievement is defined, in professional development priorities, and even in students' perceptions about which classes "matter" most. Artistic work is one of the lowest priorities.

This hierarchy does not serve children well, however, and we are well positioned to make change. To do so, I want to acknowledge the considerable obstacles that might stand in our way and explore how they influence our decisions in the classroom. I want to provide a defense to help teachers and education leaders look these obstacles in the eye, dismiss them as out of touch, and embrace imaginative writing as a central component of English Language Arts.

The Arts Are More Important Than Ever

Where does this devaluing of arts in education come from? At best, it seems to stem from a belief that artistic abilities are not helpful to students in the professional world—that they equip only a very select few to earn a living. Although it certainly is difficult to be a professional artist in our society, increasingly, the skills and sensibilities of the arts are in demand across a range of careers—from business to engineering to communications to medicine.

A friend of mine, for example, writes "teaching cases" for schools of business and government at Harvard University. Her job is to look at the data from ongoing research projects, interview the researchers involved about what they are seeing in the field, and then write "cases" describing the progress. Research students and outside stakeholders read these documents to learn about the project.

The skill she relies upon most? Good storytelling, because the goal is to get nonresearchers interested and paying attention to the details of a study so they can learn from it. She explained it to me this way:

> Developing a teaching case means working with professors and researchers to figure out how to tell the story of what's happening in a way that helps other public managers understand and apply whatever concepts the professors are interested in teaching to the case and ultimately to their own worlds. Then I write the case in a way that hopefully reads like just good storytelling but also serves those particular pedagogical purposes.

It's worth noting that this piece of work is contracted out to my friend, who has an MFA in creative writing and the skills to deliver the teaching case product. It seems reasonable to infer that many of the researchers aren't equipped to do this quickly and effectively, though it would be an asset to their work if they were.

Lawyers use a similar storytelling process. They use the evidence available to develop a story that convinces others of a person's guilt, innocence, motive, level of consciousness, and culpability in a legal case. Advertisers, web designers, and business owners create stories about their products and services for many critical functions—luring customers to want a product or creating a sense of trust in a business, for example.

I'm highlighting the art of storytelling in these examples, but visual, musical, and dramatic arts are equally valuable across a range of professional contexts for the same reasons. The point is that art influences our thoughts and feelings, and influence is power. People who bring artistic abilities to their line of work add value in almost any field.

Twenty-First Century Problems

Today there is an even more urgent reason for young people to develop their creativity: the automation of rote tasks by computer-based programs. Retail jobs are diminishing while self-checkout and online shopping rise meteorically. Self-driving cars (though I am personally not a fan of the idea) are apparently in our future. Online correspondence limits jobs in the postal service. E-Z Pass is replacing toll-takers. And so forth. This reality dramatically changes the sorts of jobs that humans are needed for.

I first encountered this argument in Daniel Pink's seminal work, *A Whole New Mind: Why Right Brain Thinking Will Rule the Future*. Pink describes the two main kinds of work that will gain, rather than lose, value in the current and future eras: work that is "high concept" (creative, dynamic, idea based) and work that is "high touch" (person-to-person, empathy and trust-based). He goes on to illustrate six human capacities most valuable in the new economy. They are design, story, symphony (bringing together disparate pieces to create something whole), empathy, play, and meaning. In his chapter on design, Pink argues that the future of our society now depends on "having artists in the room." In relation to story, he explains that because facts are readily available to anyone who is digitally connected, it is our ability to tell stories about the information and to make an emotional impact that is valuable in the economy.

The tendency to view the arts as unhelpful to people as they navigate the professional world is a vestige of past eras. I believe this was always a limited way of seeing the world, but it held some truth when jobs in factories and basic accounting abounded; today in the United States, however, the same belief couldn't be further from reality.

Power Dynamics and Art

In education, it's helpful to continually ask the question, who gains or loses power from a given decision, policy, or trend? The stance that art is not worthwhile for children may come from a misguided, but well-intentioned place. However, this position can also represent a less benevolent agenda: a desire for an education system that creates conforming and compliant students, who will grow into citizens who maintain the status quo, rather than participating actively and critically in democratic processes. The status quo can be an attractive place for people who want to protect their existing power (with or without conscious awareness of this bias). For people from oppressed groups the status quo is often not a safe place, and an education system that perpetuates existing inequities is a tool of oppression as much as anything else.

What's the connection? Art tends not to adhere neatly to established norms. The arts help us see possibilities, alternate realities, and divergent perspectives. They prompt us to question our views, expectations, and identities. Art is powerful! It's so powerful, I can say without exaggeration, that it saves lives. Art has not only saved my life several times, but it has changed my life, indelibly, over time, by influencing my emotions, world view, and decisions. Art doesn't exercise much of its power directly. Artistic works and movements are subtle and unpredictable, like a can of worms difficult to contain or control once opened. (Though, if the can wants to open, it will find a way!)

Those who desire control have a clear reason to marginalize the arts. Author and sociologist Eve Ewing summed it up in a *New York Times* opinion piece, "Why Authoritarians Attack the Arts" (April 6, 2017). As Hitler and other dictators understood, she explains:

> . . . artists play a distinctive role in challenging authoritarianism. Art creates pathways for subversion, for political understanding and solidarity among coalition builders. Art teaches us that lives other than our own have value. Like the proverbial court jester who can openly mock the king in his own court, artists who occupy marginalized social positions can use their art to challenge structures of power in ways that would otherwise be dangerous or impossible.

If we believe in a democratic society that celebrates and protects the basic freedoms of everyone in it, then art (including literature) has a clear place as a reflection of those freedoms as well as an agent of critical reflection and change.

The role of art in education within our democratic nation is not as secure as it should be, though—and this is not a recent development. Schools and their traditional structures often resemble a more authoritarian society than the democracy we ideally wish to uphold through education. One of my favorite questions to ask adolescents (especially eighth- and ninth-graders) is whether they believe the institution of school is oppressive or a tool for freedom. I've had classes divide into two sides to debate the question, and later write essays on it. Most students come to see both sides as true and tease apart the complexity in their writing.

The issue at core is control. Who has decision-making power in a school? In a classroom? Who gets treated with respect? Who gets treated unfairly? Who can offer a new idea or a criticism and be heard? Who makes change?

I think every educator, student, and former student (so, everyone) knows there are educational environments with unhealthy power dynamics. It's no small problem, and it is systemic, neither beginning nor ending with teachers and students. That said, one good indicator of health in an educational environment (like the health of a democracy) is the presence of student artistic expressions. In fact, art rooms are often safe havens for students who feel oppressed in other spaces in their schools. The book *Speak* by Laurie Halse Anderson beautifully depicts a high school art room functioning as a uniquely safe place for the traumatized main character to express herself.

What about English classrooms, then? All students study works of literary art in English Language Arts class—but do they create them? If not, isn't that sort of an odd norm? All of the other arts that students study (photography, theater, music) are generally studied by practicing them directly. We do not teach children theater by having them perpetually watch plays and critique them.

What are the fears at play when educators—teachers, school leaders, and policy makers alike—decide that there isn't space for students to create in the literary genres they read?

I'm guessing that if you are reading this book, you are not an educator bent on maintaining the status quo. You want to see students think critically about the world around them, and you want to help them in their process of finding themselves and setting and accomplishing their goals, even if they defy your own expectations of them or personal preferences. For me, some of the best experiences of teaching happen when students surprise me. Sometimes it's with a single comment or a sentence in a paper I would never have imagined coming from that student; other times it's more monumental, say, in a major identity shift in the middle of the school year or in an email or surprise visit years after moving on from middle school.

Human growth follows patterns, but it's also quite unpredictable. We don't have power over when each baby begins to walk, and we don't have the power to decide when a student will find joy in reading or writing. We have influence, not control . . . and that's a beautiful thing.

Developing the skills to truly support rather than control learning is a central challenge of teaching. After all, teaching is also an art—one that we navigate in real time by moving between reality and possibility, interior and exterior identities, individual and group dynamics, leading and letting go. Learning and leadership, too, can be approached as art forms: note the many "The Art of . . . " books written on these very topics. Thus, the separation of art from the core of education and its essential outcomes is artificial.

Moreover, by squeezing art out of education, we reinforce existing hierarchies and resist change. Marginalized people will always pay the greater price for this. Conversely, when arts are supported, everyone benefits. When the Works Progress Administration paid artists to create between 1935 and 1943 through "Federal Project Number One," our country developed beloved literature by writers like Ralph Ellison, Zora Neale Hurston, and Richard Wright, painters like Jackson Pollock, Diego Rivera, and Mark Rothko, modern dancers of Martha Graham's school (including my grandmother, who did not become famous but nevertheless spent some years dancing professionally), the iconic photography of Dorothea Lange and Walker Evans who documented the Depression Era in rural America. These and countless other artists put the United States in the position to influence culture all over the world—an investment and legacy that lasts to this day.

WHY WE COMPROMISE CREATIVE WRITING

In the context of teaching English, a discipline that encompasses a wide array of skills and understandings, I believe that teachers and school leaders receive tacit messages from policy makers that artistic production is not important or academically rigorous enough to be worth the finite amount of time we have. While nearly everyone agrees that writing creatively can be a positive experience for children on a personal level, it's common to discount its value in the mission of preparing students to be college and career ready.

A metaphor for this paradigm would be that creative writing is the dessert of ELA, and reading and analytical writing make up the main dinner course. In this mental model, imaginative writing may be tasty, but it's neither essential nor nutritious. I believe this is the prevailing cultural attitude in schools today—especially at the middle and high school levels. While most English teachers aren't necessarily buying it, we are nonetheless influenced by the norms around us.

Traditionally, teachers have not been decision makers in education policies, even in matters of curriculum and instruction. We have varying levels of autonomy in our own classrooms. Sadly, it's quite common for us to carry out plans that are not aligned to our beliefs and understandings about student learning. Pressure to comply with policies and expectations is often as strong for teachers as it is for students.

After years of following external guidelines, we can arrive at a point where the habits and skills we've developed don't even match the kind of teaching we once thought we would do. Some teachers willfully resist expectations they don't agree with; others bend but don't break, maintaining certain limits. Every one of us makes compromises of one kind or another.

For a long time, I now know, I held an unconscious assumption about creative writing: Though I loved teaching it, I assumed that to emphasize it in my class would mean sacrificing my students' other more "academic" writing. I never consciously decided this, but I gleaned it from cultural messages in education and beyond, that separate arts from "hard" academics. I never truly examined that assumption and the ways it had informed my choices with students . . . until, about five years ago, I started envisioning writing this book, and I had occasion to ask, *What if I tried actually prioritizing creative writing? What would happen?* I realized I didn't know the answer.

Even though I was a teacher who had always pushed boundaries and fought for practices I believed in and against those I didn't, my mental constructs were still heavily influenced by the norms around me. In effect, I didn't recognize certain compromises I'd made, and I'd never even imagined the possibilities that might come if I released myself from them. I will share what happened next later in this chapter.

It turns out, creative writing is a common area of compromise for teachers, and the reasons for this are built into our education system and the culture inside and outside of it. I gave an anonymous survey to ELA teachers around the country about creative writing in their classrooms. The survey was circulated via my blog, website, Twitter, and other social media.

The majority of participants, who were teachers and a few ELA coaches, agreed there were numerous social, emotional, and academic benefits of creative writing for their students. The majority also said they include one to four poetry or fiction writing opportunities in their classes annually. However, when I asked whether the statement, "I would give students more opportunities to write fictional pieces if I felt I could," is true for them, seventy-two percent responded yes.

Participants were invited to select all that apply from a list of impediments. The results are below.

- Time: 69%
- Not a priority of administration: 29%
- Common Core Standards don't require it: 28%
- Scripted curriculum doesn't emphasize it: 21%
- Not relevant to college and career readiness: 16%

The remaining responses were write-ins, ranging from "no impediments" to "my own fault for not pushing it" to "school culture doesn't appreciate it" and "focus on test prep skills."

The most interesting response, though, is the widely held perception that there isn't enough time for teachers to do the amount of creative writing they believe would be ideal. This implies that many teachers are not exactly being forced to make this compromise. Just like I had done, they are choosing it, most likely because (1) they've internalized the priorities of the system in which they teach, none of which emphasize artistic production in ELA, and (2) they don't see an immediate enough connection between the skills developed through creative writing and those of their most urgent priorities.

Let's unpack those most urgent priorities of K–12 English Language Arts and how we typically act on them.

CURRENT TRENDS IN WRITING INSTRUCTION AND UNINTENDED CONSEQUENCES

Walk into an English department meeting or professional development session, and the likelihood that the focus is text-based analytical writing is high. Perhaps teachers are discussing close reading strategies that lead to better textual analysis. Or they are trying out a new acronym to help guide students through writing analytical paragraphs. This imaginary meeting may or may not take place in a district that is currently using Common Core Standards—their influence is present either way.

Certainly, the ability to read carefully and critically and write cogently about it has always been an essential outcome of a quality education, and a particular responsibility of English teachers to teach. But the common standards have, in effect, posited that in order to prepare students to be college and career ready, text-based analytical writing *is the key lever to engage.* Though I don't completely disagree with that assessment, it's a limited conclusion to draw from a complex situation, and it creates some unintended negative consequences.

On the positive side, as I noted in "Decoding the Common Core" (Sacks, 2015):

> The new standards seemed better aligned to my teaching . . . in their emphasis on developing students' critical-thinking skills, rather than on helping students generate specific types of work products. I saw a push to have students do more of the thinking in the classroom, especially by interpreting texts for themselves and by using evidence to support their arguments.

The standards seemed to remind us that students are capable of more sophisticated thinking and writing than they are often expected to do.

However, the heavy focus on analytical responses to texts seems to assume that analytical writing skills are more important and useful than those of narrative and other literary forms. As I've said already, narrative writing is both important and useful. For all of the reasons that artistic sensibilities are valuable in the marketplace, the ability to tell stories and to consciously impact a reader's perception and mood with word choices pops up in all sorts of work, including, ironically, nonfiction writing.

The bigger problem, though, is that the overfocus on analytical writing in K–12 education also rests on an assumption that the *means* to strong analytical writing by the end of high school is a steady diet throughout schooling of . . . analytical writing.

Instead of building standards that are carefully in sync with the developmental trajectory of confident readers and writers, it appears that the authors of the standards looked at what students needed to be able to do with texts in college and just "backwards planned" down to first grade, assuming that learning is an entirely linear process (Sacks, 2015).

As a child, I was an eager writer (and reader) of fiction and poetry. Lo and behold, as an adult I write (and read) almost exclusively nonfiction! I share that to illustrate that the human mind and its development are complex. The pathway to competent writing is generally not a straight line.

Developmental Matters and Common Core Writing

What does a nonlinear learning process look like? One example in which we intuitively understand how normal this is, is driving. Everyone wants informed, skilled drivers on the roads, but we know better than to begin drivers' education in first grade to accomplish that goal. Young children are not developmentally ready to learn to drive—they are neither physically, cognitively, nor emotionally able to operate a car. Teaching the skills that are generally studied in drivers' education to young children would be a waste of everyone's time. It could also be confusing and anxiety inducing for children to be forced through activities that are beyond their developmental readiness levels.

Can't we start early, though, teaching developmentally appropriate, related skills that might improve driving readiness for those learners down the road? Of course. These activities—like developing spatial awareness and coordination through gross motor activity and learning about street signs and pedestrian safety—benefit the child in a multitude of endeavors other than driving, both present and future. They help lay a foundation for some of the skills associated with driving a car, but they are much broader than "little-kid" versions of driving cars.

Developmental theories help explain why this is. Though we're always learning, we move through distinct developmental stages. According to Jean Piaget's theory of cognitive development, each stage is characterized by specific concepts an individual is trying to learn. For example, in the concrete operations stage, roughly from age seven to eleven, one major concept children are working on is concrete logical reasoning, such as understanding why, when we are standing across from each other, my left hand is in front of your right hand. At the close of this period, in early adolescence, they enter the formal operational stage, where they begin to develop abstract conceptual and hypothetical thinking. A lot of abstract tasks not only won't make sense to the pre-operational child, but they also won't be helpful yet, because the child is working on concrete logic, a necessary precursor to thinking abstractly.

Now let's consider an example of what happens when an ELA objective is out of synch with cognitive development. In fifth grade, CCSS.ELA-LITERACY.RL.5.6 requires students to "describe how a narrator's or speaker's point of view influences how events are described." This standard points us toward a pretty abstract way for readers to engage and respond to a story, at a time when even the most advanced students are just beginning to enter the formal operational stage.

The pre-operational reader generally engages directly with the events and characters of the story, responding to them and assimilating them into their mental maps as they would real people and experiences. They know the story may not be real, but that's not of particular interest to them, because it's abstract. Adding the layer of who is telling the story, and what might be different if someone else were telling it is an abstract concept.

Teachers can certainly lead students to make statements that might qualify as evidence of meeting this standard, but often, the excessive scaffolding needed to do so takes the rigor out of the task. Most of the critical thinking is actually coming from the teacher. This undermines the original purpose of the standard, which was to build students' abilities to critically analyze the point of view of a text. Consequently, many learners disengage from the process, as it has become mainly an exercise in compliance and has little meaning for them.

Yet, students do learn something from repeatedly being in the position of having to follow their teacher's thinking—they learn dependency and self-doubt, rather than the critical skill the objective describes. This is the consequence of what I call the "big thinker" syndrome in *Whole Novels For the Whole Class* (Sacks, 2014), in which the teacher is not just the leader of the class, but also the one whose thinking is most prominent. It is a conventional role for a teacher and oh-so-easy to fall into, especially in situations when both teachers and students have little decision-making power over the learning tasks of their work.

The fifth grade example above was in relation to a reading standard, but reading standards are often the drivers of writing tasks. The Common Core writing standards are more general in what they ask students to do in response to literature— essentially to support claims with evidence and analysis. The anchor standard CCSS. ELA-LITERACY.CCRA.W.1, which applies across grade levels reads, "Write arguments to support claims in an analysis of substantive topics or texts using valid reasoning and relevant and sufficient evidence." Since reading standards are so often assessed through student writing, writing prompts frequently use the language of a particular reading standard and ask students to make an argument in response, using evidence from the text. Thus, fifth-grade students will likely be asked to compose formal paragraphs about how the narrator's point of view affects the way the events in the text are described.

On Task, But Off Course

In today's schools, students experience a steady demand of text-dependent analytical writing prompts. These tasks might appear to increase students' levels of critical thinking about texts, but they often rush students to practice skills they aren't cognitively ready for and which don't interact in a meaningful way with their humanity.

We now meet many students who seem to be adept at structuring an argumentative paragraph, quoting from a text, and explaining what they think it means. But so many teachers I know are also noticing that many of these paragraphs are disappointingly superficial in content and formulaic in their style. Students are working through those guiding acronyms, checking off the boxes to complete the task, but they are missing the subtleties in the texts, missing elements needed to adequately answer the question, and they aren't paying attention to their own language choices and how their ideas are coming across to a reader.

The effects here are as adverse as those of any misguided, ineffective teaching practice—and the stakes are extremely high.

At the same time, the common standards movement has deemphasized creative writing in its many forms in English Language Arts classes. In only one out of the 10 anchor standards for writing that span kindergarten through 12th grade are students, possibly, involved in imaginative writing. That single standard (CCSS.ELA-LITERACY.CCRA.W.3) is phrased, "Write narratives to develop real or imagined experiences or events . . . " That means that a student could conceivably meet all standards without ever having written a poem or a fictional story.

The trend away from imaginative writing is disappointing, but it's symptomatic of a larger cultural problem of devaluing the arts in our country and in education. This cultural characteristic holds some sway over all of us.

There is some good news though. It is possible and, I believe, highly effective, to meet these very Common Core Language Standards and the state standards they've influenced with a program that includes a large dose of creative writing. We can actually make some of the abstractions of the analytical standards concrete through imaginative writing. I'll go into this in Chapter 2.

THE SHIFT STUDENTS NEED: RELEASE FROM COMPROMISE

In my thirteenth year of teaching, I followed my curiosity about what might happen if I prioritized creative writing and ventured into a new realm. I had sensed it was there all along, but I'd never fully stepped into it because of all of the figurative caution tape I had yet to name.

A combination of factors propelled me to change. For one thing, I was finally over the hump of the sleepless nights of early parenthood. I had also gotten to know my school and students enough to feel confident to try new things. I was working a .8 schedule, which gave me designated time in my week to write, and thus, more mental space all around. Finally, I was seriously contemplating moving on from classroom teaching at the end of that year.

There is something about teaching like it's your last year—it was like flipping a switch in my brain. I developed a heightened commitment to being present each moment of teaching, and I leaned into my relationships with students. I had enough of a foundation in my practice—in terms of curriculum, tools I'd created to solve common problems, understanding of standards and assessment, routines and classroom management skills, and a general sense of pacing—to fall back on. That freed me to take risks and to listen to a wiser, calmer part of myself when making decisions as the group leader.

The risks I took fell into a few categories. The first was time. I stopped trying to rush through units and lessons. I decided instead that doing things well and deeply was worth our time, even if it meant not always finishing projects neatly before a vacation week, or not sticking to everything on my initial curriculum map of the year.

On a day-to-day basis, this meant that if there was a fire drill in the middle of an intense class period, I saw the humor in it just like students did, rather than silently cursing the alarm. When we returned to the classroom, we still picked up where we left off—this time without frantically trying to make up the time. When topics bubbled up in class that energized students and were relevant and important to their lives, I allowed time to discuss them, sometimes creating space to explore further the next day, rather than proceeding with my original plans.

Some might worry this shift would undermine the sense of urgency in learning that many educators view as crucial to motivating students. In fact, my ability to exercise a different kind of a judgment around the use of class time—less rigid and busy and more caring and focused on the learning opportunities of a given moment—seemed to send a message to students that what we did in class was *very* important. Student "buy-in" was extremely high. I had always been student-centered in my methods, but never as consistently in my own presence and understanding of the big picture of what we were doing and why it mattered. I had let go of an additional layer of control so that students had a greater hand in co-creating "what we did" daily in class.

I had seen incredible outcomes from the creative writing I'd done with my students since my very first year of teaching. I thought, *what would happen if I pushed this farther than I ever have before*? If ever there was a time to try following my hunch about creative writing, this was it.

I knew in my mind and heart that more opportunities to write imaginatively would have a positive impact on students then and for years to come. I also knew I could switch up the balance at any time to make sure students were getting what they needed. That's what a responsive classroom is, after all.

My shift toward more imaginative writing was an augmentation of what I had always done—but I let go of my sense of worry or guilt about it. Instead of feeling like I was stealing time away from teaching the essay (centering the essay as the major writing form), I allowed creative writing to share the center stage of our studies, along with all types of reading and expository writing.

I didn't announce to students in any formal way that creative writing would be central to our learning together. I didn't plan a huge creative writing unit either. I simply allotted ample time for exercises we'd always done in connection with each novel study (more on this in the coming chapters). I paid special attention to the focus and excitement I saw in students when we did so, extending the time when I saw fit.

I devoted more class periods than ever before to students sharing their work with the class, pausing to discuss what we noticed in each other's work, which has become a key component to the method and its positive outcomes.

This all felt risky, because no one—I mean *no one*—tells English teachers that we should spend more time on imaginative writing. We are not often explicitly forbidden from doing it, but the common core movement and academic tradition in general push analytical writing. We hear subtle comments that imply creative writing is not real, worthwhile work. The common core standards' single gesture toward narrative writing ("real and imagined") is often interpreted to mean once a year is adequate, and that the skill can just as well be accomplished through nonfiction narrative writing, whether personal, historical, or journalistic. These forms are valuable, but not *more so* than fiction or poetry writing (which is completely missing from the standards), especially for children.

Imagine for a moment if someone proposed that secondary English teachers should have students write just one essay in an entire year. The response around most any table would be overwhelming disapproval because everyone knows that students can't learn a form by trying it once a year. ELA standards are not a collection of content that students can learn once and then file away; they are processes and skills that we develop cyclically over time, always revisiting in new contexts.

As I embarked on my experiment of prioritizing imaginative writing in my classroom, it occurred to me that, at worst, I would tip the balance too far—I would give students the chance to develop some mastery of the single writing standard that would never be tested (in New York, at least) and was unlikely to be prioritized again in any core class they would take in their secondary education. And this might come with the cost of students stagnating in other writing skills over that year. I decided that this worst-case scenario was not ideal, but it was also not truly worse than its opposite—tipping too far in the other direction and never giving students the chance to work to become adept at imaginative writing, which is the norm throughout their education. I dove in, seeking a new balance.

MY JOURNEY TO FULL INCLUSION OF CREATIVE WRITING AND AFFIRMING RESULTS

You don't know what's at the horizon line until you try going there. The year that unfolded was wonderful in many ways, and the quality of our work exceeded my expectations. Students were more motivated and focused than in years past on *all* the work we did—not just the creative writing. Through steady practice crafting fictional pieces in conjunction with our novel studies and later with poetry, students developed both their writing voices and their personal identities to a greater degree than I had seen before. The social benefits were multifaceted, as they had always been; but it seemed that the more attention I paid to my students' social–emotional growth as individuals and in community with one another, the more apparent the growth became. (What we give our attention to is what grows.)

Finally, what happened to the aspect of this shift I had questioned the most? The choice to prioritize creative writing *as much as* expository writing did mean cutting back some of the time I had previously devoted to other types of writing. Amazingly, it also seemed to benefit my students' analytical paragraphs and essays. I noticed a difference in the way they approached writing arguments in my formative assessments early in the year. They seemed more present in their writing, somehow. Overall, their writing was making more sense. They made steady progress, taking in the lessons I had always taught on paragraph and essay writing, with a tad more interest than usual (it seemed to me). I will discuss the reasons this might be the case in Chapter 2.

That summer, additional confirmation of the effects of my integrated program came in the form of students' scores on the 2017 NY State Common Core ELA Exam: 98% of this cohort made at least "one year" of growth on the test (maintaining the score they had the year before one year younger), and 48% gained one or two levels, making two or three "years" of growth according to the logic of the test. This cohort of eighth-graders had been making progress in their average proficiency levels since fifth grade, but the jump in eighth was notably larger, more than double the progress in each previous year, and in sharp contrast to the overall negative trend among eighth-graders throughout the city. Though my students had always shown at least decent growth on standardized tests, this year's was more pronounced than that of classes of students from previous years (all data is available at www.nyccharterschools.org).

It was the exact opposite of the outcome I had feared.

The following year, I did leave the classroom, only to do an about face a year later and return to the same position at the same school. My return to teaching was unexpectedly difficult for me personally, and it also happened that my school was going through a rough spot that affected teacher working conditions and the learning environment for students. I continued my practice of a heavy dose of creative writing. You'll see that while my own school's averages dropped significantly that year (not surprising given the challenges we faced), my own classes of eighth-graders soared. (The state test was canceled in 2020 and 2021 due to the pandemic. In 2022 my students took the test again and did well, but I can't create a similar chart comparing it with their own past performance, because that would be going back three years.)

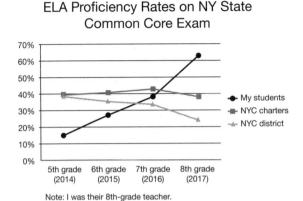

Figure 1.1: My students' ELA proficiency rates on the NY State Common Core Exam 2017

I am certain that the choices I made in my teaching practice impacted these results, but I also doubt any one factor is responsible for them. I won't claim that *simply increasing* the amount of creative writing in any ELA class will definitely lead to higher student achievement on standardized tests. But I can say this: In my experience, any claims that spending significant time on creative writing is a waste and a disservice to students when it comes to the realities of high stakes testing are untrue.

Whatever image we are fed about what rigorous work in English Language Arts is supposed to look like does not hold up in real life—likely because that image is a simplified "kid" version of what college scholarship traditionally looks like, rather than a range of more authentic activities that *lead* children and adolescents along a path to full intellectual and social–emotional development.

It's a good thing that the traditional image of academic rigor for young people is a falsehood. We don't have to choose between happy or successful children. We can fuel the soul and challenge the mind at the same time. We can permit ourselves to teach creative writing as an essential.

As ELA teachers, we can facilitate creative writing so that it plays the role of both the dessert AND the vegetables. In order to pull that off, we need to be intentional about the context for these tasks and how we guide them. I'm not suggesting that we turn ELA class into an art class at the expense of other fundamental objectives. Being mindful of and dedicated to the many demands of English Language Arts, **we can utilize imaginative writing to help meet more of them, more effectively, in the same amount of time we've always had**. That may sound crazy, but time is not the insurmountable barrier I once thought it was.

If creative writing is to compete for space and time in English Language Arts class, we must approach it with an understanding of the following:

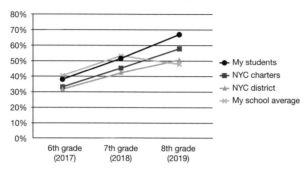

ELA Proficiency Rates on NY State
Common Core Exam

Note: I was their 8th-grade teacher.

Figure 1.2: My students' ELA proficiency rates on the NY State Common Core Exam 2019

1. It is the art form central to our discipline.
2. Students urgently need it in their lives as an outlet for their personal identity and social–emotional development.
3. It is a vehicle to achieve greater equity and empowerment for all students in a post-industrial world and to foster understanding across differences.
4. It's vitally connected to the call for students to build stronger analytical reading and writing skills—and this concept is key to tackling the time issue.

In Chapter 2, I'll introduce the model I use for integrating imaginative writing into my English Language Arts program, share one of my highest leverage teaching practices, and explain why it helps students academically so much. I'll describe how the first few months of my curriculum flow with imaginative writing integrated into our literature program.

2

Harnessing Imaginative Writing for Academic Development

THE (MISSING) LINK BETWEEN IMAGINATIVE WRITING AND CRITICAL READING

The earliest piece of writing I can remember producing was a story, written in phonetic spelling on small pieces of scrap paper, stapled together. Mimicking as best I could a "real" picture book, I called it "Yuc, Yuc, u Slug," and it was based on an experience I'd had the day before, when my best friend and I turned over a large rock and found beneath it . . . a frightful slug! This must have been in late kindergarten or early first grade, as my writing development closely mirrored my reading development.

Throughout my childhood, I wrote many stories and poems, and in all of them I can see the combined influence of the reading I did and my own lived experiences. The same is true for many of my students. Toward the beginning of the year, I ask students to tell me about their reading and writing histories, and I get to hear the memories they have of early stories they've written. Some even bring them in to share, reminiscing about the fun they had.

As students progress through a traditional education, though, their reading and writing experiences become increasingly lopsided. They *read* works of fiction and poetry throughout, but they must make a dramatic shift away from the imaginative writing of childhood toward analytical paragraphs and essays. The common core standards movement has compounded this effect by emphasizing analytical writing at much earlier ages, while not explicitly requiring fiction or poetry writing at any age. I know kindergarten teachers who now prompt students to answer questions about an author's choices during story time, while creative writing is taking even more of a "back seat." For many reasons detailed in Chapter 1, this is a mistake—especially if we want students to read and write more critically.

Imagine you're taking a ride in the back seat of someone's car and you're asked to offer a critique of their driving. However, you have very limited experience as a driver yourself. You might be able to describe how the ride feels to you—bumps, turns, acceleration, sudden stops—and perhaps formulate some opinion about the driver based on these sensations. However, you wouldn't be able to analyze what the driver is doing (or not doing) to create the effect you feel as a passenger. When the driver shifts into low gear to go up a hill in the snow, for example, you don't notice. Even if you did, you'd find it difficult to understand why this was an effective choice without having experience with the particular problem the driver is solving.

When we ask students to be critics of literary art without giving them consistent, relevant experience writing literary pieces themselves, we put students at a similarly awkward disadvantage as the backseat driver in the previous analogy.

We also stunt students' writing styles and voices when we don't encourage them to write in the genres they read and try their hand at imitating elements they enjoy. The key to developing a writing style, many writers agree, is in the ear. Even if it's silently reading the words on a page, we develop our style by hearing the words flow and assessing whether they sound good, like the writing of authors we love to read. Similarly, when we learn to speak a first or second language, we need to hear the language spoken a lot by others, and then we begin to try using the words for ourselves.

The bizarre reality of most of our developing young writers is that they read and hear fiction, but must write (speak on the page) analysis. That incongruity is a handicap on students' development as confident writers whose voices come through on the page.

If we give literary writing a promotion in our curricular hierarchy—from the margins into a key role that students regularly take on—we can shift this imbalance. We can empower students to explore language and literary elements through both their receptive and productive modes, listening/reading and writing/speaking. We can do this in a program that is as intellectually rigorous as it is joyful.

In this chapter, I will share:

- The curricular framework that supports integrated creative writing into my literature program
- A key techique I use for harnessing creative writing to teach literary elements
- How integrating literary writing into literature study creates balance in terms of a) the receptive and productive language development of our students in

relation to literature and b) the convergent and divergent thinking demands of our courses

- An outline of the first several months of reading and writing in my classroom to illustrate how imaginative writing fits

FOUR ESSENTIAL ROLES: A CURRICULUM MODEL FOR TAPPING INTO THE POWER OF CREATIVE WRITING

Powerful creative writing experiences don't happen in a vacuum. The practices I share in this book and my arguments for them have taken shape in the context of my own classroom, which centers on a robust whole novels and independent reading program. Imaginative writing is an integral component of my overall literature program—rather than a separate writing curriculum piece.

To create this model, I investigated the relationship between imaginative writing and the other strands of my curriculum. I noticed that the practices of reading books, talking and writing *about* them, writing our *own* fictional pieces, and sharing and discussing them with classmates were all very much intertwined.

I first envisioned these as curricular threads that I wove together throughout the year. While I like that image from a design standpoint, I wanted to name *what students do and experience within this curriculum.* Rather than abstract strands that I am weaving for them, my students actively embody a variety of roles, including writer of literary pieces. They embody each of these roles, not just once, but successively over a year or more.

The term *role* is helpful to me because it suggests the ongoing practice of becoming skilled and experienced at something, rather than quick touch points of exposure. There are many more roles students can take on in the ELA classroom—journalist, linguist, researcher, for example. The roles I focus on here are not meant to encompass all that students do in English Language Arts, but they are the essential roles of the literature program that is at the center of my curriculum.

Here are the four interconnected roles that fuel a balanced, student centered literature program. Each role strengthens a student's capacity in the other three.

Figure 2.1: Four Essential Roles

Table 2.1: Descriptions of Roles

Role	Description	Domain
1. **Receptive Reader**	Each student has an ongoing relationship to reading, which includes preferences for certain books, authors, and genres; and has a personal, subjective experience with each literary work they read, based on the text as well as their own lived reality, beliefs, and memories.	Individual/ Personal
2. **Member of a Reading Community**	Each student engages in reading alongside peers, shares, and discusses responses with others, and, in so doing, gains a deeper understanding of a literary work—its structure, characters, conflicts, themes—and the range of responses that one text can engender in its readers.	Social
3. **Literary Critic**	Each student closely reads and rereads texts to interpret themes; to study an author's craft and evaluate its impact; to consider the messages and biases of texts; and to discuss, debate, and write about them.	Intellectual
4. **Writer of Original Literary Pieces**	Each student knows what it's like to play and create in a literary world, to channel their ideas, experiences, and perceptions into stories, poems, and other literary forms; makes decisions and utilizes tools to create a convincing experience for readers; and knows the feeling of having others read what comes from their imagination.	Creative

The Fourth Role

In this model of four roles, the fourth role, writer of literary pieces (i.e., stories) is very often missed or underdeveloped in English Language Arts courses. Here are some ways this can look in a curriculum program.

All but the last scenario misses out on the many benefits I've found come from purposefully and continually integrating creative writing practice into our students' development as readers and writers. In an integrated program, the fourth role is both informed by the other three roles (reader, community member, critic), and fuels each of them. The connections among them become stronger with practice.

Integrating Imaginative Writing Into Literature Study

In my classroom, the whole novels method provides a structure for integrated reading and writing in a literary community. I share this method in detail in *Whole Novels for the Whole Class: A Student-Centered Approach* (Sacks, 2014b), and you can read a summary below.

More broadly, here are the key curricular components that lay an important foundation for students to realize the potential of the fourth role within a literature program. Imaginative writing can be engaged literally at any moment—but I have found that the impact grows with these pieces in place.

1. **Students read a lot of literature.**
   - They read books of their choosing, which allows students to follow their interests, develop enjoyable reading lives, and recommend books to their peers.
   - Students participate in group novel studies with the class that allow for shared experiences and deep discussion of characters, themes, and craft.
   - The texts students read are often contemporary young adult novels, featuring a range of diverse characters, written by diverse authors.
   - The diversity of authors and writing styles provides students many models of who can write and what they can write about, which influences students in their own writing.
   - Roles: reader and member of reading community.

2. **Students discuss literature, sharing their genuine responses with the community.**
   - Through discussions and other formats, students are able to voice their authentic responses to texts, ask questions, make connections, and develop

Table 2.2: Common Positioning of Imaginative Writing in ELA Curriculum

Position	Description	Pitfall of Approach
Missing	Omitted from literature program altogether, deemed unnecessary or an unaffordable luxury, often for students who are "behind" on traditional basics; could be consciously planned or just how things "end up."	Misses the opportunity to use/practice the art form at the center of our discipline and all of its benefits; sometimes out of synch with stated values of educators.
Occasional	Included occasionally as a fun activity to punctuate a core curriculum, but not seen as serious work; little investment of time or pedagogy.	Not enough time invested to see benefits; underdeveloped pedagogy in creative writing; assignments may not connect meaningfully to standards.
Standalone Unit	Included in a serious way, but configured as a standalone unit on fiction writing, often separated from literature study.	Lacks reiteration needed for students to develop skills and depth of experience; lacks integration needed for conceptual understanding that connects this role to students' critical reading and writing.
Option for Students	Included as an option, as part of an independent writing workshop or project-based approach, in which students choose which genres to write in throughout the year or in various projects.	Students' choices and their outcomes vary greatly; some students might write one fiction story and one poem, while others might choose these genres more frequently.
Integrated into Literature Studies	Included seriously as a major component of literature study; a modality students enter into in response to reading as easily as they do analytical writing about text; relevant skills spiraled throughout the year.	Can result in decreased time spent on other kinds of writing; may conflict with traditional or mandated curriculum plans.

critiques of them. This is in contrast to a program where students are focused on reading to answer comprehension questions and/or to learn which points the teacher believes are important.

- Each student's distinct voice, opinions, and experiences are welcomed into the community; membership in the literary community also means learning from the voices, opinions, and experiences of others.
- Roles: reader, critic, and member of reading community.

3. **Students engage with the literature they read through writing on two levels.**
    - Expository: Students explore ideas and *write about* the texts, informally and formally based on questions and topics they are curious or passionate to explore. Students' writing about texts is influenced by and also feeds our discussions of texts.
    - Imaginative: Students creatively *interact with* the texts, by adding to them, adapting them, mimicking them, and borrowing authors' techniques. Students' imaginative writing is fueled by our reading of fictional (and poetic) works—and it becomes new material for our literary community to enjoy, think about, and discuss.
    - Roles: **reader, critic** (discussing and writing critical responses to texts), **writer of literary pieces**, borrowing, playing with elements of the text, **member of reading community**, now responding to classmates' creative pieces, . . . and sometimes **critic** again, describing, analyzing classmates' pieces.

The four roles become cyclical. By adding students' own literary writing into the flow, we can learn more from the reading, writing, and thinking we do. We add another powerful dimension to our community of readers and writers.

SUMMARY OF WHOLE NOVELS METHOD

Big Idea: The method is organized around the concept that students should read the whole novel before analyzing it. Novels are works of art that create an immersive experience. In the whole novels method, we support students to read the whole book, and then step back and look closely at pieces of it with the "whole picture" in mind. We begin with highly accessible, relatable books and move into more complex texts over the year, as students gain stamina and a familiar process for reading whole novels.

Structure of Reading Process: Students receive a copy of the book, with a pacing calendar, to read each day. There is class time for reading, and students must finish the remainder of the day's reading at home.

◊ Students are allowed to read ahead using the calendar as a minimum. For those who finish early, I offer a number of suggestions for their continued reading.

◊ Students respond to the text with sticky notes as they read. The goal is to get them to pay attention to their own thoughts and record them. This habit can be applied to any text, rather than teaching students to become dependent on teacher questions.

◊ We focus on one literary element that is well-developed in the novel. One note per day is a structured note, in which students track the element using guidelines I provide.

◊ Students engage in small group activities that allow them to engage with one another to build comprehension and read more deeply. These can be differentiated based on students' needs or interests in relation to the reading.

◊ We offer supports for students depending on their needs. These include audiobooks, frequent teacher conferences, partner reading, and teacher-facilitated small groups.

Whole Novel Discussions: When we reach the due date for completing the book, we are ready to begin discussions. Students drive the content of the discussions, and teachers play a facilitator role.

◊ We discuss with half of the class at a time. The other half of the class works independently on a creative writing assignment.

◊ We begin with a Go-Around. Each student must say something about the book—something they liked or disliked, a character or section they have a comment about, something that confused them, a connection, a sticky note they want to share, etc.

◊ I take notes on what everyone says, projected for students to see.

◊ After the Go-Around, the discussion is open. Topics of interest and debates emerge.

◊ I encourage students to turn back to the text to reread relevant sections to clear up confusion and deepen the discussion.

◊ Each half group meets two to three times for continued discussions. Students receive a copy of the notes to review each time.

Writing: In each novel study, students write both creative and expository pieces.

◊ We begin creative writing pieces connected to the story a day or two before discussions begin. Students work on these between discussion sessions.

◊ I generate essay questions from the topics students were most interested to talk about. Students write essays during class.

◊ The study concludes with a share of the creative writing pieces, using a process shared later in this chapter.

THEORIES CONNECTING IMAGINATIVE WRITING WITH CRITICAL READING

Reading and writing are connected in myriad ways. As common as it is to talk in the literacy field about the connections between reading and writing development and the implications for our instruction, I've rarely if ever heard the argument that *creative writing*, specifically, is fundamental to our development of *critical reading*. More often, we hear the reverse, which is also true—that reading widely and observantly helps develop skill and style in narrative writing. I'm here to say that, perhaps counterintuitively, creative writing practice is absolutely a benefit to students' critical reading—and therefore, their analytical writing as well.

My mentor at Bank Street College, Madeleine Ray, advocates strongly for imaginative writing as a powerful way to interact with stories and learn about literary forms. Her teaching got me started on many of the practices I share in this book. The theoretical texts she assigned in her children's literature course help to make these connections clearer.

Much of the thinking that supports creative production as a central part of engaging in the world of literature and developing literacy comes from an older era: theorists such as Arthur Applebee, Northrup Frye, D. W. Harding, Bruno Bettelheim, and Wolfgang Iser in the 1960s and 1970s built on earlier twentieth-century theories of John Dewey—"learning by doing"—and Louise Rosenblatt—the subjective experience of reading.

One of these important texts is *The Child's Concept of Story: Ages Two to Seventeen* by Arthur Applebee (1978). Applebee's entire process for assessing what children understand about stories is illustrative of the connection between story production and story knowledge. He analyzed how his subjects responded at various ages to the prompt, "Tell me a story." He looked at which formal elements children included in their responses and at which ages these tended to enter into their narratives. The stories that the children shared in response were made up—original imaginative productions! Yet, they reflected elements of stories they were accustomed to hearing or reading. The complexity of these responses increased with age.

Applebee's research reminds me of a time I saw my daughter, who was nearly three, open a picture book she did not know very well and pretend to read it. She began, "Once upon a time . . . " even though the book did not actually begin that way. She turned the page and saw a picture of a turtle and said something like, "There was a turtle . . . " and she mumbled some gibberish about the turtle. She turned a few more pages and then said in an exaggerated storytelling inflection, "But *one dayyyy* . . . " and she went on to create her own spontaneous version of the entire picture book.

None of the sentences she uttered was in the book—only the main character of the turtle was borrowed. But she had recognized patterns from numerous other stories she'd heard, including the phrase, " . . . but one day," so often used in children's books to introduce a conflict. She was learning *and* practicing this conceptual understanding by making up a story. She was playing in the world of this book's illustrations, and beginning to speak the language of story.

When learning a new language, our development of both listening comprehension and speech are equally important. These receptive and productive tasks are connected as we learn how the story world works as well.

Glenna Sloan of Columbia Teacher's College built on the work of her contemporary, Northrop Frye, who theorized about the essential role of literature in human experience in her wonderful book, *The Child as Critic: Teaching Literature in the Elementary School* (1975). Sloan did what almost none of these theorists had: she made concrete suggestions for teachers to apply the research findings in their work with children. Here's how Sloan discusses the role of writing fiction in a literature curriculum:

> Composing is an important aspect of the critical experience. Knowledge of form and structure of story comes first hand from the attempt to write a story, particularly if the student tries to match the *structure* of a myth or fairy tale, perhaps using realistic incidents from [their] own time. Writing should come after exposure to forms, for literature grows out of literature itself, and children should not be expected to compose in a vacuum. . . . In elementary school, children should

write story more than discursive prose, for it is through story that the child orders his experience and orients himself to the world. (pp. 106–107)

Sloan understands why imaginative writing has such a strong impact on students' critical reading. By writing stories, students participate directly in the world of literature, learning about its elements through imitation and experimentation. This direct participation is an application of Dewey's concept of learning by doing. She also touches on why story writing is so powerful to my students' identity development. Stories help us "order" our experiences and position ourselves in the world.

THE DRIVER'S SEAT: A HIGH LEVERAGE TEACHING TECHNIQUE FOR FIRST-HAND EXPERIENCE WITH LITERARY ELEMENTS

One of the vital ways my students regularly take on the fourth role in my classroom is by adapting pieces of the stories we read. As Glenna Sloan argues, new stories grow out of existing stories, and almost never do I ask my students to "compose in a vacuum." This process concretely connects reading and writing for my students and helps them practice applying literary vocabulary to name what they've done.

To illustrate, here is a peek into my classroom during a creative writing share toward the end of a novel study. This process can be used with a story of any length; I'll go into detail on how I craft assignments in Chapter 5.

◊

It's March and my eighth-graders have finished reading the novel *My Heartbeat*, by Garret Freeman-Weyr. While half of the class discusses the book, the other half of the class works independently on an imaginative writing assignment; they must put themselves in the role of author and write one scene in which they alter an element of the novel. The assignment choices include adding a character, changing the point of view, changing the setting, giving a "boring" scene "a makeover" by writing it in a more exciting way, and the most popular option—killing off a character.

I always introduce the assignment to the whole class at least a day before discussions begin, so that I'm available to help students get started. The creative but focused nature of the task easily catches students' interest, and once they have their footing with an idea and at least a first sentence, students of all levels dig in with excitement.

"SILENT GROUP" WORK

Your Task: Write a fictional scene based on the novel *My Heartbeat*. The scene must be *at least* one page, but you're encouraged to write more.

Expectations: Your scene should show creative thinking about the book, using elements of the author's style. Use proper punctuation and paragraphing, paying special attention to how you punctuate dialogue. First draft due Friday.

#1: Give a Scene a Makeover! Pick a scene from the novel that you felt was boring. Rewrite it in a more compelling (interesting) way. Give it a title and explain which scene you're rewriting at the top of the page.

#2: Kill off a Character! Pick a character from the book. Write a scene in which that character dies. Make sure to use dialogue, description, and detail.

#3: Add a Character! Make up a new character for the novel. Write a scene in which your character enters the novel. Make sure your reader can really picture your character. What does he or she say to the other characters? How do they meet? What kind of personality does this character have?

#4: Change the Point of View! Pick a character from the novel who is NOT the main character. Rewrite a scene from that character's point of view. (This can be done in either first person or third person.)

#5: Change the Setting! What would happen if this story took place in a different place or time? Rewrite a scene from the novel in a completely different setting. You may change other things in the scene too. Remember to use dialogue, description of setting, and detail.

After several days of half groups alternating between discussions with me and the creative exercise independent work, we come together as a whole class to read the writing pieces aloud. After each reading, I will ask listeners to jot down notes and then share on the following prompts:

1. Based on what you heard, what did the student choose to do differently than the original author?
2. What literary techniques or elements stand out to you in this piece?

Preparation

Before we begin, we brainstorm together a menu of techniques and literary elements we know about—like dialogue, descriptive language, interior monologue, and foreshadowing. These become a reference for students when answering the second question. Some of these we've practiced in previous fiction-writing assignments; others we've only discussed as readers. I write the items on the board and students record them in their notes. Throughout the readings, we add to this menu as students' pieces spark more ideas.

Introducing Read Aloud

I ask students to read aloud without introduction or explanation for this particular assignment. This is not meant to conform to traditional writing workshop protocols, where the author sits silently as the group discusses the work (critiqued by Felicia Rose Chavez in *The Anti-Racist Writing Workshop* for its uncomfortable and damaging erasure of the author, who is sitting right there). In this case, I want to give the listeners a chance to answer the first question "cold"—to identify the choices the student made in relation to the original story for the intellectual practice that affords them as critical readers. Once students have had a chance to do that, the author may explain anything and participate in the rest of the activity.

Joyful Listening and Analyzing Elements

The scenes are genuinely fun to hear, especially because we're all familiar with the original text and enjoy being surprised by new directions students take. Many opportunities arise to discuss the choices of each writer and their impact. Jonathon, for example, has changed the modern setting of the novel to 1894. In the actual book, the narrator's brother, Link, is struggling to come to terms with his sexuality. Here is an excerpt from Jonathon's scene:

> "I'm not gay," Link said. "James is." My heart dropped. I suddenly began to fear for James' life. The year was 1894. Any openly gay person could be killed by angry mobs. Being gay was not only a sexuality, but also an open bounty on your head for anyone to take. I now realized why Link wanted to deny it . . .

After he reads, I ask students to jot down responses to the two questions in their notes. What did Jonathon change? Which elements or techniques stood out to you in his piece? Immediately, students note that he changed the setting. It's a good moment for students to review that time period is an aspect of setting.

Connecting to Standards

In addition to setting, several students also noticed a shift in the conflict. "The conflict got bigger," one student says, "because of the time period." Here, the student has tapped into an authentic opportunity to see how different literary elements can impact one another. The Common Core ELA Standards emphasize this concept. In fact, the seventh grade reading standard RL.7.3 asks students to "analyze how particular elements of a story or drama interact (e.g., how setting shapes the characters or plot)." In this case, one student's creative writing offered a powerful springboard for other students to build critical understanding of literary elements.

As more students share, we hear a number of carefully foreshadowed tragic deaths of various characters. (As I said, killing off a character is a popular choice.) Many students only just realize that they've effectively used foreshadowing when we take the time to note it. They've heard the word before, but now they have an example from personal experience. This chance to share and discuss raises students' awareness of how literary concepts work and helps them name their own techniques.

Introducing New Terms

We hear Soraya take the point of view of the unpopular, overbearing father character. In the book, his homophobia is clear—he expects Link to be heterosexual at any cost—but we only hear his voice through dialogue told by Ellen, the first-person narrator. Soraya explores this father's emotions and internal conflict: "I see Link asleep on the couch. His eyes have dark circles under them, and I begin to wonder if it's because of me. I begin to wonder if his stress was always caused by me . . . " she writes.

Students first note the strong interior monologue in Soraya's scene. Then someone adds, "It's like she made a whole character out of the father." I want to push this idea further. I write "character development" and "complex character" on the front board in our list of literary terms. Character development is a word we've used before, but didn't make it into the earlier brainstorm. "Complex character" is a new term.

"Why isn't the father a 'whole' or complex character in the book?" I ask.

"Because Ellen is the narrator, so you really can't tell what the father is thinking," a student answers.

"Given that," I push. "What could an author do to write a book that has several 'whole' or 'complex' characters?"

"You could switch off narrators," one student suggests.

"Like in *Wonder*," another adds. Multi-character narration is an increasingly popular format in young adult literature today.

"Or you could write in third person," another student offers. Once again, students' experimentation writing fictional narratives creates opportunity for them to notice how authors' choices around narration and point of view impact the reader's experience of the story, and often, the complexity of characters.

Author–Audience Interaction

Another interesting moment comes when Lana allows a classmate to read her scene. (This is always an option for students.) It is quite intense; every word seems carefully thought out. It begins with Link studying with excruciating focus for a math test. Then she writes this:

> I stood up, ready to go to James's house, when Link's head fell loudly onto the table.
>
> "Link!" I yelled, running to him. White bubbles foamed out of his mouth, and tears trickled down his face, mixing with sweat from earlier. His body was shaking aggressively. Link's eyes began to roll back into the inside of his head when I hurried to pick up my phone. I dialed 9-1-1, and the ambulance soon arrived.

As we listen, I catch Lana scanning the faces in the room with a look that is hard to read. The scene continues as we follow characters to the hospital. Then, in the same serious tone, we find out that Link has a tumor in his brain. At that point, James, his best friend, starts coughing uncontrollably and admits he has cancer. There are some gasps from the class. Lana's face cracks a slight smile. The situation gets more and more extreme. Several students let out laughs, but Lana's narrator never breaks character. When we discuss afterward, students immediately remark on the strength of her descriptive language. "I notice that some people laughed. Did Lana use humor?" I ask. Students are quiet, and I imagine they are unsure as to whether their laughs were appropriate.

"Not exactly, but it was still funny at times," someone says.

I probe. "Lana, did you expect people to find your scene funny?"

"Yeah, kind of," she says, with a mischievous smile.

"It was tragic, but . . . " another student says, trailing off.

"There was something not completely serious about it, right?" I offer. We discuss tone, and I end up introducing the term *satire* to describe the effect of Lana's scene. In a way, after hearing more than a few tragic death scenes of characters by other students, written in serious tones, Lana seemed to be satirizing us!

In this activity, students practice many Common Core standards in reading. Depending on the assignment, the response guidelines I create, and the particular choices students make in their work, the class might be working on any of the following standards or others:

◊ RL.8.3a: "Engage and orient the reader by establishing a context and point of view and introducing a narrator and/or characters; organize an event sequence that unfolds naturally and logically."

◊ RL.4: "Interpret words and phrases as they are used in a text, including determining technical, connotative, and figurative meanings, and analyze how specific word choices shape meaning or tone."

◊ RL.5 for Grades 9 and 10: "Analyze how an author's choices concerning how to structure a text, order events within it (e.g., parallel plots), and manipulate time (e.g., pacing, flashbacks) create such effects as mystery, tension, or surprise."

◊ RL.6: "Assess how point of view or purpose shapes the content and style of a text."

NOW I GET IT: A CONCEPTUAL UNDERSTANDING OF THE AUTHOR'S ROLE

Every student approaches the assignment differently, and as we listen to them read their pieces, the concept of the role of the "author" is suddenly very tangible. It's often challenging for young people to remember there is a real person with a real life behind a novel or any text, who uses their imagination and makes all of the decisions! Reading fiction is such a powerful virtual experience that kids tend to interact with it as if it were an extension of their own lives, rather than the brainchild of a stranger.

For young children, this distinction isn't very important: a story should simply be enjoyed! And that is a developmentally appropriate positioning for children in the concrete operational stage, as Piaget defined it. But as we help students become critics, the concept of an author becomes essential. In this activity, the authors are the classmates sitting right in front of us, making the complex concrete.

Students rarely get to experience firsthand such an immediate interaction between author and audience through text as they do in the group share of their scene writing exercises. As members of a literary community, students gain awareness of their own choices and intentions as they write stories. They encounter, first-hand, the problems authors face in crafting stories, and they discover and experiment with literary techniques to solve these problems. They become more keen analyzers of other authors' choices and intentions when they read.

Returning to the analogy of the driving critic who lacks driving experience, a student without genuine experiences creating literary art can easily be left to look to the teacher for "answers" as to what authors are up to in their use of literary techniques. I've seen this cause frustration in classrooms, as it diminishes our students' opportunities to activate their own critical thinking in this area. Imaginative writing indeed contributes to students' development of literary analysis skills.

DIVERGENT AND CONVERGENT THINKING AND THE MEANING OF RIGOR

Integrating the fourth role (imaginative writing) helps coordinate receptive and productive language development: reading/hearing and writing/speaking. It helps students become active, experienced agents within the world of literature. Another way that imaginative writing positively impacts the academic experience of students is by helping to *balance the divergent and convergent thinking demands* we make of them.

Convergent thinking, the opposite of divergent thinking, was first coined by psychologist Joy Paul Guilford. It is what the mind does to solve a problem that is well-defined and requires a correct answer (Guilford, 2018). Convergent thinking can be easy or difficult, depending on the task. An easy question that requires convergent thinking might be how many U.S. presidents have been female? A more difficult one might be, how much should you invest monthly into an account with a four percent interest rate at age twenty-nine in order to retire with money to live for twenty years? Or, where in the novel does the protagonist begin to change?

Divergent thinking, on the other hand, is what the mind does when a problem has many possible responses or solutions. Brainstorming, risk-taking, making unexpected connections, following curiosity, imagining alternative ways of doing something, and creating something original, all involve divergent thinking. A divergent thinking task could be, how could your community increase the number of young people who have gotten their COVID vaccine? Or, if we were going to rewrite the ending of this novel, what options would we have and how would they impact the theme of the book?

Our traditional schooling model, often called a factory model, heavily emphasizes convergent thinking. Standardized tests and IQ tests almost exclusively test convergent thinking. In a study on the two types of thinking, strong convergent thinkers on average had much higher course grades and less of a problem doing homework than those participants who were stronger in divergent thinking (Luendendok, 2019).

Course grades likely emphasize convergent thinking because of how simple and efficient it is to measure single-answer questions organized around specific knowledge than it is to organize and measure complex processes and creative productions.

Even if the reason for the emphasis on convergent thinking is expediency, we can't discount the values being perpetuated here: conformity over diversity; fixed knowledge bases over dynamic change; mimicry over creativity; dependency over risk-taking.

Intelligence, however, relies on both convergent and divergent thinking, which are very much connected in the real world. There is a false dichotomy that "book smarts" equal convergent thinking and creativity is all divergent thinking. In fact, doing high-level academic work requires both. The same study (2019), for example, showed that strong divergent thinkers had notably higher reading and word fluency scores than those with low divergent thinking. The people we regard as geniuses tend to be strong divergent thinkers. At the same time, doing valuable creative work requires both kinds of thinking—any artist or inventor knows that divergent ideas are only part of the work—executing them within real parameters requires plenty of convergent thinking-driven work based on the selection and application of a range of established techniques. Intelligence, I believe, is really our ability to integrate and apply the two types of thinking, moving between them in response to the situation.

There has been a strong push in the last decade for educators to make sure our curriculum content and methods are "rigorous" for students. It seems like this word is used with the intention of describing intellectually challenging tasks that push our students at or beyond their zones of proximal development. Pushing students beyond their zones of proximal development is not recommended by psychologists or learning experts. Nonetheless, we are often pressured to do it in schools based on "bars" set via standardized tests, bell curves, and other external influences. In education, the word *rigor* has come to describe a task or mode that is considered difficult for typical students of their respective age group.

In addition to putting a premium on that which is developmentally difficult, ideals of rigor in education tend to be biased toward convergent thinking. If you ask a group of adults to, say, write a short play about a current issue in the world or in their lives, they will likely find that a very difficult and demanding task. But teachers know this kind of assignment in a classroom can often come under scrutiny for not being "rigorous" enough—not because it is easy, but because it channels divergent thinking, which is misconstrued as easy.

The term rigor in education has come to describe tasks that are difficult for our age group and require demanding amounts of convergent thinking.

BALANCING DIVERGENT AND CONVERGENT THINKING IN THE CLASSROOM

I remember high school biology, the class famous for being the hardest one we'd encounter in high school. It turned out to be a lot of direct instruction and memorization. I didn't find it so hard, but it was time consuming as anything. It made your brain hurt to cram those vocabulary words on flash cards into your memory each week. I did the work, and I managed to learn some important concepts that stay with me even today—but I didn't come away with any interest in biology, nor did I gain any understanding of how actual biologists work. This is an example of an overload of convergent thinking—every class period, every unit, for the whole year.

The class was a gatekeeper of sorts, a test of extreme convergent thinking. While I was lucky enough to be able to keep up without it ruining my year, many were not for reasons I now know are not tied to their intelligence. It's not natural for the teenage brain to stay in that convergent state for so long.

On the flipside, divergent thinking by itself is unsettling and falls flat for most students. I remember early in my career, I gave students in an elective class an exciting creative task. I put them in groups and told them, "Imagine you have the opportunity to start your own business. 'The bank' will loan you money to do it if you come up with an innovative idea, a name for your business, and plan for how you will get it started." And then I pretty much told them to begin. I imagined we would work on this for weeks and end up with amazing proposals.

A small number of students seemed to thrive on the challenge and lack of structure. They came up with interesting ideas and then were able to organize their plans with their groups. But most groups generated super basic ideas, and they quickly declared themselves "done." I spoke with each group, asked questions, and encouraged them to build further on what they'd started. But overall, I was disappointed with the results.

I'm sure many other teachers have made this kind of rookie mistake. You give students a large task that has exciting potential. You give them total freedom over their process and product. You think students will love this and do amazing work, but they don't.

So what went wrong? How would you have scaffolded this project for students?

The students needed reference points for how to begin, and where they might need to end up. They needed some examples of innovative business ideas and models for how the ideas could be organized and presented. They could have benefited from having the task broken down into steps. They might have done better if the focus of the business were limited in some key way: Create a business that solves a problem or need in your community, for example. This doesn't mean that I would have to come up with all of the framing. We could have developed the assignment and process together as a class, found examples together on the internet, and then turned the work over to small groups.

The steps we take as teachers to help students meet the challenge of a task that requires substantial divergent thinking help because they introduce convergent thinking into the process. I'm using convergent thinking in a more general sense than its original definition. While we may not be working on tasks that have a single correct answer, we're moving along a continuum in that direction. We're taking something ambiguous with no clear parameters and making decisions that anchor and focus the work. That focus becomes a lens through which to see multiple possibilities for a more specific question. After looking through that lens, we make another decision and the work focuses a little further; we generate a new set of possibilities, make a new decision, and so forth.

In this way, creative work involves a cycle of repeatedly opening and then focusing the mind, diverging and converging, moving toward a bigger vision while creating and organizing each detail along the way. Project based learning, done well, is a wonderful mix of divergent and convergent thinking. Creative thinking and true scholarship in any discipline go hand in hand.

I hold the concepts of divergent and convergent thinking when I teach—it's one way that I continually assess my planning with the goal of keeping students intellectually engaged. I strive for a balance between the two—within each class period, within a particular project or unit, and even over the course of the school year. I make a point to notice how and when different learning experiences challenge students to use both modes of thinking, and I look at how individual students respond to each challenge. These observations help me differentiate my instruction—to introduce more convergent or divergent thinking, depending on the individual and context—to reach more students.

IMAGINATION HELPS BALANCE THE MEAL

When students experience a curriculum that allows for an energizing and productive balance of divergent and convergent thinking, they notice that it feels right. They are excited to explore ideas and just as excited to bear down and sustain focus on a specific task that feels relevant.

In the whole novels method, students have the chance to read a novel for enjoyment and respond authentically to it; to then share unfiltered reactions, questions, and concerns with their peers; and investigate them together following their curiosity, convictions, and disagreements. They emerge with serious motivation to pick an idea about the book that has come up in discussions and write a formal argument essay about it. Writing those builds on the initial divergent thinking of the discussions, but then students employ convergent thinking to make their argument using the best evidence and analysis they can in support of their claim.

In a similar way, when students are writing fiction in my class, their relationship to more traditional academic tasks shifts. Fiction writing requires students to use their imagination, see possibilities, take risks, and make decisions that have immediate impact on their writing and its effect on others. In this context, which privileges divergent thinking, I find that students are quite eager to work on things like punctuation and sentence structure, which can otherwise be frustrating or "boring" to some students, and where there is generally a right and wrong way to do it.

That's because imaginative writing balances the meal. Students become hungry for left-brained convergent-thinking work that is relevant to their task, because (1) they know it helps them move toward the bigger vision they're invested in, and (2) because their brains are not already filled to the brim with it.

→ Exercise: Think a moment in your curriculum of your school year so far that seems heavy with demands on students' convergent thinking. How do students feel? How do you feel? What adjustment could you make to add divergent thinking into the unit of lesson? What about specificity imaginative writing?

HOW IT COMES TOGETHER: FOUR MONTHS OF CURRICULUM WITH FOUR INTEGRATED ROLES

How does curriculum flow when imaginative writing is integrated into a literature-based English Language Arts classroom?

To illustrate, I'll take you through the **first three to four months** of the school year with my eighth-grade students. Each year, my curriculum choices vary, but I tend to use a similar trajectory for the first couple of months and then depart from there based on what I learn about my students, what's new in YA literature, and other school-based factors that come up. Pacing changes somewhat each year based on scheduling.

These examples provide a general picture of how creative writing fits into the program, integrating with the other three roles to help the ebb and flow of divergent and convergent thinking. I will go into more detail on designing these and other imaginative writing assignments, the skills and concepts I teach and assess, and materials I use in Chapters 5 and 6.

I. Folk Tale: "The Treasure"

Oral Storytelling: Our first story of the year is a folk tale, told aloud. I usually tell this one because it comes from my own Jewish cultural background and I know it by heart—and my students enjoy discussing it. It's the story of Isaac, a poor man who lives with his family in a cottage at the edge of a forest in Poland. He dreams for three nights in a row that there is treasure buried over two mountains and across a bridge. He journeys to look for it, but a "bridge keeper" asks for a toll in order to cross the bridge. He can't pay it, but he tells the bridge keeper about his dream and offers to split the treasure if he can cross without paying. The bridge keeper laughs and allows it, only because he says it would be entertaining. Isaac doesn't find the treasure. Just as he gives up, the bridge keeper laughs and tells him about his own dream that the same treasure is over two hills behind the oven in a poor man's house. Isaac runs home, shakes the oven, and finds the treasure. (Role 1–Reader/Listener)

Three Ways of Thinking Lesson: After they listen to the story, I ask students to share their responses: what do you think, notice, or remember about it? I write down each comment in a numbered list. Then we categorize them into literal, inferential, and critical thoughts. (This lesson is detailed in Chapter 3 of *Whole Novels For the Whole Class*.) The session is very open and allows for some divergent thinking about the story as well as simple recall. The categorizing activity is more of a convergent thinking piece. Although we debate about many of the students' responses, we attempt to agree on the most accurate categorization for each one. (Role 2–Member of Reading Community, Role 3–Literary Critic)

Some years, at this point, we jump to creative writing. One year, for example, I left this assignment on a day I was absent. Students dug right into it, even without me present. (Role 4–Writer of Literary Pieces)

Pick ONE option. Write a story or scene in your notebook that is **about two pages (or more)**.

Option A: Pick a character from "The Treasure" other than Isaac. Write a part of the story (or the whole thing) from that character's perspective. You may make up additional details related to this character, but you cannot change the details we know from the original story. For example, you can make up what Sarah does during the day, but you can't change what's in the original story, such as how she responds to Isaac when he tells her his dream.

Option B: Write a modern-day version of this story. You may change and add details to accomplish this task—perhaps the family lives in an apartment in Manhattan in your version.

Option C: Start from the point where Isaac sets out to look for the treasure. Change what happens from there. For example, maybe the bridge keeper is interested in the treasure. Maybe the treasure is actually there. Maybe there is no bridge keeper. Maybe the bridge keeper tells him his dream but it's something else. Maybe something happens in the forest . . . use your imagination.

Other years, we move into our second text before doing imaginative writing, so that we can focus on applying the three ways of thinking to it. Then we jump into the fourth role—with creative choices related to either story.

II. Read Aloud: The Hundred Dresses

<u>Prologue</u>: As a prologue to this text, we discuss the question of what makes "a classic." I introduce the writer Italo Calvino's poetic 14 definitions of a classic from his book, *Why Read the Classics?* (1991). We discuss it and create a list of classics we're familiar with in various genres: books, songs, movies, television shows, sneakers, etc. Students usually mention popular fairy tales and this leads to the notion that to be a classic, a story must be passed down from one generation to the next. (Harry Potter books are just now becoming modern classics.) Given that, all folk and fairy tales can be considered classics. (Role 3–Literary Critic)

<u>Read Aloud</u>: I introduce *The Hundred Dresses* by Eleanor Estes as a classic, first published in 1944 and still widely read. I tell students, after we read this book we will consider why it has endured, while others from the era are no longer in print.

This illustrated novella is the story of Wanda Petronski, an elementary student who wore the same dress to school each day, but said she had one hundred dresses at home. It is told through the eyes of her classmate, Maddie, who stood by while Peggy and other girls played "the dresses game" with Wanda, asking her repeatedly how many dresses she has and laughing at her response. Then Wanda wins the drawing contest, drawing 100 unique dresses, but she is not in school to receive her award. Her father sends a letter to the teacher, explaining that they have moved to "the big city," where no one will make fun of their last name. The girls reckon with feelings of guilt and responsibility for Wanda's departure. (Role 3–Literary Critic)

<u>Habits of Response Practice</u>: Every student has a copy of the book to fol-
low along as I read aloud. We pause every so often, and I ask students to
write an open response on a sticky note—whatever they are noticing, wondering, or thinking about as they read. We share the notes and practice applying literal, inferential, and critical categories to them as we did with the
folk tale. (Role 2–Member of the Literary Community/Role 3–Literary Critic)

<u>Students Cocreate Imaginative Writing Prompts</u>: I ask students to help me
brainstorm a list of creative writing assignments in connection to this book or
"The Treasure." I record the list on the board, while students copy them into their
notebooks. The requirement will be to write a scene of one page as a minimum. I
steer them away from expository writing tasks, since we will get to that after our
discussions. (Role 4–Writer of Literary Pieces)

Here is an example of one of our brainstorms:

- Rewrite a part/scene of *The Hundred Dresses* from another character's
  point of view (Cecile, make up a classmate, Ms. Mason, Peggy, Wanda, Old
  Man Svenson).
- Rewrite a part/scene of "The Treasure" from another character's point of
  view (bridge keeper, Sarah, one of the children, one of the townspeople).
- Change the ending and, therefore, lesson of one of the stories.
- Change setting; modern version of *The Hundred Dresses* or "The Treasure."
- Write the beginning of a sequel of *The Hundred Dresses* with Wanda's new
  life in the city and/or Maddie's life after Wanda has left.
- Add a character to either story—write the scene where that character
  enters the story.
- Merge the universes of the two stories!
- Change the conflict of *The Hundred Dresses* (e.g., Wanda wants to draw
  motorboats, not dresses).
- Change gender of main characters and other details.

Having students come up with the choices gives them more agency over the work
and keeps things fresh. It also helps them imagine possibilities in fiction, which is
what authors do.

Being open to students' suggestions can lead to unexpected places! When a student first suggested "merging the worlds" of two stories, I was instantly skeptical.
I had a reaction of fear—*they will be unsuccessful and it will be a waste of time*, I
was thinking to myself. Reluctantly, I ended up telling them that, though I thought

it would be a much bigger challenge than the other choices, if anyone wanted to try, I would support them.

Oh, how wrong I was! Thank goodness I did not succumb to my own fear, because the students who chose that assignment wrote really interesting pieces. They felt proud for accomplishing the task, and as it turned out, once they came up with their basic idea, the writing was not particularly harder than that of the other choices.

Creative Writing Time: Everyone gets a class period to get started on their chosen task. Then, writing time continues while half of the class is in discussions of *The Hundred Dresses* with me. We do just one day of seminar-style discussion for each half group—two periods total—for this novella. (Longer novels usually get three discussion sessions per group.) Then, we spend another day on the creative writing as a whole class.

My goal in this agreement is for students to get their narrative voices flowing, for them to try out an idea in the fictional world of the story they've chosen. Having the original text of *The Hundred Dresses* to refer to is helpful, as students can begin by borrowing Estes's third-person narrative voice from the page and diverge from there. I offer one mini-lesson on paragraphing in narrative, so that students are moving away from writing in solid blocks of text.

We end up with a great variety of pieces. Apna writes a modern version of "The Treasure," with a twist. Isaac is now a workaholic father, trying to reach his dream of success as defined by money. He neglects his family, though. In the end, he realizes he's been working for the wrong dream, goes home, and embraces his children.

Jesus writes about a modern-day Isaac who follows a dream and buys a winning lottery ticket, then loses it and must find it to cash it in.

Tai writes a shocking "merge worlds" tale. We start out hearing a first-person narration from the perspective of Old Man Svenson, a mysterious minor character in *The Hundred Dresses*, who was the neighbor of Wanda. Svenson is talking about Wanda's family and what happened to them. Then, he mentions a treasure and betrayal by his best friend in the old country. If we are reading carefully, we can infer that Old Man Svenson is actually Isaac from the folk tale, now living in the United States after his treasure was stolen by his best friend, the butcher (also a minor character from the tale).

One student rewrites a scene so that Wanda stands up to the girls who are teasing her about the dresses. It's so satisfying to read, because it fulfills a common wish people have while reading the book.

We also hear a modern version of a schoolyard scene from *The Hundred Dresses* in which the three main characters are male. The teasing is about sneakers.

Brandon writes a version of "The Treasure" in which the bridge keeper ventures back through the forest with Isaac. The genre changes when night falls and they encounter monsters.

Devya writes a 17-page modern version of *The Hundred Dresses* where Wanda is a despondent teen who is bored in school and rejected by her peers. She sneaks out of class and wanders into the basement. It turns into a horror murder mystery when she happens upon a dead body.

The variety is tremendous, and the divergent and critical thinking students use to achieve their visions is inspiring. (Role 4–Writer of Literary Pieces)

→ **Share session:** Sharing our writing in the literary community is very important, but we ease into it. We do some partner sharing during the writing process. Sharing with the whole class in this first assignment is usually voluntary. We listen for enjoyment and then discuss what the student writer chose to do with the original story. That process allows students to go back into a convergent thinking process to identify the decisions their classmates made in their pieces. (Role 2–Member of Reading Community/Role 4–Writer of Literary Pieces)

<u>**Three Ways of Thinking and Analytical Writing Assessment**</u>: We spend two days reviewing the three ways of thinking, analytical paragraph structure, in preparation for an assessment. This is a convergent–dominant thinking process. In the assessment, students must categorize sample student responses to *The Hundred Dresses*, with corresponding page numbers in the book, into literal, inferential, and critical thinking. They need to explain their designation using evidence from the book. Then, they write a formal paragraph on a critical question related to *The Hundred Dresses*. (Role 1–Receptive Reader; Role 3–Literary Critic)

III. Novel Study: *The House On Mango Street*

Some years this is our first novel study, and other years it's our second one. *The House On Mango Street* by Sandra Cisneros is a novella, structured as a collection of short vignettes about the main character's life on Mango Street, on the south side of Chicago. In the first chapter, the main character, Esperanza, describes her disappointment in the house her parents buy, and she vows to one day have a house of her own. The vignettes then jump around to portray various pieces of her life and those of her neighbors and friends on Mango Street. It's not a plot or even character-driven story, though there are layers of meaning within each vignette and in the book as a whole. We focus on elements of setting, descriptive language and theme as we read.

Prologue: To get into the element of setting, we read the opening of Ray Bradbury's *The Martian Chronicles* aloud together (the first chapter and about half of the second chapter). We highlight language that describes this imagined setting of Mars. I remind students that, unlike in movies and television shows, everything in a written story must be created—painted, almost—with words.

Students who are interested in *The Martian Chronicles* can opt to read this book as a Seeker Opportunity—a component of the whole novels program for faster readers—when they finish *The House On Mango Street*. (Role 1–Receptive Reader)

→ **Setting Creative Writing Exercise:** Students then select a setting—real or imagined—and write a description of it, with the goal of making the reader vividly imagine it, as if they've been transported there. We turn this into a bit of a game, by not explicitly naming the setting in our pieces. When we share, listeners can try to figure it out themselves, like a riddle. I also suggest playing with point of view. For example, students can write a pet's description of their living room, or made-up creatures that live inside school lockers, observing school hallways during class change. Students may choose to describe a perfect day at the park, life on an island, the subway, or the inside of the refrigerator from the point of view of a rarely used condiment.

This is a one-day writing activity. Students start in class and take it home to finish. I encourage illustration. The next day, we have an optional share. Students listen and guess what setting the writer has created. This can be done in pairs, small groups, or whole class. The goal is to appreciate descriptive language of setting. (Role 4–Writer of Literary Pieces)

Reading *The House On Mango Street*: Students receive a schedule for the reading of this book. We read some of its short chapters, called vignettes, aloud together. Students also have time in class to read independently. I pair students up to read aloud to each other as well.

As students read the book, I have them notice and record their thoughts, questions, opinions, connections, etc. in what we call "Open Response" sticky notes. I also have them record topical themes (e.g., family, friendship, shame, hope, sexism) and interesting language in special sticky notes, labeled "Theme" or "Language" notes. We work on some of these special notes together to create models. Students have time to read the book in class. It is 110 pages, so it takes just over a week to read. (Role 1–Receptive Reader; Role 2–Member of Reading Community)

→ **Rewrite a Vignette**: During the reading portion of the novel study, students try writing their own version of a vignette from the book. For example, the vignette called "My Name" is all about the main character's name, where it comes from, how she got it, how she feels about it. The chapter "Boys and Girls" begins, "The boys and the girls live in separate worlds." I suggest students borrow and adapt the title and/or first line of a vignette they like, then move forward writing their own version of it, using details from their own lives. I model starting my own version of the first vignette, "The House On Mango Street," but mine is called, "The House On 92nd Street." This is an in-class exercise. We write and end class with a partner share, then volunteers reading what they have so far with the class. (Role 4–Writer of Literary Pieces)

Theme Scoring Mini-Project: Toward the end of the reading calendar, we start a mini-project to track themes across the book. As a class, we create a color-coded list of the common themes that pop up throughout the book. Then in pairs, students are assigned one to two vignettes to analyze for major and minor themes. They must create a simple visual representation of the vignette with color-coded border and lettering for major and minor themes. Then we put up all of these visuals in sequential order so that we can observe and discuss patterns in the thematic development of the story. (Role 2–Member of Literary Community; Role 3–Literary Critic)

→ **Variations on a Theme Vignettes Project**: In this creative writing project, students borrow elements they've been observing in *The House On Mango Street* and apply them in their own creative pieces. They choose a theme that is present in the book. They must write three different vignettes that each address their chosen theme in some way. They use a consistent first-person narration. They do not need to create a plot; the emphasis is on descriptive writing, use of figurative language, and developing the theme by focusing on different aspects of it in a realistic setting.

Everyone gets started on the same day, with teacher help. Then, students write independently, while half of the class discusses the novel with me. I teach a mini lesson on writing figurative language. Students must try to include figurative language in two of three vignettes. (Role 4–Writer of Literary Pieces)

Discussions of *The House on Mango Street*: I facilitate discussion with half of the class at a time. The other half works on their vignettes project. They type on Google Docs, so I am able to view their work and leave feedback that afternoon. In my inclusion classes, I have a coteacher who works with the writing students, while I am in discussions.

The next day we switch groups, and we repeat this process so that each group gets three days in discussions and three days of writing time. The homework for the writing group each night is to finish one of their vignettes. The homework for the discussion group each night is to write a paragraph on an analytical question we come up with in the group, based on the trajectory of our discussions. Discussion sessions include a dynamic mix of divergent and convergent thinking. (Role 2–Member of Literary Community; Role 3–Literary Critic)

Author Interview and Writer's Craft Collection: We conclude the discussions by watching an interview with the author, most of which are available on the internet. In some cases, we have been able to meet the author, in person or virtually. After seeing and hearing the author speak about their writing, we note the strengths of this author in a special "craft section" of the notebook. Across the year, we collect craft elements from the writers we study. (Role 3–Member of a Literary Community; Role 4–Writer of Literary Pieces)

Essay Writing: Based on the content of discussions and the homework questions students cocreated with me, I generate a list of essay prompts about the book. They may also propose one of their own, but must check it with me. Students have a day to select a question and plan, and then 1–2 days of quiet in-class writing, after which the work is collected. Later, students will look at some exemplar essays, reflect on their own writing, and set goals for what to work on in their next essays. (Role 3–Literary Critic)

→ **Vignettes Project Community Share:** We end the unit with our first formal community share. I ask every student to select one of their three vignettes to read to the class. I'll share more about how I set up the classroom to support this sharing in Chapter 3. We listen and note the theme(s) we notice and lines or sections that "stand out" for their descriptive, figurative, or emotional impact. More than anything, though, these readings are special to hear because we get to know each other on a deeper level than students normally reveal. (Role 3–Member of a Literary Community; Role 4–Writer of Literary Pieces)

IV. Novel Study: *The Absolutely True Diary of a Part-Time Indian*

Written by Sherman Alexie, this novel is the story of Junior, a Native American boy living on the Spokane Indian Reservation in Washington State, where Alexie himself grew up. The protagonist has a chance to leave the reservation to go to high school in a neighboring "white" town. He gets into conflicts with his best friend and others on the reservation as well as the students at his new school which, at core, are about identity, culture, and power. The story includes frequent comic graphics, which add content. We take about three weeks to read this book, though some students read more quickly and move on to read additional books by Alexie and other Native authors.

Prologue: We watch the film *Smoke Signals*, written and directed by Sherman Alexie, and shot on the Coeur D'Alene reservation with a Native cast. This helps students gain an understanding of the setting and culture represented in the film and the book before we start reading. It gives us a chance to discuss what a reservation is and connect to their social studies course work. I have students do a theme analysis mini-project in small groups on large chart paper. The group must identify a topical theme and three parts in the film where the theme is present. For each of these parts, they must explain what's happening and what this moment seems to be showing about the theme. Finally, they assess the three examples and write a "theme statement." I have students present their charts to the class, speaking through their theme analysis and three supporting examples. (Role 1–Reader/ Viewer; Role 2–Member of Reading Community; Role 3–Literary Critic/Scholar)

Reading *The Absolutely True Diary of a Part-Time Indian*: We focus on the element of conflict in this novel. I introduce the categories of character vs. character, character vs. self, character vs. society, and character vs. nature in a lesson that uses examples from *Smoke Signals* and the other books we've read. I introduce a process for breaking down a conflict: what does the character want or need? Who or what gets in the way? Which category of conflict is this? And, what changes, as a result?

Students continue to record sticky notes with their "Open Responses" as they read. They also use the above process to write "Conflict Notes." Later, students work in groups to analyze a conflict from the book together that has multiple layers— meaning it can be looked at as a conflict between two characters but also manifests as a conflict with society and/or the character's self. (Role 1–Reader)

→ **Conflict Story Writing:** In this project, students create a very simple story plot around a character who has a conflict. They map out the conflict using the same process they used to analyze conflicts in the novel. Each section of the visual map becomes the focus for a "chapter" of the story. They write three chapters of one page each—or more if they choose. Some students write twenty-page stories.

Everyone gets started on the same day working on their plans. I do a lesson the next day on punctuating dialogue, and we review the skill at the beginning of class for the next several days. After a day of planning and a day to get started writing all together, we begin discussions of the book in half groups, while the other half writes.

We repeat this until each group has had three discussion sessions and three writing sessions. Discussion groups have paragraphs to write for homework; the writing group has a chapter to finish each night. My homework is to review stories for half the class that wrote that day on Google Docs and leave comments.

This is our first full story of the year. Students take the opportunity to write what interests them, often in the genres they like to read (or view) most. We have everything from a bank heist gone wrong, to time travel to learn from one's past mistakes, accepting help to overcome an eating disorder, a friendship falling apart, coming out as transgender to a parent, heroism among warring tribes and deities on an island, a superpower a character would rather not have, and on and on. (Role 4–Writer of Literary Pieces)

Author Interview and Craft Summary: We watch an interview with Sherman Alexie and note his craft strengths in notebooks. (Role 3–Literary Critic/Scholar; Role 4–Writer of Literary Pieces)

Essay Writing: We review our essays and goals from the essays on *House on Mango Street*. I generate essay questions again from the discussion transcripts. Students have a day to plan and then two periods to write. I collect and set these aside again for a self-reflection exercise after this unit is done. (Role 3–Literary Critic/Scholar)

Dialogue Punctuation Quiz: I give a brief formal assessment of students' ability to punctuate dialogue correctly in a narrative. (Role 4–Writer of Literary Pieces)

➔ **Conflict Story Share**: For this project, some years, I ask students to prepare a chapter of their story to read to the class. Other years, we share in a silent reading gallery format. Everyone leaves their printed story on their desk spot with a "guest book." I add one or two extra stories, either from another class or a previous year to empty desks. Everyone gets up, moves to another student's desk, and reads their story at their own pace, leaving comments in the guest book. When they finish, they may move to any empty desk and read the story that is there. This can end with students volunteering to read a favorite section of a story they read and/or nominating a few students to read their entire story to the class.

During our remote year, we gave students the option of reading a chapter of their story to the class over Zoom, or creating a slideshow about their story idea and writing process, including challenges and a brief excerpt. (Role 4–Writer of the Literary Pieces; Role 1–Receptive Reader; Role 2–Member of Reading Community; Role 3–Literary Critic)

◊

This has been a walkthrough of three to four months of my eighth-grade English course, in which the fourth role, imaginative writing, is a central, integrated component. I haven't included every single thing we do in the class, but this comprises the main engine and bulk of our work. Many of the pieces mentioned in these descriptions will be covered in more detail in subsequent chapters.

UPDATING MY GOALS: THE WHEEL TURNS FOR EVERY STUDENT

In *Whole Novels for the Whole Class* (Sacks, 2014), I created this diagram to illustrate the process students are involved in when they read and respond to novels.

It begins with an author writing a piece of literature. The literary work is transmitted to a reader, who experiences it uniquely and has a subjective response. In a classroom community, readers then share, examine, and compare their responses. This prompts further investigation of the text to pursue questions

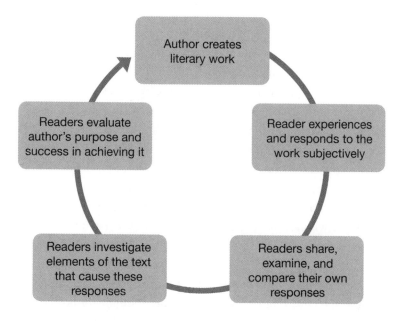

Figure 2.2: Whole Novels Reader Response and Analysis Cycle
Used with permission of John Wiley & Sons, from *Whole Novels for the Whole Class: A Student-Centered Approach*, Ariel Sacks, 2013; permission conveyed through Copyright Clearance Center, Inc.

about it and look closer at how the text is functioning to create the impact it has on readers. (e.g., Why did most of us hate this character until the final scene? Or how did this character actually die? Who pulled the trigger? Or why do some hate and others love this character?) Finally, we get to evaluating the messages of the book, the purpose the author seemed to have in writing it, and whether we agree with the messages and/or feel the author was successful. The process is aligned to standards, but we leverage the *subjective* experiences of a community of readers to pose questions and identify purposes for closely reading and analyzing the work.

In this vision, the end point is formal critique and evaluation of a novel, the author's purpose, their craft choices, and their impact.

During the pandemic summer of 2020, I was leading a virtual workshop on whole novels for the staff at a middle school. They were radically changing their program to allow one teacher to teach the same group of students in person all day long to minimize the possible spread of the virus. This meant all teachers suddenly needed to teach English. When I presented the above image, one of teachers asked, "But, is that the only place the cycle could lead to? Aren't there other possibilities?" I loved this question. She was absolutely right that analysis and evaluation as the end point is a limited way to conceive of literature study. It was probably not coincidental that this teacher was an art teacher.

This teacher's question along with my own experiences have led me to see that within this same cycle, there can and should be a concurrent process that moves toward students writing their own imaginative pieces, then responding to each other's work, and reflecting on their impacts.

When we add students' creative writing to the cycle, it's as if they jump into the diagram and take another lap around it. Empowered by their own imaginations, they become the author named in the first step, "Author creates literary work," as the cycle makes its next turn. The steps that follow—readers experiencing the author's story, sharing responses, examining the elements, critiquing the decisions and messages in the story—are all now in relation to the original creation of a student writer, rather than a professional author.

In this way, the wheel turns for each student in the class, simultaneously, as if it has twenty-odd gears. Students practice the same skills of critiquing elements of the professional author's writing on their classmates' work. They get to reflect on their own decisions as writers and the way they've impacted their peers. They get to be powerful and vulnerable at the same time. It is demanding and fulfilling for both mind and soul.

Later, when students jump out of the author role and read a new book, they have a more acute lens through which to view the work, and an appreciation for the skills and ingenuity of great writers.

We can apply this same concept to music. Analyzing the structure of a symphony as a listener may not help you very much in playing in an orchestra. But, having played in an orchestra gives us a significant advantage in taking apart what we are hearing when we listen to an orchestra. We can much more easily pick out the distinct voices of instruments. The cadences and dynamics are more obvious when you have actually followed a conductor's lead as a musician. The difference between adagio and allegro are made concrete when you've played both many times.

Students start having more intense experiences as they read now that they are reading as writers as well. The reading, writing, speaking, and listening aspects of English Language Arts become far more connected. Finally, with students contributing creatively as well as analytically, the classroom community and each student's role within it takes on a more inclusive and empowering shape.

3

Empowering Students' Social-Emotional Development

I DISTINCTLY RECALL when my daughter, as a baby, became conscious enough of her surroundings and her own body to decide she hated her car seat. She would be perfectly happy until the car door opened, and it was time to strap her into that contraption. The howls of protest were formidable and unnerving!

Children instinctually grasp for autonomy—as much as they can handle within an overall supportive environment—to explore and practice the things that interest them. Those interests almost always serve a developmental function. Around that time, my daughter was practicing body movements leading up to crawling. No one told her she needed to do those things; the drive is innate.

When young people feel their autonomy threatened, they do what they can to defend it. In my daughter's case, the car seat cramped her style, and she used the only tool she had against its oppressive control—her cry. She lost the battle for obvious reasons; safety had to prevail. But know this: if there were any safe alternative to forcing her into that car seat, I would have signed up so fast! Her cry was that effective. I'm sure many parents have been faced with that very same thought.

When children get older, they seek more autonomy; they become more aware of the places they have power and the places they don't, and they become more sophisticated in the strategies they use to get it. The kinds of power they want change with age as well. When, at age three, my daughter's pediatrician asked her which ear she wanted her to check first at an annual visit, the choice sparked her interest. The strategy is developmentally appropriate, and my daughter bought in. An eight-year-old, who can tie her own shoes and read a book, would probably not find that a meaningful opportunity to practice autonomy, and a twelve-year-old, who is concerned with identity and social hierarchy, might dismiss the question with some prime sarcasm.

My mentor, Madeleine Ray, has always been insightful about children and power dynamics. "You want to know why so many kids love video games so much?" she asked our conference group of pre-service teachers at Bank Street College in 2005. Yes, we sure did want to know. The typical answers to this question tend to be soft putdowns, reflecting a deficit lens: they're lazy; they are addicted; they don't know how to do anything else; they don't care to do anything else.

"Power," Madeleine said, simply. It made sense. In video games, young people get to make decisions that, in the virtual world of the game, are important. They carry "life or death" consequences, though the context is overall a safe one (at least in the physical sense). They get to practice decision-making and become more effective at it through repetition.

Practicing decision-making is what children want to do in real life, but they often lack positive outlets for doing so. There are some decisions that are not age-appropriate for kids to make, of course, like my daughter with her car seat. Other times, adults exert unnecessary amounts of control over young people for various reasons.

Remember wanting to be older so you could decide to eat cake whenever you wanted? Presumably, by the time you were old enough to decide, you understood something about nutrition and the tradeoffs involved. On the other hand, did you ever know a child who had good reason to want to run away from home, but couldn't because they also depended on that home, and where else would they go?

In both cases, children come to know that they lack power—and that greater independence is key to gaining the power they want. The skills that allow independence are attained through practice, taking risks, making decisions, and learning from what happens. School can and should be a safe and exciting place for young people to develop their independence through age-appropriate activities. And when classrooms don't offer ways for students to develop their power, they often seek it out in unproductive or unhealthy ways.

One of the great benefits of letting students write imaginative pieces of their own is that we put substantial decision-making power in their hands. This power changes and enriches students' relationships to writing and literature; it shifts social dynamics in the classroom when students share their writing; and it becomes a vehicle for students to explore their identities, possibilities, and challenges in the relative safety of the virtual world.

In this chapter I will discuss:

- The nature of the power inherent in creative storytelling
- How we can create conditions that support imaginative risk-taking
- Embracing the dual purposes of supporting academic and social–emotional growth
- How to respond when students choose to write about traumatic experiences

STUDENTS FEELING POWERFUL IN THE DRIVER'S SEAT

One year, I had a class of twenty-eight eighth-graders, twenty-three of whom were boys. It also happened that the visible social leaders in the class were all male and tended to act out in ways that challenged my authority and expectations of them. Each of these six or so leaders had their own set of circumstances. They were not especially similar, but for the fact that they wielded influence over other students and were often motivated to derail the class.

Tommy, I remember, was one of the influencers. He was so angry—among other things, about a lack of attention from his busy parents—that he lashed out in school. He had good days and bad days. Sometimes he arrived in a good mood. He would get excited about his work and motivate a bunch of his classmates along with him. He beamed when he received recognition for his effort and ideas. Other days, he was in a bad mood. He wouldn't say hello at the door and resisted any of my efforts to connect. He would carry on loud off-topic conversations with classmates in the middle of class. He ignored the usual redirections, and if I forced the issue, he was likely to erupt in anger. Sometimes he'd quietly pick on other students who were trying to work. Other days he arrived so tired, I had to continually try to keep him from sleeping. Tommy was white and nearly six feet tall with a muscular build at age thirteen. He was treated as a young man by strangers, but was as inexperienced and emotionally young as the rest of his peers.

Raymond faced a different set of challenges. Gang violence was a reality in the area where he lived. We knew that he risked being beaten up on his way home if he walked past dark, which was the case in the winter when he stayed late to participate in sports. With his classmates, he was kindhearted and friendly. Everyone knew his charisma and infectious smile. For all his smiles, Raymond had a deep sadness; he'd lost people close to him to gun violence and incarceration, and he was worried about his future.

Adding to the turmoil, Raymond struggled to read. He had experienced interrupted schooling while he lived in a rural area of Ecuador during three crucial years while his peers were learning to read. His education and literacy were entirely in English, but at home his family spoke Spanish. He had some decoding skills, but the effort it took him to maneuver through all the reading required in a school day was often more than he could stand. The supports at our school did not seem to be enough.

His school identity vacillated wildly between bright-eyed optimism—being eager to please and make himself heard—and anger and defeat—"I hate school; there's no point." Probably every adult in the building tried convincing Raymond that with consistent effort, he could grow and succeed, and the work would eventually get easier. Somewhere in these conversations, he often made a comment like, "I'm probably gonna die anyways, or go to jail. What's the point?" He stared straight at you when he said this, neither smiling, nor frowning.

Under the right circumstances, with the right supports, he made progress in his assignments, but the social makeup of this particular class presented extra obstacles for him. If Tommy or any of the other leaders started creating distractions, Raymond jumped at the chance to catch a break from his work.

I saw this group of leaders vying for power, challenging my authority and the general expectations of the school, and competing with one another to determine who had the most influence. Meanwhile, other students were frustrated and angry with them—and at me, for not being able to set firm limits.

It was a tough year. I was not a new teacher, and I thought I had some classroom management chops, but this class caused me to doubt myself daily. My approach to classroom management relies substantially on fostering a community among my students, who then *choose* to take part, to accept my leadership, and to assume some leadership of it as well. I believe this approach prepares students to participate actively in a democratic society. It also supports the kind of collaborative and critical academic work that develops intellect and crucial skills in today's job market.

However, for most of the year I could not figure out how to create a community with this group. I tried many different tools, some of which worked, but only temporarily.

I tried a more top-down approach to behavior management, for example. But a more top-down model favors more controlled, individual processes—and an overemphasis on convergent thinking. The shift seemed to improve matters for a short period of time, but soon it limited the kind of work we could do. The work became boring for students and that set the distractions and frustration cycle right back in motion.

Meanwhile, I'd set aside some of my key principles to make that change, so the steps forward we took in productivity and decorum were also steps backward in terms of students taking ownership of their work and community. Back to square one.

I never really solved the puzzle of that class, but the brightest moments always came on the days in which students were involved in imaginative writing. Throughout the year, we worked on several shorter pieces and took the time to share them. Once the students got into the writing process and past the fear of "getting started," those days were joyous. I took note of this, but didn't make any bigger changes in response. (This was several years before the year that led me to write this book.)

At the end of the year, we conducted a whole novel study of Orwell's *Animal Farm*, which the class appreciated most of any book. For those who haven't read it, *Animal Farm* is an allegory in which farm animals overthrow their human owner and attempt to create an egalitarian utopia—"Animal power!" they cry. One of the pigs carves out a leadership role for himself. Gradually, he becomes a dictator and establishes pigs as the ruling class. At the end, the pigs are indistinguishable in their behavior and values from the humans who ruled before them, and life for the other animals is as bad or worse than it had been before the revolution.

Following this novel study, we embarked on a longer fiction project. Borrowing the major theme of power from the novel, each student would write an original story that explored in some way a theme of power. Together, we built a general plot framework, based on novels we'd read and some picture books I introduced. Students came up with their own concepts, wrote outlines, and spent about two weeks writing.

This was June. Given the year they'd had and the general dynamics of middle school behavior in June, especially "graduating" eighth-graders, this could have been our most frustrating, raucous two weeks ever. Instead, it was our best two-week period of the year. The feeling in the classroom was a relaxed, productive hum, with occasional humorous interruptions. For once, though, such interruptions didn't throw everyone off track.

Students' engagement in this creative process was more powerful than the urge to play the social hierarchy game of the classroom. The reason for this, I believe, is that writing fiction offers a great deal of power to the author. A video game creates a virtual reality and offers a player a role as a character. In fiction writing, the author plays god, creating the virtual reality and the fates of everyone in it. I believe that when my students entered deeply into this role, they no longer felt the need to grab at power in other ways.

This example shows how creative control was healing for a particularly needy and vocal group of students; but every child needs empowerment. Even those who appear to be adept at school and comfortable within its structures struggle inside in ways they might not share with us. All children have a developmental need to shape their autonomy and identity under safe parameters. Fiction writing answers that call for adolescents like little else.

The Risk and Empowerment of a Creative Stance

What is the power inherent in storytelling and story creation? How, exactly, does a student's sense of their own power shift when they transition from reading, responding, and critiquing to actually writing fiction? Remember, this shift is fairly rare in schools, especially past elementary grades.

I personally experienced a similar shift in a totally unexpected context. I was working with a personal coach, whose help I needed in making an overwhelming life decision. The coaching was a three-month process. A key piece of the work turned out to be finding ways to connect with my core self in order to make the decision that was most aligned with that person. (It actually worked, by the way!)

Sometime in the third month, I had a vivid dream. I don't have these often, so when I do I try to tease out their significance. I "read" the dream as a message of sorts from my own psyche. In a ton of detail, I recounted it to my coach. It involved a beach, three lionesses walking along the sand, and an enormous sea dinosaur prowling in the shallow water of the ocean shore.

In my description, I was able to put language to the feeling the dream gave me. Looking at these powerful creatures, which seemed to be blocking my path toward the water, I was filled with an intense mixture of fear and awe. Articulating that alone was helpful. My coach asked me what I thought the various characters might represent. Again, it was helpful to probe those layers.

I desperately hoped the conversation would lead to her offering an answer to the big question on my mind: *What did the dream mean? What was it telling me to do?*

She caught me completely by surprise when, instead, she asked, "So, if you were to direct the rest of this dream, what would you make happen?" I laughed, because I would never have asked this question of myself, and that amused me for some reason. I had been so caught up in interpreting the dream, as if that were the only option for how to handle it. Her question challenged me to work differently with the material I had, to be both imaginative and true to myself.

An answer to her question popped into my head almost immediately, but it seemed a little crazy; I dismissed it. I took some time to think further, but I ended up returning to that very first inclination. In my continuation of the dream, I took a walk with the lionesses on land, and then I approached the sea dinosaur, climbed on its back, and took a ride in the ocean. In both cases, I took what felt like huge risks to move past my fear to engage with the creatures.

My imaginative risk-taking occurred on two levels: first, as a character in the dream world, I risked my physical safety; but also, as a writer or creator, I was trying something that seemed "unrealistic" or even "stupid" to my rational side. I risked my own self-judgment and, in my mind, that of my coach. In my extended dream, each relationship unfolded in its own way and served a figurative purpose in relation to my life circumstances. I had to overcome my fear and judgment to connect with the power of these creatures, and, thereby (in my imagination), develop aspects of my own power.

"Rereading," discussing, and interpreting my original dream helped me make meaning of it and think about my situation through the lens of the dream, but that lens was more of a *mirror* than a *map* for my life. Creating the rest of the story, however, helped me see beyond my "stuck" place to a stronger version of myself. It was a little like activating a superpower. In superhero stories, the power is something that's always been there, but finding it is a process of self-discovery and evolution.

My experience rewriting the dream parallels what I see happen for some of my students when they write a fictional story that, by virtue of their own choices, explores an aspect of who they are. As they make decisions in the virtual world, they are processing and articulating things they often wouldn't dare to do in the real world.

For example, I have had more than one student who seems to be struggling with their gender or sexuality choose to write a story about a character who comes out as gay or trans. The details may be imagined, but the conflict is intimate for the student. Just playing out this story and being able to look at it on the page is empowering. But kicking it up a notch, some students have read their stories to the class—and received heartfelt applause!

I remember a student who struggled with feelings of insecurity around his family's financial situation—especially the external signs of it, like not having new clothes. He decided to write a story in which the protagonist is a "rich" teenager who meets a homeless teen. Despite the protagonist's disapproving parents, the rich teen decides to befriend the poor teen, and the two begin an adventure.

This student used his imaginative writing to do a brilliant thing: through his main characters and their exaggerated rich/poor dynamic, he created the compassion for himself that he needed from the kind of person he feared would never offer it in real life.

Neuroscientists have found that stories function as virtual experiences that are stored in the brain just like real memories are. The "experience" of embodying the rich teen who did *not* judge the poor teen helped my student shift the negative image he had of himself. Incidentally, this student also struggled with insecurities about his academic skills, but he emerged from this assignment very proud of his work. The academic and social–emotional aspects of school are always connected.

The ability to make choices, to play out future possibilities, imagine consequences, and be heard through their creative writing empowers young people, who often have limited power in their own lives—by virtue of being young, as well as other individual and societal circumstances. I've noticed a pattern of students flipping a situation that's causing fear to one that vitalizes through storytelling. Creative power builds us up and can heal in a multitude of ways.

For children who are dealing with trauma, mental illness, or facing systemic oppression, finding their intrinsic power is an even more urgent need, because their power is continually undermined by the adversity in their lives. Engaging in imaginative writing, by its very nature, allows us to support the social–emotional development of our students in so many different ways, without dropping academic work.

CREATING CONDITIONS FOR CREATIVE RISK-TAKING

All of this potential has profound implications for our teaching, the way we position ourselves as guides, instructors, and mentors, and the way we respond to students. While it opens the door, simply adding a creative writing assignment to each novel study isn't sufficient to guarantee best results.

In order for students to benefit most from creative work, to develop their power in that context across a year, they need to feel comfortable taking risks in our classrooms. Creative writing practice on its own helps students take risks, but the conditions surrounding the work, the way a student feels in our class, can expand or hinder their willingness to open their imaginations. Their feelings are both generated in each moment *and* built cumulatively over time—a mix of past and present experiences in school, in our subject, and in our particular class. Our leadership style and the messages we send through our choices influence students' mindsets.

Here are some general guidelines for building a safe, trusting space for students from day one, not specific to creative writing work. For this section, I tapped the collective knowledge of accomplished teachers I connect with online. Many I know from the former Teacher Leaders Network, a national group run by Center for Teaching Quality, and others are former colleagues in NYC schools or classmates of mine at Bank Street College.

One note: I'm well aware that creating an emotionally safe environment in school is easier said than done, as my earlier example of a challenging class shows. We never finish learning how to do this, because groups of humans are so complex and varied. What I do know is that I kept trying with that group. I never gave up what seemed to be in my locus of control, and, at the very least, my efforts allowed for some excellent days now and then. There's always something to try, and demonstrating perseverance is also a lesson we teach through our example.

Build a Safe Space for Risk-Taking

Model being wrong. We send messages to students through our own behavior, whether we're conscious of them or not. For students to feel comfortable being wrong, we need to counter longstanding traditions that shame students. We can start with ourselves.

- When you find you're wrong about something in class, don't try to cover it up or move forward too quickly—embrace it as a teachable moment! Show how you can learn from this mistake, be curious about it, laugh at yourself if it fits the situation, apologize if that's appropriate, and invite students to help you figure out what's correct or works best.
- Ask for help: For example, after misspelling a word, I might say, "Can somebody look up the spelling of 'definitely' for us right now, because nothing looks right as I'm writing it on the board! I'm confused!"
- Apologize and move on: After raising my voice at the class, I have said, "I'm sorry, I was too harsh on you all. I see now that tone wasn't helpful. Could we take a deep breath and return to the activity for five more minutes, everyone putting in their best focus?"

Make "being wrong" part of the learning routine. When a student misunderstands something, if we embrace it, the question or mistake creates an opportunity for everyone to learn and for us to teach better.

- There is a famous video on The Teaching Channel called "My Favorite No," which has inspired many teachers to share, celebrate, and talk through a great "mistake" made by a student (omitting the student's name). Check out the video to get ideas.
- Instead of focusing on sharing correct responses to questions or perfect exemplars, NBCT kindergarten teacher in Los Angeles, Jane Ching Fung, selects work that is "almost there," again without the student's name. The class works together to "highlight the positives and then add the one thing they could do to make the work a YES."
- Another California NBCT, David Cohen, shares that in his AP English class, when a conversation stalls—perhaps because students feel uncertain and insecure to take a risk—he asks for students to share definitely wrong answers, then notes that "everything is okay" even after wrong answers arise, and we applaud whoever has volunteered to be wrong.

Model taking risks. If everything appears to go exactly as planned each day, students don't get to see the creative risk-taking that is surely part of every teacher's practice.

- Instead of pretending our in-the-moment changes are part of the plan, invite students into the process sometimes, revealing the risk you're taking:

"I have an idea . . . instead of sharing all together right now, could we try breaking into groups for five minutes first? I'm not sure whether to have to you share with students who wrote on the same topic or different topics first. Any thoughts on this?" I might say.

- Or I might share that "I've never read this book with students before, and I'm not sure what you will think of it. I'm curious and a little nervous," which is how it feels to take a healthy risk.

Prioritize community in the classroom. How we treat one another and how we respond when someone is harmed is key to whether the students perceive our classroom to be safe for them.

- Deanna McBeath, a middle school STEM teacher in Chicago and a former classmate of mine at Bank Street, recommends something that our mentor, Madeleine Ray, emphasized relentlessly: "Consistently model repairing social–emotional ruptures in the moment, making this a priority over academic curriculum especially early in the year . . . . Mainly I call students out in the moment and coach them on how to reframe their language to make it more kind—anytime I hear something that is potentially an 'ouch/oops' moment that needs addressing or reframing, I help them do that right when it happens." Deanna has trained with Responsive Classroom and recommends their resources for teachers wanting more information on this kind of approach. I've trained with Developmental Designs on similar content and recommend their workshops.
- Deanna also recommends "cultivating a culture of positive good humor and camaraderie through laughter and games." I heartily agree. I keep a collection of old school board games in my classroom closet. I'm always surprised how much fun a random period (after a testing day, for example) of board game playing is, elevating our moods and relationships. We also play a whole-class version of Taboo which brings out laughter and teamwork.

Make your classroom inclusive and safe for students from marginalized groups. I'm going to delve into this big topic more as it relates to teaching literary writing in the next chapter. In general, here are some suggestions.

- Use and teach inclusive language that recognizes and embraces differences in the room. Saying "families" or "caregivers" instead of "parents" helps remove stigma and feelings of alienation for students who aren't raised by their parents. Using students' preferred pronouns and learning to pronounce all names correctly are necessary steps to forming positive relationships with the students in question *and* setting a tone of respect and belonging to everyone in the room.

- Address it when hurtful language is used between students. If a student uses the word "gay" as a putdown, for example, address it right away. "First of all, no one can speak for anyone else's sexuality. Each person is welcome to speak only for themselves," I begin, which cuts a lot of the tension already. "Secondly, it sounded like you used that as a putdown, and that makes me sad. We absolutely can't have that here. Do you know why?" Have a conversation about how people of all sexuality and genders as well as race, religion, and ability are welcome in our school and classroom. This may seem obvious, but speaking it makes a difference.
- Don't allow students to use the "n-word" or other racial slurs in class, even among themselves—and don't read these words out loud if they show up in texts either. (Check out the chapter on this in Dr. Kimberly Parker's book, *Literacy Is Liberation: Working Toward Justice Through Culturally Relevant Teaching*.)
- What students say outside of school is not in our control, but we can set clear norms for language use in our classes and hallways. Most schools have rules in a handbook about discriminatory language, but having a conversation and even doing research together about why—where these words come from and how they've been used to dehumanize, exclude, and harm whole groups of people—provide important context for students to understand and buy in to the rules.

Build choice and decision-making into students' work on a regular basis. Students need practice making choices, managing their time and resources, and identifying their questions. This is simply good practice for engaging students fully in their education and preparing them for the real world.

- Many wonderful educators have shared methods for allowing students greater choice in their learning. Check out the book list on the next page for more resources.
- Experience making choices in learning builds comfort with taking risks. It's part of a project-based or student-centered learning process. Deanna describes, "So many students are so used to being told exactly what to do every second of the day that they don't know how to self-initiate or ideate in relation to their schoolwork. Sometimes they need several days of me steadfastly refusing to tell them exactly what to do on a project before they kick into action and follow through on one of their ideas." We need to give them practice, in small and large doses, with this exact struggle across the year, so they learn to move through uncertainty and act on their ideas.

Strive to be a collaborative problem-solver rather than a punisher (or a rewarder).

Again, this is a big topic. I'm not a purist—I believe punishment-like consequences are sometimes appropriate. However, this is the approach I believe generally benefits students as people and learners, as well as the imaginative work of this book.

- A culture that relies on punishment tends to inhibit students in critical thinking and creativity. Students look for the right and wrong things to do and say, rather than developing self-awareness within the context of the school community and their learning tasks.

- Adolescents, in particular, often respond to a punitive system by thinking critically about the system, looking for hypocrisy or unfairness among its upholders, for holes to get around rules and assert power that way. When punishments are strictly doled out, we shut down conversation about the issues at hand and the result lacks student voice.

- Many "misbehaviors" can be reframed as opportunities to collaboratively problem solve. For example, student "J" has just asked a question that makes it clear they weren't listening to my directions—at all. This is extremely annoying to me, and I'm tempted to reprimand J, but instead I want to publicly seize this teachable moment, since it was a very public error and other students are rolling their eyes at J's gaffe. I say, "Look, everyone has been in J's situation before—you weren't paying attention for whatever reason, and then you have an important question to ask. This even happens to adults sometimes in meetings, myself included. What advice can we give J or any one of us for how to best handle this situation next time?" Students offer excellent suggestions about polite and discreet ways to get what they need in this situation.

- My choice helps students activate compassion rather than judgment, and critical thinking with a purpose rather than a simplistic right–wrong mindset. Had I responded with a reprimand, I would have lost the chance to problem solve with the class. J would have felt shame, and this could have a negative ripple effect for J and other students about asking questions in my class. It sends a message that the mistake was not allowable, and that it's better to be quiet than risk a mistake.

Book List for Building a Safe Classroom Space

- *Building a Community of Self-Motivated Learners: Strategies to Help Students Thrive in School and Beyond* by Larry Ferlazzo
- *Punished by Rewards* by Alfie Kohn
- Developmental Designs—*Origins Curriculum*

- *Discipline Over Punishment: Successes and Struggles With Restorative Justice In Schools* by Trevor Gardner
- *DIY Project Based Learning For ELA and History* and *Just Ask Us: Kids Speak Out On Student Engagement* by Heather Walport-Gawron (aka Tweenteacher)
- *Textured Teaching: A Framework For Culturally Sustaining Practices* by Lorena German
- *Shift This! How to Implement Gradual Changes For Massive Impact in Your Classroom* by Joy Kirr
- *Literacy Is Liberation: Working Toward Justice Through Culturally Relevant Teaching* by Dr. Kimberly Parker
- *Assessing with Respect: Every Day Practices That Meet Students' Social and Emotional Needs* by Starr Sackstein
- *The Flexible ELA Classroom: Practical Tools for Differentiated Instruction in Grades 4–8* by Amber Chandler
- *Meet Me in the Middle: Becoming an Accomplished Middle Level Teacher* by Rick Wormeli

TAKING RISKS, EXPLORING POSSIBILITIES, AND FACING CHALLENGES IN THE SAFETY OF THE VIRTUAL WORLD

When we give decision-making power to students and support their imaginative risk-taking, outcomes are less predictable, of course. They require us to listen and observe students carefully and weigh our priorities when we respond. I spoke to my former colleague and fellow Bank Street graduate, Renata Robinson-Glenn, who teaches social studies and incorporates fiction writing into her curriculum throughout the year. She said to me, "Do you know why so many teachers don't teach creative writing more than a little bit? Because they don't want to deal with what comes out when they do . . . when students write what's on their minds and what they're going through. It can be a lot to handle." How to deal with what comes out truly is a learning process for teachers and requires a slightly different mindset than working on expository writing normally does.

The stories students write in my class are almost never explicitly autobiographical, but students explore situations that matter to them. They usually reflect elements of the worlds they actually know and live in—but in the story world, they can take risks and determine fates they wouldn't be able to do in the real world.

To make the most of this, we need to be aware that students are doing work that serves an academic purpose and, usually, a personal one too. This is always true, but more explicitly so in imaginative writing. Through virtual worlds, students may be building their identities and exploring problems close to them. The ambiguity of fact and fantasy in the virtual world makes it a less vulnerable place for young people to explore personal issues than in nonfiction forms like memoir. In fact, I tell students, fiction is a place where it's actually appropriate to lie! Tell your biggest, best lie if you want! As Albert Camus said, "Fiction is the lie through which we tell the truth."

Our role as teachers in the *personal* aspect of our students' fiction writing is mostly as a kind witness to their process; but being conscious of it and knowing the value of students' creative exploration of complex issues in fiction helps to inform how we respond.

Raymond

Here's an example of a situation where the fictional and real worlds collided intensely in my classroom. We were working on those "power"-themed stories in the class I described to you earlier, after reading *Animal Farm*. Raymond (remember him?) was sitting next to Jose. Jose had a mostly happy-go-lucky attitude in school, and the one thing we all knew about him was that he wanted to be a police officer like his uncle. He reminded us of this almost daily. He wrote "police officer" on most of his notebooks, alongside his name. He and Raymond were casual buddies in class.

I already knew Jose was writing a story about a young man who became a police officer, because he asked me as soon as he began the project if he could write about a police officer. I was pretty sure he knew he didn't need my permission to make that decision, but I assumed he asked me because he wanted those around him to know.

When I took a look at Raymond's plot outline, I saw that he'd gotten farther than most of his classmates in mapping out the rising action. He was almost at the climax. I asked him to tell me about his story. "It's about this kid," he began. "He lives in a tough neighborhood, and he wants to run away from home and join a gang." He paused and looked at me as if to check if I was going to object this topic. I could have asked a million questions, but I wanted to hear from him first.

I gave him a look to say, "Go on, I'm listening."

"So, he joins the gang, and at first it's good," Raymond continued. "But then he gets in trouble with the police." Raymond's voice got louder. Though he began at a whisper, his volume was now high enough for the entire class to hear . . . and he had their rapt attention. For better or worse, I did not ask him to lower his voice.

"The police are chasing me," Raymond continued, unconsciously making the switch to first person. "And then they chase me down an alley way. But I have a gun . . . . And then I shoot! And I kill Jose!" He stopped talking and turned to me with a look of surprise at what he'd just said. This was not written on his paper.

He and I were both aware of the class and Jose sitting right next to him. I froze, too, my thoughts racing. I was worried about what the rest of the class was feeling. Part of me wanted to admonish Raymond for suggesting violence toward another student, but something didn't feel right about that.

Then, Raymond broke the silence. He put his arm around Jose, and gave him a vigorous shake of a hug. "You know I love you, Jose," he said with his winning smile, arm still around him. Jose grinned right back and put his arm around Raymond.

"Of course, man. You know I love you too," he said.

There was palpable shock and relief in the classroom. In this moment, both Raymond and Jose had played through in their imaginations one dramatic possibility for how their paths could cross in the future, for an audience of their peers. I think we were all equally aware that the gunshots could have gone in the other direction as well. This was June of the summer police shot an unarmed teenager named Michael Brown in Ferguson, Missouri, which sparked national attention on police brutality toward people of color and the Black Lives Matter movement. It was theater of the realest kind—the kind that may only happen in classrooms, in which teachers have the rare privilege of playing a role. Though my role was mostly passive, I had given students space to imagine, and I had allowed Raymond to share with a diverse audience.

> In fiction, students can learn from taking risks that have personal significance. This helps develop what CASEL defines as **responsible decision-making**: "**The abilities to make caring and constructive choices about personal behavior and social interactions across diverse situations.** This includes the capacities to consider ethical standards and safety concerns, and to evaluate the benefits and consequences of various actions for personal, social, and collective well-being."

One such consequence was the way that choice could alter his relationships with many of the people he was friendly with at school. The chance for Raymond to take that risk in his writing mind and share aloud with Jose and the rest of the class led to a loving and empowered outcome. Some years later, when I no longer worked at that school, I received an email with a graduation announcement and class photo for this group of students. Scanning it, I spotted Raymond and Jose standing right next to each other in caps and gowns, tall and grown up, smiling ear to ear. My heart swelled, especially for Raymond, who had not given up on school.

I share this story as an example of how young people can explore possibilities in their writing, but also as an example of an unpredictable moment that challenged me as a teacher. (At the time, I was blogging regularly, and so I wrote about it right away. That is how I remember the details pretty well.)

My choices that day mattered in the outcome. Let me unpack a few of those.

I don't censor story content. I tell students, any idea is a good idea if you're willing to commit to it. I make a point to show them I mean it. "Oh, your protagonist is an egg? Cool! Tell me about it." I have a few minimally invasive rules that are designed to help students avoid common pitfalls (covered in Chapter 5), but the topics and details of stories are the domain of each student writer. In Raymond's case, I think he wondered briefly if his topic was "school-appropriate." "Literature is life," I also tell students. "Authors write about real life and imaginary life and so can you." The only rule Raymond did break in his think-aloud of his story plan is using names of classmates for characters, which I would remind him of later.

I keep in mind the social–emotional significance of the writing experience and feel free to prioritize this when I believe it will benefit the student. Most teachers care on a deep level about their students' social–emotional development; however, our primary and default role is as a teacher of our academic subject. For that reason, it's important to consciously give ourselves permission at times to focus on a students' personal development in our class. These two sides are not separate anyway, but our classroom decisions often favor academic processes over social or personal ones. What we pay attention to grows, though. Our attention to the social and emotional growth of our students creates more growth . . . and that growth improves academic outcomes as well.

As Raymond shared his story idea with me, raising his voice enough so that the whole room could hear, I made an intuitive choice not to prompt him to lower his voice. Normally, since students were working independently, I'd have wanted this to be in a quieter tone so as not to distract the others. Given Raymond's delicate, often strained relationship with his work, his excitement about this project seemed more important in that moment than the need for a quiet work space. I felt that his enthusiasm could have a positive effect on others in the class and that him having an audience for his story idea, whether he was consciously looking for it or not, could be motivating for him.

And so, I weighed my options in a split second and took a risk, which we do all the time in teaching. When Raymond went off-script and said, "And then I shoot Jose," I was shocked. I worried I had made a wrong choice and didn't know how to remedy it. I think Raymond, too, was intuitive in that moment, and he saved it as only he could with a loving gesture toward Jose. I'm grateful to him for that. If this had happened today, I might have opened up a class discussion about the interaction, allowing students to speak on the thoughts and questions it brought up.

Don't assume students' fiction is autobiographical; don't assume it isn't. Writing stories has often been a vehicle for my students to experiment with the choices they are grappling with in their real lives. The genre allows them to do this without the vulnerability of writing directly about their most personal dilemmas. For the most part, I've found that students instinctively understand this about the genre. Some aspects of a story might reflect the writer's own life and other aspects are made up. They also seem to understand that parsing these distinctions isn't important. I've never, in nineteen years of teaching, had a student pressure a classmate to reveal which parts of their story were real. As a pattern, that's kind of remarkable. It speaks to the universality of our relationships to stories and our understanding of how they function. It helps that we see this same mix of real and imagined details in the literature we read by professional authors when we listen to them speak about their work in interviews.

Playing out hypothetical scenarios in story form helps young people better understand themselves and their predicaments, and prepare for the future. A socially isolated child, for example, wrote an incredible story about a character who retreats daily to an imaginary world where she enjoys the company of a long-time imaginary friend. She retreats further and further into this pretend world and isolates herself from friends and family. Until one day, the imaginary world literally cracks and her imaginary friend disappears. She's stuck in the real world and must gather up the courage to face it. Although I doubt my student had an actual imaginary friend in middle school, I believe she created a kind of mirror for her isolation in this character and then played with the possibility of coming out of her figurative silo. I believe that the work she did to envision this and write through the fear, probably moved her closer to the reality of doing so.

I remember the student whose main character builds up the courage to tell her mother to stop pressuring her to be thin. I'll never know for sure if that was her personal situation, or one she had seen in someone else, or just something that seemed important in the world—but I know she chose to imagine it with a great deal of empathy. She played through that conflict in story form so convincingly that I know the imaginative work will serve her in that situation or a similar one down the line. Fiction is such a powerful place to explore the world, our identities, and the choices that form them.

At the same time, I remember a student writing about a main character who is the son of a high-level drug dealer in a "cartel" type organization. He wrote convincingly of the emotions of trying to have a "normal" teenage life, while the family was hiding this dramatic other reality. I was vaguely curious as to whether any of this reflected the students' actual circumstances. I mentioned it to another teacher who knew the family better. My colleague laughed. "Not a chance!" she said. "As far from it as you can imagine." As I got to know the student better over the year, I could also laugh at myself for wondering this. And I discovered he was a huge fan of the show "Narcos." Sometimes students write from life; sometimes they imitate stories they enjoy, which have nothing to do with their own lives; and sometimes there is a combination. I share this just to balance out the picture—to remind us to keep our judgments and assumptions at bay.

The National Board for Professional Teaching Standards recognizes the aspect of accomplished teaching that is knowing our students and supporting them as growing humans, and the special potential of our subject for doing so. In the set of standards specific to teaching English to early adolescents, the first one includes this description:

> To build trusting relationships with their students, accomplished English Language Arts teachers honor their students' passions and concerns . . . . Accomplished teachers use [their knowledge of students] to establish appropriate outlets as needed for students. For example, a student struggling with a loved one who is experiencing a terminal illness might benefit from reading a novel about a character in a similar situation, and might even use the novel as the gateway to conversations with the teacher about this issue. However, accomplished teachers are sensitive to their students' individual temperaments; they understand when to intervene directly and when to act more reticent in order to respect a student's privacy. Although teachers observe professional boundaries and remain in adult roles in all relationships with students, their professional status does not prevent them from being accessible, caring, and eager to share knowledge that will empower students. (p. 23)

→ **Exercise:** Think of a time you paused your academic objective to give space to the social–emotional growth of a student or group of students. Describe it. How did your choice impact the student(s)?

THE POWER OF CREATIVITY IN HEALING TRAUMA: LESSONS FROM THE MEDICAL PROFESSION

A great many of our students have experienced trauma in their lives. According to the U.S. Department of Health and Human Services' National Child Traumatic Stress Initiative, more than two-thirds of young people reported at least one traumatic event by the age of sixteen, which includes physical, sexual, or psychological abuse; community or domestic violence; neglect; sudden loss of a loved one; natural disaster; or war. One in seven young people reported experiencing a form of child abuse.

Traumatic stress can weigh heavily on children and adolescents as they form their identities and world views, relationships, cognitive skills, and school habits. While schools alone cannot and should not be expected to solve all of the problems our students face in a fractured world, schools have an important role to play in helping students work through trauma, since trauma impacts learning and since educators are key figures in the development of the children we serve.

Creating art of any kind has a therapeutic effect and can be used to work through traumatic stress. Even just a small amount of artistic production has been shown to lower cortisol levels (the stress hormone) in study subjects. Writing has additional therapeutic benefits, though. "Narrative therapy" involves patients in writing directly about trauma, which works because storytelling helps humans to order our experiences. When we have painful facts and no coherent narrative about them, our brains tend to suppress these facts and that worsens the traumatic stress. (Markman, 2009) Recently, the medical profession has been a space for experimentation with "expressive writing," a protocol developed by Jaime Pennebaker for treating psychological trauma. Health care professionals, stressed and grieving during the COVID-19 pandemic, were the subjects of a new study, which showed that three sessions of expressive writing about their experience significantly reduced PTSD, depression, and symptoms of psychopathology (Procaccia, Segre, & Tamanza, 2021).

Pennebaker's task is different than what we do in fiction writing in English class—mainly because my students only write about their trauma of their lives in general if they choose to do so. If they choose it, they may be the only ones who recognize what they're doing. Finally, in fiction, they can mix reality with fantasy. This alters the nature of the writing, but adds an imaginative element which holds other benefits.

I want to be careful not to suggest here that creative writing in English classes should be considered a formal part of a therapeutic program for trauma-affected students (though this might be a worthwhile area for research). Based on my teaching experiences, creative writing under the right conditions has a positive effect on the overall well-being of any student, and can specifically become a medium for some to process traumatic events. I think the key is that the student chooses to do so without any prompting whatsoever. Of course, whether we've built trust and a safe classroom environment is a major factor in whether a student might make that choice.

SUPPORTING STUDENTS WHO CHOOSE TO PROCESS TRAUMA THROUGH IMAGINATIVE WRITING

I usually don't know for sure if a student is writing through personal trauma, but I pay attention to my intuition. Along with other details I may have about the student,

I often get a strong sense of when this is happening. I consider it an honor if a student feels comfortable enough to risk writing about a traumatic experience in class, and it's an honor to be able to provide students with tools to do so. I've often been inspired by the ways my students have engaged bravely and creatively with their pain, transforming it through language and imagination.

I can best describe my role in these situations as a witness. I've created conditions and a task, but my student is the one leading now. I don't attempt to have a conversation about personal experiences that may or may not be incorporated into their writing. I'm not a therapist, and this is not my business, unless the student chooses to talk to me about their experience.

At the same time, I know that my presence is important. I'm not there by coincidence, but as a function of my role as teacher and caring adult. I think about a *New York Times* article, "What Do Teens Want? Potted Plant Parents." The author uses the metaphor of a potted plant to describe the ideal role for parents of teenagers to play. According to the author, decades of research confirm the value of parents "simply being around." A recent study found that their physical presence, even with minimal interaction, has a profound effect on adolescent health. Teens want autonomy, but also the security of their parents' "quiet and steady presence." (Damour, 2016). I am pretty sure students feel similarly about teachers at least some of the time. I feel like having a quiet and steady presence is often the right approach when a student writes through trauma. This is not a time to meddle, but neither should we leave the scene completely. Stand by, take note, and step up if we're called to do so.

Khalil

I don't believe in having favorite students, but Khalil was one eighth-grader who stood out from the crowd. What I appreciated about him was how bright and academically engaged he was, how socially mature he was, and how he somehow also managed to be viewed as "cool" in an environment where many students felt pressure to rebel in school and underperform in order to achieve social status. Khalil, it seemed, had cracked the code, and was flying above that harmful dichotomy. He was a positive leader, I imagined nothing would get in his way in life.

That's why it was especially heart-wrenching the beautiful spring afternoon we found out he had been attacked on his way home from school by some neighborhood boys he didn't know.

After that his attendance declined sharply. He stopped doing homework. He did the minimum to get by in the class. It was tragic, given how he had been just months before.

All of the power that he had felt through his intellectual and social engagement at school had not been remotely adequate for facing the dangers in his outside environment. What was he to make of that? What could I say to convince him it was worth keeping up with his schoolwork, that the pathway of education would lead somewhere good, when it couldn't even get him home safely? I desperately wanted to solve the problem or help in some way, but I was not equipped to do so, a white, young female teacher from suburban Boston. Perhaps another teacher might have known what to say. Maybe today I would have been able to find the right words.

In 2010, I gave a presentation at The Big Ideas Fest, in which I told Khalil's story adding my own fantasy ending: my imagined ending was that our school collaborated with community members to create a safe-walk system for students coming home from school. While writing this chapter, I remembered something about the real ending to that school year that hadn't seemed relevant to the focus of that talk.

Toward the end of the year, we were writing full-length stories. I remember noticing that after months of lackluster participation, Khalil was engrossed in his writing. I hadn't seen that look of concentration on his face for a long time. I did not want to call too much attention to it and interrupt a good thing, so I left him alone. He wrote with intense focus for days. I remember coming around briefly to his desk and glancing at the writing. I could see that there was harsh dialogue and fighting happening. There was description of setting, something I'd emphasized in class, which was a Brooklyn neighborhood. It looked to me like he was writing the experience.

I was right. He turned in a twenty-page story, well beyond the minimum length requirement. In it, the protagonist (a boy from Brooklyn) gets jumped twice. The third time the boys attempt to "run his pockets," he's ready for them. He fights back with superhuman strength. If I still had the story, I'd like to reread it for more detail, but what stuck out to me in this memory was that Khalil found an outlet for his pain, a place where he could process the experience and reclaim or reimagine part of himself through it. Even though the ending was a fantasy, like all literature, it served as significant virtual experience for him. It was the first time in class I saw him shake the cloud off and move forward.

I remember an educational clip I saw decades ago (in middle school health class, actually) about abuse. The video showed footage of a rape victim in a therapeutic setting, hitting a pillow with a bat as hard as she could; she was virtually beating her rapist (who was not present), crying and yelling at him. It wasn't real, but it was a way to release anger and regain some sense of her power. I believe Khalil's choice to beat up the boys who assaulted him in the story world worked along similar lines.

Many students who choose to write about traumatic experiences in fiction are exercising aspects of self-management as defined by the CASEL Framework, in the most challenging context: They are "Showing the courage to take initiative" and "Identifying and using stress management strategies," even if they don't do so intentionally.

What I offered Khalil through this assignment was a space to work creatively through his trauma on his own terms. It was completely his choice and I mostly left him alone as he worked. Before his attack, I might have chosen to confer with him more to coach him on craft, but in this case, I felt it would be an unnecessary intrusion. I witnessed his momentum and felt proud of him. His own imagination would provide what he needed in that moment.

Paul

Paul was another well-adjusted, high achieving student, who experienced sudden tragedy. Out of nowhere, his mother died of a chance health incident that came with no warning whatsoever. One day, she was his healthy and vibrant primary caregiver, and the next day she was gone forever.

Paul was devastated. He was grieving the unfathomable loss and simultaneously transitioning to living with his father and stepmother. He had been so stable and self-aware, and now he seemed unsure of how to behave in his new reality. In class, he usually went through the motions of his schoolwork, but looked shaky and sad. Sometimes, he lay his head down on the desk for a while (totally uncharacteristic for him until now). Occasionally, talking with classmates, he'd smile and seem to forget for a brief moment.

I had expressed my condolences over email and again when Paul first returned to school. He thanked me politely. As time went on, I wanted to say something more to him, but I wasn't sure how to reach out. I felt for him. Maybe because Paul was Jewish and I am too, and my parents had been divorced like his were, I could more viscerally imagine myself in his place, losing my mother at that age. I wasn't a therapist, of course. I didn't feel like I had much more to offer than a simple message that I cared. Not knowing what to say, I never approached him to talk about it. (One of my colleagues lost a parent at a young age and had some in-depth conversations with Paul.)

One day, though, I found an opportunity to say something more to him. Here's what happened. We were transitioning from reading poetry to writing poetry. I had students working in stations, each one designed to inspire poetry through a different form or modality. The stations were meant as exercises to generate ideas, not formal assignments.

Paul had been reluctantly trying to get through the work that day, but with more discomfort than usual. I could understand why, since poetry taps our emotions more than most tasks. Paul sat at one station (I don't know which one) with his head down, but I could see a look of agony on his face. I came over and saw that he'd written something on his notebook page. One phrase: "God doesn't see me," it read.

I felt tears well up in my own eyes.

I didn't want to cheapen his expression with advice or any kind of academic feedback. I also couldn't tell him, *Yes, god sees you*, or *No, god doesn't*. I didn't want to ask him to *tell me more*, either. He had said plenty, and I understood his meaning.

I took out my pen and just wrote in the margin: "<u>We do</u>." I underlined it for emphasis. This was what I had wanted to tell him all along. I see you. I feel for you. Everyone in this class does. I cannot speak to you about god or why this would happen to you or anyone. But I know that we all here care. I knew that Paul would understand what I meant. I looked him in the eye briefly. Empathy was all there was to give.

The space to write poetry opened a line of communication normally closed in our daily school routines. Without it, Paul probably wouldn't have articulated that thought (part of the narrative he would slowly piece together about what happened to him), and I wouldn't have found that medium for expressing my support to him. It was tiny in the face of his loss, but it was a step in processing it.

Thalia

Finally, I think of Thalia. She was a quiet, perceptive young teenager, who could have excelled academically; but something major was in her way, and no one knew what it was. She was chronically absent from school, and her mother simply said that she was unable to get her daughter out of bed in the morning. Having to leave the house early herself to keep her job, she was at a loss for what to do. We knew there must have been more to the story, but couldn't get any further than that.

Thalia was preoccupied during class and had difficulty focusing on most any assignment, especially when she'd been absent and was missing important context. She often had a glazed over look. She would smile and nod when I tried to work with her, but there was a distinct lack of real engagement.

The school had taken measures to help her over the years with no real progress. She was tightlipped and mistrustful of counseling.

In English class, we were outlining stories. The element we had studied in our last novel was conflict, and we were focusing our outlines around the development of a character with a conflict. Thalia sat with her blank paper. I went over the directions again with her, but Thalia still couldn't seem to get started. I came back in a few minutes and offered to help. She came up with a female protagonist with a name, but said she could not think of a conflict. I gave her a few examples from other students. Together, we reviewed some of the major conflicts in the books she'd read that year. Still, she was stuck. I sat with her and let her think. She usually had better focus when an adult was right next to her.

Finally, after quite a while of silence, Thalia asked, "Could the conflict be that her parents abuse her?"

"Yes," I replied. "That is definitely a conflict." I told her to write it down on the corresponding part of the outline organizer. I could have pushed for detail, but given the topic she'd chosen, I felt it was important that she set the pace. We moved on to working on some other fields of the outline. One section asked for other characters, including a helper character. She wrote down the parents, who were obviously characters in the story, but not exactly helpers. Then she got stuck again. "What about friends?" I asked.

"See, she can't really make friends," she said, pausing. "Because, you know, she can't really talk about it." Her face wobbled the slightest bit as she spoke, as if to fight back tears. She looked down. At that point, my gut told me we were talking about something at least partially real for Thalia.

To be clear, a student's choice to write about abuse does not mean the writing is from personal experience, and we shouldn't assume it. Some of these heavier topics are quite popular in young adult literature today, and students tend to mimic the genres they like to read. We also shouldn't assume it's not personal. The total picture of what I did know about Thalia, combined with the intuitive feeling I had as she talked about her character made me feel as if she was writing about a personal struggle—a deep, ongoing trauma.

It was still just a sense, but it was strong enough for me to adjust my approach to allow for this possibility. Potentially, this was a very courageous step for her to talk with anyone about this, even in an indirect way, and especially with an adult at her school. I was aware that behind each of her words and choices could be layers upon layers of emotion. She was stepping up to a plate that held both danger and possibility.

In class, we analyze conflicts in terms of (1) what the character wants or needs, and (2) who or what stands in the way, and (3) what changes. Thalia and I broke down her protagonist's conflict like this: (1) she wants to live a normal, happy life and have friends, like other teens do. (2) her abusive parents get in the way of this; she's miserable and can't make real friendships.

Then we got to the question of what changes.

I don't expect students to fully resolve the conflicts in their stories—real literature doesn't always do that anyway. Instead, we just say that the conflict must bring about some kind of change, and students have choice there. It was challenging for Thalia to figure this third part out. If parts one and two were close to reality, this was where she needed to use her imagination and write something that hadn't happened. (Kind of like me deciding the rest of my dream with the sea dinosaur.)

Many of her classmates were writing about conflicts between characters, in which the characters themselves change. At the end, there is a confrontation and reconciliation; or the main character has a realization, matures, and comes to see the whole situation differently. Neither of these possibilities felt appropriate for the unacceptable reality of a minor living with abusive parents. There was probably little chance of getting the abusive parents to change; little chance of a true reconciliation. And this also wasn't a situation where the protagonist was at fault and needed to change her outlook. No, she was a victim and needed real, physical liberation from that.

Thalia looked as unsure as I did. She could have her character run away, of course, but where would she go? What would become of her? I felt like I needed to throw her a line, to allow her to move forward in the story. I was also reluctant to suggest that she make the character get help through a counselor; even though this might have been the most appropriate real-life scenario, I thought it would push her away from the creative process.

"What if you change her age from fourteen to seventeen?" I said. "She would then be about to graduate high school. She'd be old enough to get a job and her own apartment, or an apartment with roommates." Thalia nodded.

"That's a good idea," she said with a little bit of a smile. We talked a little more, and she was ready to write.

Unlike with most assignments that year, Thalia wrote the entire story. It didn't offer a lot more detail than the ones we had discussed, but it was clear and convincing. She even managed to weave in a subplot in which her character makes her first real friends—they become "helper characters." In the story, she tells the new friends about her situation at home, and they are the ones who physically help her move out of her parents' house in the end.

I shared my concerns about Thalia's home situation with the school social worker, but there was nothing concrete to report beyond the choice of story topic. There have been times when I have asked students directly about disturbing content in their creative writing and sometimes asked them directly to talk with the school counselor about what they'd written. This is usually when I see a story focused on self-harm or physical harm to others.

Thalia had already had ample opportunities to talk to the school counselors over the years and had shown every time that she had no interest in opening up about whatever was going on. Maybe I could have gotten her to talk more to me, but this just as easily could have backfired, triggering her mistrust—and my primary job was to be her ELA teacher.

I felt instead that she had taken an important step within the safety of the story world: she had taken a look at her situation from a distance; the distance between art and reality. From that distance, she developed empathy for herself through creating the main character of her story who was not to blame for her problem. Finally, she imagined a way forward toward the life she wanted.

Art opens up new portals of emotion, consciousness, and communication. The literary arts are our precious superpower. So often, they throw us a lifeline when we need it most. As teachers of English Language Arts, we have the opportunity to provide space and support for students who open the door to write creatively about trauma in their lives. The choice should be entirely up to the student, and in my estimation, we should generally stand witness at a distance as they direct their own processes, unless they ask for help or seem stuck. The only exception, of course, is if we suspect harm to self or others.

If A Student's Writing Concerns Us, When to Get Help

When students write about troubling content, the ambiguity of the story world complicates our role. What if a student writes about harming themselves, for example? Simply, we can't assume the writing is based on their own experience; but we also can't assume it isn't. Self-harm is a prevalent issue for adolescents, and it's also present in the literature and television stories they consume. It can show up in their creative writing for either reason. When a student's writing causes us to worry that they might be in danger, there are a few different initial steps we can take.

> **Know your legal responsibilities and your school's specific policies.** Your state, district, and school all have policies around what to do if you think a student may be at risk for self-harm or harming others, or in danger in another way. Find out what these policies are and make sure to follow them. If you aren't sure, because of the ambiguity of the fictional world, its best to err on the side of caution. If you want to first get more information, the following are some steps you might take before making an official report.
>
> **Talk to the student.** Ask to chat with the student privately after class. Share that you felt concerned for them when reading their story, and you don't want to assume they are okay if they aren't. "Do you know which part I'm talking

about?" you might add. The message should be one of simple concern for their well-being. See how they respond.

Consult with a school counselor or wise colleague. Sometimes I read something and can't quite tell if there's cause for concern. In this situation, I show it to a school counselor or wise colleague to get their opinion. They may know the student better or a counselor may know the signs better and be able to make a determination about next steps.

Talk with the student's caregiver. Depending on the nature of your concern, you may want to first share with the student's caregiver. As a parent, I would certainly want to know if my child was writing content that concerned my child's teacher. Sometimes, parents can give us additional context for the situation and would be grateful for the chance to talk with their child about what they're going through. However, this is also a step the school will take if we make a report. So our choice here depends on the level of the communication we want to have with the student and their family. It's also possible to send a quick email that says, "I just want to let you know. I had some concern about something your child wrote about in their story today. I shared it with our school social worker, and they will be following up with you about it."

If you feel that your student may be in danger, you're likely required to report it to school personnel based on your school's policy and to local authorities if your student is a target of abuse or neglect pursuant to mandatory reporting laws. It can be beneficial to let the student know: "After reading your story, I was worried about you. Do you know why I felt that way? . . . So, I let [school counselor] see what you wrote in your story. [Counselor] will be reaching out to you today. I hope you can understand why I felt worried about you."

If you work with adolescents, you know that they have big emotions, that bouts of temporary depression are common, and that many teens even find an attraction to depressive or "emo" art. This is important to keep in mind as we read student fiction; but it doesn't mean we shouldn't also take it seriously if students write about self-harm, depression, or suicide.

Valeria

In spring of 2021, my school was still entirely online. I taught online sessions daily with each class, and I viewed student writing on Google Docs. Valeria, an eighth-grader, was writing a story with a first-person narrator who was cutting herself. The description was so vivid and the emotions seemed so real, I was worried as soon as I started reading it. The character then writes a long note, which is apparently a suicide note. It rails on the adults in her life who never took her pain seriously. It was Friday afternoon when I read this first scene and Zoom class was already over. I paced around my living room, where I worked from my computer all year, debating what to do next.

I texted a school counselor but she was on a bike ride with spotty connection. Thankfully, due to pandemic funding, we have two additional counselors this year. I emailed both of them—do either of you work with Valeria? No immediate reply.

I emailed an administrator at my school who handles student issues. I pasted the story text in the email. No immediate reply.

I emailed the student: "Hi Valeria, I took a look at your story and have to say I feel a little worried about you. Can you give me a call?" I left my phone number. No immediate response.

Maybe I was too pushy. No student should have to call their teacher on a Friday afternoon. I sent another email: "Hi Valeria, only call if you would like. But maybe you could email me back and let me know how you are. I know you are writing a fictional story, but it feels so real to me as I read it. It has me concerned." No immediate reply.

In a panic, I called her parent. No answer. I decided not to leave a message. Soon, I received a message from the administrator, who agreed this warranted concern. She got in touch with Ben, one of our counselors, who was able to get in touch with a parent and arrange a video call meeting with Valeria.

He then gave me a call. In his professional opinion, though the story was vivid and troubling, after speaking to her, he was confident that she was in a stable mental space and not at risk of harming herself. She explained to him that so many teens she knows are going through mental health crises. This was especially true during the height of the pandemic. Valeria only wanted to show what some people are going through. Ben said that she was joking and laughing by the end of the conversation.

I received a flurry of emails from Valeria:

Hi Ariel,

Sorry for worrying you. I'm doing fine. My story is being based on other real stories of kids who have and/or almost lost their lives to suicide. My character is a representation of how those kids might have felt. Once again so sorry for worrying you. I am doing fine.

Hello Ariel,

I am doing well. I feel fine mentally and physically. Sorry I worried you once again. My main thing I'm focusing on in writing this story is making the reader feel how this character is feeling. As you said in your email it felt so real as you read it. That was what I wanted to do, make the reader understand how

they are feeling. But once again I'm doing fine :). Thank you for checking in and
seeing if I'm okay <3. Sorry for concerning you like this.

I wrote back:

> Hi Valeria,
> I'm very relieved to hear it. You are a very good writer!!!
> I did reach out to a school counselor before I heard back from you. They
> might reach out to you too. Sometimes students look for help in different ways
> and it's been such a difficult time. I did not want to guess that you're fine and
> be wrong (like in your story!). Please don't take that as a judgment on my part.
> Just caring.
> Ariel

> Hi Ariel,
> Everything's fine—I understand why you were worried, I should have told
> you before what I wanted my story to be based on. I just got off of Zoom with
> the school counselor so everything's fine there. Thank you for caring and say-
> ing I'm a good writer, I appreciate that very much when people say I'm a good
> writer—it makes me want to continue writing.

I was so relieved. Even though this case turned out to be a false alarm, I know that
reaching out for help was the right thing to do. It occurred to me later that, while the
story was apparently not a literal cry for help, Valeria was writing about something
she had at least partially witnessed in others, which can be traumatic. The chance to
speak to an adult about it may have been helpful to her anyway. Beyond that, Valeria got some positive attention on her writing. Ben, the counselor, also remarked on
how strong it was. All kids need positive attention, and more so in the isolation of
pandemic remote learning. Her dramatic story was successful in that.

Esther

The practice of reading for an audience can open up more ways for some students
to process trauma. For example, during our year of remote learning, Esther wrote
a story about a protagonist whose best friend has cancer. As she continued writing,
she added a backstory: The protagonist had lost her older cousin to a heart condition a year before. The narrator reveals this story through flashbacks as the current
story with the friend unfolds. I didn't know Esther's family well, because I met her
remotely that year, and it was her first year at our school.

We held our story share session over Zoom, in which each student reads a section of their story for the class. Esther chose to read the section in which her protagonist remembers her brother's death in the hospital. She began reading, and at first, it sounded like her internet was spotty. There were more pauses and her voice sounded strained. I realized she was crying. She said she was sorry, and I offered to pick up and read for her. She said, "Yes, please." Some students posted heart emojis through the chat window.

I tried to read this scene, and I was shocked to find that I too got tears in my eyes and had to pause many times to keep my composure. More heart emojis. The writing was so vivid and sad and beautiful. The sense I had that this was Esther's own truth made it much more intense. This was compounded by the fact that several students in the class had experienced devastating losses during the pandemic and, in their pain, were isolated from the in-person community and routine that school usually offers.

At the end of the period, I had a brief conversation with Esther through private chat. She confirmed that these flashbacks were of her own brother. I offered my deepest condolences and told her I was honored that she chose to share this and let me read her words to the class. I told her a lot of students were in pain over losses, and her courage in sharing hers had no doubt made others feel less alone. It also drew empathy from everyone listening at a time when genuine human connection beyond our homes was rare.

4

Utilizing Imaginative Writing as a Tool For Equity and Community

So, who gets to write fiction? I recently spoke to a neighbor, a white woman who works as a food journalist, about the topic of this book. She listened and said, "I see what you mean. I was an English major. I loved literature; but I never tried writing fiction. Not because I wouldn't have liked it, but because I never thought that it was *for* me, never really considered that I *could*."

The same is almost true for me, but for the influence of my grandmother, who was a teacher and passionate about developing imaginative writing in young people. I lived in the Boston area and she lived in Jersey City, but she played a vital role in my reading and writing development, mailing me books that she'd chosen just for me and encouraging me to write creatively. She would listen on the phone as I read her my poems and pieces of stories, oohing and aah-ing in the way perhaps only a grandparent can. She was the person who opened the gates for me, with her consistent message that my imaginative writing was important and wonderful.

Most children receive an implicit message through their schooling that writing fiction is not an available path for them, simply because they have almost no invitations to explore it. This is true for our general population, *and* it is even more so the case for children of color, LGBTQ+ youth, and others whose identities are historically underrepresented in literature and publishing. Through the tradition of the "canon," the implicit message to children of marginalized groups has been that writers are usually white, male, cis-gender, often wealthy, and that literary topics and styles are confined to those which these writers have chosen.

Growing up one of very few Jewish students in a suburban public school system, not one book I read for a class was by or about a Jewish person. I didn't question this. I pushed myself to identify with the fiction assigned to me; I developed a love of F. Scott Fitzgerald's sentences, Shakespeare's drama, and Thoreau's philosophical meditation on Walden Pond. But let me be honest: There were many books I "fake-read" for school, doing just what was required to receive a good grade.

By contrast, when my grandmother sent me a copy of *The Mozart Season*, by Virginia Euwer Woolf—about a girl who, like me, played violin seriously and had a confusing relationship with her family's Jewish heritage—I experienced a totally different version of reading. I was absorbed and swayed by this character who was more like me than most people I knew, and in ways I'd never seen in a book or any other media for that matter. In today's language: I felt seen.

That feeling of connection while reading welcomes young people into a world of literature and puts us in community with its authors as well. When we extend this community by inviting students to write their own imaginative fiction, we have the opportunity to facilitate a profoundly inclusive and equalizing process.

This process in the classroom is a means to achieve greater equity in education (and beyond) on several levels:

1. Big picture, we are developing more diverse pathways into writing as a profession. This will help fuel the movement to diversify publishing and connect new generations of readers with writers who will, in turn, make them feel seen. For young people from marginalized groups, this opportunity has been denied at greater levels than for the general population, which is a disservice to us all, and should prompt teachers to take action in the place we have most influence: our classrooms. We are gatekeepers for each of our students. When we open those gates and encourage students' writing, we can impact the course of their lives and, quite possibly, the lives of their future readers.

2. By centering imaginative writing in our classes, we are placing a tool of freedom and empowerment in our students' hands and helping them discover how to use it. For students facing systemic oppression, tapping into their own powerful imagination through writing can be a vehicle to envision possibilities that transcend unjust realities—which ultimately benefits us all in our shared humanity. Creative writing can also provide a safe space to be vulnerable and process difficult feelings and experiences, which can be hard to come by in the "real" world, where the safety of people from oppressed groups is continually threatened.

3. When diverse students share their imaginative writing with one another (and all classrooms are diverse, even if not visibly so), their stories create virtual

experiences for their classmates. Sharing stories builds empathy and connection, helping to upend biases and stereotypes students often hold about one another. Our classrooms are, in many ways, ground zero for creating a more just, loving society if we take up the call. Sharing creative writing in a classroom community is a key tool for this progress.

The power in storytelling as a tool to advance equity in our classrooms has special implications for our teaching, especially our work with BIPOC students and others who are marginalized. To successfully enable each layer above, we have corresponding responsibilities as teachers.

In this chapter, we'll look at:

- How creative writing practice can help challenge racist and biased traditions in schools and literary communities
- How we can develop ourselves as antiracist, antibiased educators to best support and learn from our students' creative work
- Structures for sharing student writing in class and how this facilitates connection across racial, cultural, economic, and other persistent divides
- How to lead and grow through difficult moments

THE HUMANIZING QUALITY OF STORIES

Most of us were taught some version of the Golden Rule: Treat others as you would like to be treated. Versions of this concept of reciprocity and the value of kindness show up in religions all over the world. In schools, the Golden Rule is used almost universally. Our consciences tell us to be kind to others, or as a minimum, not to harm others. Yet, people participate in the oppression of fellow human beings. How do we reconcile this contradiction?

Oppression, in its many forms, operates by dehumanizing whole groups (or categories) of people: poor people, people of color, immigrants, women, Muslims, Jews, gay people, gender nonconforming people, disabled people. The dehumanization is fueled by negative stereotypes: "People from X category do such-and-such bad thing." These messages can be blatant or subtle, but they perpetuate misunderstanding and mistrust of the targeted group. This creates a sense of separation from the group and ultimately allows people to think of whole categories of people as being less human, less worthy of kindness, compassion, and justice. This is why segregation is such an effective way to uphold racism—separation allows negative stereotypes to persist without being challenged or even acknowledged.

The moment we see individuals from groups we are used to labeling "other" as humans, whom we understand and relate to, we are on a path to challenging and rejecting oppression. The stories of many former white supremacists, such as Christian Picciolini and Angela King, who founded Life After Hate, show how for each of them just one genuine connection with a person of color sparked their process of questioning and unravelling the ideology on which their white supremacist hate depended. The work of Darryl Davis—a Black musician, who has struck up relationships with white supremacists and convinced over 200 KKK members to leave the group—tells a similar story from the other side (Brown, 2017). We are living in an era in which hate is amplified online. Real human connection is powerful and needed.

Stories have unique power to capture our imaginations and influence our thoughts and emotions. Storytellers have the ability to humanize people, including themselves, for a wide audience. By contrast, those who are silenced in storytelling realms are vulnerable to others telling their stories in ways that perpetuate stereotypes and continue to dehumanize them.

Stories both reflect and influence human societies. By limiting which children are supported to craft stories, we limit those children's ability to illuminate and influence their worlds; we also limit ourselves from seeing their humanity in the stories we consume. When we make that decision for Black and Brown children, which is often in the name of closing the so-called achievement gap, we actually help to uphold racist structures, which systematically undermine people of color and cut us off from one another. Including creative writing in the education of children of color is imperative for all of the reasons that apply to everyone—plus the weight of oppression, past and present.

CREATIVITY IS NOT A LUXURY: IMAGINATIVE WRITING FOR ALL STUDENTS

I know that some educators will agree with me about the importance of creative writing for young people to a point, but argue that for students who are struggling with basic literacy skills, writing imaginatively is a luxury they can't afford. I want to challenge educators in and out of the classroom to step away from this mindset. It may come from a well-meaning place, but its impact is to weaken educational outcomes, separate people along problematic lines, and exacerbate existing inequities in our education system.

What is commonly referred to as the achievement gap—between white, affluent, English-dominant, typically developing students and basically everyone else—has been identified and measured almost exclusively by performance on standardized tests. These measurements, and all of the data and implications that result from them, are already outdated when it comes to their purpose: to equip students with the skills of today's job market. Yong Zhao (2017) explains that for more than twenty years, the United States has been suffering from "achievement gap mania," in which all educational resources have been devoted to "narrowing the chasm in test scores and graduation rates between students of different backgrounds, especially income and race." But, he writes, "it hasn't worked." During the era that began in 2001 with the federal No Child Left Behind Act, the "performance gaps" between rich and poor, and children of color and white students in the United States *as measured by the tests*, have actually widened.

Furthermore, Zhao argues, the initiatives designed to close these gaps have "narrowed the scope of schooling," turned education into test prep, demoralized teachers and students, reinforced a deficit mindset while concealing the real causes for educational inequality, and "deprived many children, particularly those whom the campaign was supposed to help, of the opportunities of a real education" (Zhao, 2018).

Meanwhile, leaders across industries have been lamenting the need for employees with "the most important competency, strategic priority, or point of competitive advantage: creativity," according to research by Innovation Advisor and author, Larry Robertson. He argues that we need to "assimilate insights into how creativity can become more than just a gift we admire in a rare few, but instead a practiced skill that becomes our collective habit. We all have the capacity for creativity. Understanding that . . . raises the odds that the future we lead ourselves to will be one in which we thrive" (Robertson, 2017).

Schools in which students were not performing up to designated proficiency standards on tests are the places where test preparation and the almost exclusive emphasis on convergent thinking skills have become most dominant. This was a disservice to those students in a world where knowledge and contexts are constantly changing, and technology continues to replace humans in routine tasks. Zhao argues, "We need humans to be unique, creative, and entrepreneurial." And, he explains, while the West is obsessing over Asian education systems of China, Hong Kong, Singapore, and Japan, after their stunning 2009 PISA test scores (which far surpassed those of most Western countries), Asian nations are enthusiastically seeking knowledge of Western educational traditions. "Instead of reducing academic success to test scores in a limited set of subjects . . . all four East Asian systems have been expanding and redefining education outcomes to include what are commonly known as twenty-first century skills: creativity, communication, collaboration, and higher order thinking; they are also interested in students' social–emotional and physical health" (Zhao, 2017).

The elite in East Asian countries have been sending their children to Western style schools for some time, according to Zhao. And likewise, the elite in the United States have been sending their children to schools that recognize the value of twenty-first century skills, most of which abstain from standardized tests altogether until the SATs.

This point cannot be ignored when we go along with initiatives that prescribe a far less engaging and effective brand of education for poor children of color in the United States. It does not matter how passionately their champions talk about educational inequities and closing the achievement gap. Not only does this brand fail to close the achievement gap that is defined and measured by standardized tests, it focuses on a false concept of achievement in the first place.

Creativity is a necessity for leadership and problem solving in an uncertain future. It is unethical to foster this capacity in some of our children and deny the same opportunity to our most vulnerable populations. Although I have made the point that most children lack meaningful opportunities to write creatively as part of their education, here, I'm responding to the notion that students who struggle with basic skills should specifically be denied these opportunities.

Creative writing, with its considerable academic and social–emotional benefits, must not be a privilege for the few. It must not be a white privilege. It must not be a privilege for students whose families have money to pay for tutors to help with essay writing and test preparation. In fact, while creative writing is important for every developing writer, it is especially vital for students who face systemic marginalization. At the same time, it's a tool for forging genuine connections among students from different backgrounds, who would likely not connect otherwise. Centering creative writing in ELA classrooms is a way we can shift power structures, bring people together, and literally make the world a more humane place.

WE NEED DIVERSE BOOKS AND NEW GENERATIONS TO WRITE THEM: OPENING DOORS FOR OUR STUDENTS

I first asked the question, "Who Gets To Write Fiction?" on my blog, On the Shoulders Of Giants, at Center For Teaching Quality—an organization that has created space for so many teachers, arguably an oppressed group when it comes to education policy, to make their voices heard beyond their classrooms. It was 2014, and I had just read two beautiful side-by-side opinion pieces in *The New York Times* by the late, young adult fiction writer Walter Dean Myers and his son, Christopher Myers, who is also a YA author.

Walter Dean Myers, who was one of the first African American novelists to break into children's publishing, framed his piece with the question, "Where Are the

People of Color In Children's Books?" That year, according to the Cooperative Children's Book Center at the University of Wisconsin School of Education, just seven percent of the 3200 books published for children were by authors of color. That percentage has steadily grown in recent years, but today, just about 26% percent of publications for children feature characters of color, according to Cooperative Children's Book Center, and that number includes all writers, not just writers who themselves share the identity of their BIPOC characters. Meanwhile, half of U.S. children under five are non-white, according to "We Need Diverse Books," an article published in *Writer Mag* in 2017.

In his article, Walter Dean Myers recounts his teen years, in which he went from being a voracious reader to dropping out of school and abandoning reading altogether once he discovered he was constantly reading only white characters. That changed when he read *Sonny's Blues* and met its author, James Baldwin, and was encouraged by a teacher to write stories for a magazine. He eventually found his way toward a life committed to writing books that reflect the humanity and diversity of Black people in this country. I can attest to how much his books have spoken to my students over the years in New York City—bringing them joy and offering occasion to think and share deeply on issues in their lives and communities.

Chris Myers, in his article published that day, "The Apartheid of Children's Literature," points out the narrow cast of characters in children's literature, "in which characters of color are limited to the townships of occasional historical books that concern themselves with legacies of civil rights and slavery but are never given a pass card to traverse the lands of adventure, curiosity, imagination, or personal growth." He writes that not only can literature be a mirror for children, providing "the sense of self-love that comes from recognizing oneself in a text"—but he takes this a step farther in showing that literature creates maps for children, who "are also deciding where they want to go. They create, through the stories they're given, an atlas of their world, of their relationships to others, of their possible destinations." He criticizes the publishing industry for hiding behind "The Market," making dubious claims that there is not enough interest in books featuring characters of color.

I was moved by these two pieces. Teaching in NYC public schools, where the vast majority of my students were children of color, I intimately knew how much my students' relationships to reading soared when they found books with characters they could directly relate to. Equally well, I knew the limited selection of such titles.

I felt the urge to blog a response, and wondered what I could add to the discussion. I began thinking about the implications of this issue for teachers.

Clearly, teachers must get diverse books, particularly by authors of color, into our classrooms for our students—this is imperative in any classroom, especially for teachers of primarily students of color. By doing so, we also support the publishing of books by and about people of color, affirming the very real market for them. I can only speak for New York City, but Walter Dean Myers's books were perpetually in demand, on order lists, and flying off the shelves in classroom libraries. Today, the selection of novels featuring BIPOC characters has increased significantly, but is still not enough to mirror the diversity of the real world and to balance collections that reflect years of publishing almost exclusively white authors.

The second implication I thought about was the writing instruction for young people of color. I titled my post, "Who Gets To Write Fiction? A Response to Walter Dean Myers and Chris Myers." In it, I asked, aside from publishing politics, are students of color getting enough opportunity and encouragement to write original stories?

> Perhaps all students could use more opportunity to write creatively in today's schools, but in my experience there is a lot more drilling of the basics in urban schools that serve mostly students of color than in schools that serve predominantly white, privileged students. Testing alone helps create this disparity. Test scores mirror socioeconomic status, so the focus on "test prep" is much greater where test scores are low. Schools that serve poor communities of color are under the gun to raise those test scores. Unfortunately, in such contexts, spending time on creative writing is often viewed as an unaffordable luxury. Of course, these conditions for students and teachers only exacerbate the gap in quality education and "achievement." (teachingquality.org, 2014)

Less than a year later, in response to a panel of children's books authors at a BookCon fan convention in 2014 which was entirely white and male, the hashtag #WeNeedDiverseBooks was born. Subsequently, a nonprofit organization with the same name (WNDB), was created by Ellen Oh, Dhonielle Clayton, and Judy Schricker, "to help produce and promote literature that reflects and honors the lives of all young people" toward a vision of "a world in which all children can see themselves in the pages of a book."

As an educator who is active on social media, I can attest to the impact of their robust advocacy. We Need Diverse Books has not only raised awareness of the need, but they've also led an ongoing inclusive conversation about this issue among educators, librarians, authors, readers, and publishers. They have spread the word about many wonderful books by diverse authors, and helped to tease apart issues of representation of marginalized people that arise in literature by authors who are from the dominant group. They have helped to define what diversity in children's literature means. Their programs now include financial grants to diverse authors and illustrators who are not yet published, mentorship for diverse, early career authors, and internship grants for diverse students pursuing a career in publishing.

I used to literally go to bookstores (shout out to the Bank Street Bookstore!) and scour the shelves of YA fiction, looking for books with Brown faces on the cover or by authors with names that didn't sound European to preview for my students. I would read as much as I could of each one—and there often weren't many to choose from—and then make a decision on whether to buy it for my classroom. Today, the ease of the internet and the many individuals and organizations who have taken up this issue have made it so much easier for teachers to give students access to diverse books.

While the movement to increase diversity of books in classrooms has, I believe, dramatically impacted the teaching of reading nationwide, there hasn't been a similar, complementary shift in writing instruction in K–12 education: We haven't had a movement among ELA teachers to encourage all students to write in the genres they love to read and envision the possibility of careers as authors. I am hopeful that we could be at the precipice of this change today, though.

In an article titled "We Need Diverse Books," for example, editorial consultant Marcela Landres explains that we need to begin outreach to children in order to solve the problem of "segregation in book publishing." Landres says, "If I was queen of the world . . . I'd reach down into middle grades and start a mentoring program for children of color so they could see themselves growing up to be members of the literary community, as readers, writers, and/or publishing professionals" (Hart, 2021).

Felicia Rose Chavez, author of *The Anti-Racist Writing Workshop: How to Decolonize the Creative Classroom* (Haymarket Books, 2021) emphasizes active recruitment of BIPOC students to writing workshops, especially in college, where students have to choose to join. She also advocates for the format of the workshop itself to support diverse writers. In 2022, We Need Diverse Books launched a partnership with NaNoWriMo, National Novel Writing Month, which facilitates a nation-wide project of writing a novel over the month of November with special features and community engagement for students and their teachers to encourage students of color to participate.

In addition to special programs, partnerships, and college level writing workshops, K–12 teachers can absolutely shift toward creative writing in our regular ELA classes, where students are legally required to be 180 days each year! If we do it well, with equity in mind—and I will provide more specific steps for that in this chapter—we can make a huge wave of change in the world of literature and in the culture of our schools.

When people started noticing that computer science professionals were overwhelmingly white males, they didn't just interrogate the hiring practices and working conditions of tech companies. Girls Who Code and Black Girls Code organizations also began leading the change with young people. We still need diverse books—and we need to support new generations to write them. Teachers, we're at the forefront of change. We're gate-openers, if we choose to be.

WITH POWERFUL TOOLS COMES GREAT RESPONSIBILITY: DEVELOPING OURSELVES AS ANTIRACIST, ANTIBIAS EDUCATORS

One of my mentors, educator Barney Brawer, emphasized this point to me. When we find a tool that facilitates deep and important work for young people, our responsibility in leading that work increases. We don't just let our students play around with "power tools" in the woodshop. We have to know these tools ourselves, have safety measures in place, and be aware and careful when the tools are in use.

With creative writing, which can be a powerful tool for equity, we need to be aware of the stakes for our students, especially those from historically marginalized groups, to make themselves vulnerable in our classrooms—and we need to be aware of our potential to positively or negatively impact that process.

While imaginative writing can help students challenge and resist oppressive structures, it's possible for us to undermine that process with our own behavior, often without knowing it. This caution applies to any teacher, but especially where a teacher is a member of a dominant group (white, male, heterosexual, cisgender, wealthy, able-bodied, Christian, and/or native English speaker), and their student is a member of a marginalized group. In 2022, The National Center for Education Statistics reports that children of color now make up the majority in U.S. public schools, so it would seem that a majority of our teachers are in fact teaching students of color. Meanwhile, the most recent demographic data for teachers in the United States, from 2018, shows approximately 79% of teachers identified as non-Hispanic white.

Race and other factors that determine power in our country influence our relationships with students. Our role is to help empower students within an imperfect system, but we too, are imperfect products of the same system.

To manage our own impact on our most vulnerable students—to first do no harm and to then maximize our positive influence—we must strive to develop an antiracist, antibiased teaching practice. That takes work. It isn't enough to feel in our hearts that we want equality or believe that we already have it. Educators and people in general, who have been committed to antiracist, antibiased practices know that this learning and work are never-ending. If we could end racism with a wand, an app, a conversation, a book, or a vote, we would have. Racism is complex, and evolving in how it shows up. The same is true for other forms of oppression, like sexism, classism, homophobia, religious bigotry, and anti-immigrant prejudice.

Start With Our Own Learning

As with most great challenges involving other people, the first step we need to take is with our selves. We start by learning about how racism and bias operate in our country and our communities, and reflecting on their impact on our families, personal identities, and schools. White-identified educators, especially, need to learn about racism if we want to help dismantle it.

If you find yourself thinking at this very moment, "I'm not racist," or "I'm colorblind," or "I don't come from a racist family history" and that those statements would mean you're exempt from the need to learn about racism, I'm here to tell you that it's more complicated than that, and there is a lot to learn—a lifetime, if you take the charge seriously.

I'm delving into this topic here not because I consider myself an expert on antibias, antiracist education, but because I want myself and my family to be able to live free of hate, because I am committed to creating more justice in a country built on injustice, committed to learning more and doing better at being a member of a diverse community, and because I am a teacher to many children of color of diverse backgrounds. I believe that awareness and commitment to antibias, antiracist (ABAR) practices—which overlap a great deal with generally sound, developmentally meaningful, student-centered practices—are crucial to being an effective educator for all of our students, and that's the journey I'm on.

Furthermore, I *am* making the argument in this book that imaginative writing is a tool to challenge oppression, and I'm not alone. Dr. Bettina Love, in *We Want to Do More Than Survive: Abolitionist Teaching and the Pursuit of Educational Freedom*, argues that creative thinking and "freedom dreaming" are exactly the capacities education should develop in young people so that they will be able to imagine solutions to the problems of racism and prejudice that are entrenched in our society.

I would be incorrect and irresponsible, however, to suggest that teachers can bypass learning about racism, bias, and culturally responsive teaching, and believe that creative writing on its own will bring greater equity to our students. Though artistic spaces have distinct qualities and often exist outside of or in defiance of society's norms, they are unfortunately not devoid of racism, sexism, and other forms of discrimination. Empowering outcomes are not a given for all of our students, just because we open the door to creative writing.

In a 2009 interview with WNYC, Sandra Cisneros, award-winning author of *The House On Mango Street,* talks about her time at the renowned Iowa Writers Workshop, as "rather horrible . . . " specifically because of how she was treated as a Chicana writer, a woman of color, and a working class writer. " . . . I am a writer *despite* the Iowa Writer's Workshop. It taught me what I *didn't* want to be as a writer, and how I *didn't* want to teach . . . " she says (Lopate, 2009). Cisneros explains that there are other working class women and writers of color who feel similarly about their experiences in the program, but they haven't been heard.

Pulitzer Prize winning author Junot Diaz, wrote in 2014 in a New Yorker article entitled, "MFA vs. POC" (Master of Fine Arts versus People of Color) about how deeply unsupportive to writers of color the MFA program he attended at Cornell University—as well as similar programs across the country—were. He describes how his program had few to no faculty of color and didn't see a problem with that, discouraged discussion of race and its impact on writing, and offered an education almost exclusively focused on white male writers. He wrote: "I was a person of color in a workshop whose theory of reality did not include my most fundamental experiences as a person of color—that did not in other words include *me*."

Author–educator Felicia Rose Chavez, who attended Iowa Writer's Workshop, has published a book called *The Anti-Racist Writing Workshop: How to Decolonize the Creative Classroom* (Haymarket 2021). She recounts her own painful MFA experience, echoing Cisneros's and Diaz's criticisms, and she offers solutions. She shares structures for an actively antiracist writing workshop. She developed the framework with high school and college students in response to the racism and patriarchy in the traditional structure: "a blueprint for a twenty-first-century writing workshop that concedes the humanity of people of color so that we may raise our voices in vote for love over hate" (Chavez, n. d.).

Chavez's methods, which she uses herself in college-level creative writing courses, have met with glowing responses, not only from students of color but also from workshops with majority-white participants, which supports the notion that antiracism benefits everyone.

Gholdy Muhammad, author of *Cultivating Genius: An Equity Framework for Culturally and Historically Responsive Literacy,* studies Black literary societies of the 1900s. She applied what she has learned through her historical research to create a framework for K–12 classrooms today. She makes the point well that this framework, though designed by and for Black students, is a great benefit for all students. "If we start with Blackness (which we have not traditionally done in schooling) or the group of people who have uniquely survived the harshest oppressions in this country, then we begin to understand ways to get literacy education right for all" (Scholastic Teaching Resources, 2020). The health of a group, a community, a country, can be assessed by looking at its treatment of its most vulnerable members.

I'm thinking now about the teachers at Iowa Writer's Workshop, who taught

Chavez and Cisneros, and the teachers at Cornell, who taught Diaz. Knowing traditionally white education spaces well myself, I think the likelihood is high that most
teachers there would claim abstractly not to be racist or biased against writers of
color, even when their words and actions indicated otherwise.

What this contradiction represents is something I've had to learn as a white-
identified person in diverse spaces: *because racism doesn't happen directly to me,
my own experience doesn't equip me to be knowledgeable about it.* It doesn't matter that I've experienced being "other" in certain spaces that privilege male perspectives or Christian traditions; these experiences still do not make me aware of
racism and my relationship to it. I have to seek out knowledge from people who do
know—whether from their own experiences or because they're further along a path
of learning than I am.

If I don't seek out knowledge of racism, I remain ignorant, not only about a
significant force that impacts many people around me, but about my own role and
impact within it. This limits me as a human being, a thinker, and a teacher, and
allows for the possibility of my doing harm to others and probably being blind to it.

As the poet Maya Angelou famously said (quoted by Oprah Winfrey), "You do
the best you can until you know better. And when you know better, you do better."
Educators are knowledge workers, among other things. We have a special obligation
to keep learning, to know better, especially where our lack of knowledge can harm
our students. As we involve students in the powerful tool of creative writing, we will
maximize benefits and minimize harm, if we reflect regularly on our own biases and
work to create antiracist, antibias learning spaces.

Resources on Antiracism and Antibias Practices

Because this area of learning is vast, I'm offering here a list of reading from leaders
in the field of antiracism and culturally responsive teaching in three categories: general reading, education-related reading, and literacy-specific reading. If you're new
to this kind of work, I recommend starting with a title in the first section, because
these books offer a chance to expand and reflect personally, before applying the lens
to teaching. Many of these authors have articles and excerpts published online, so
exploring online would be a great way to get a sense of each author's work before
selecting books to read.

Note: In this first section, the books are mostly focused on racism. This is partly
reflective of my own bias in reading topics—these are powerful books I can personally recommend to you. I also believe learning about racism is essential to understanding power in the United States; this learning must be consciously taken on,
because of the particularly deep avoidance our dominant culture has around it.

Knowing how racism developed and operates opens up understanding of systems of power and how these affect many oppressed groups. For white people, this is not about feeling guilty. It is about gaining knowledge, making critical connections, and accepting that we have choices in how we position ourselves in a race-based system—if we know the system and ourselves.

General Books for Deepening Understanding of Racism and Sexism

- *How To Be an Antiracist* by Ibram X. Kendi
- *So You Want to Talk About Race* by Ijeoma Oluo
- *White Fragility: Why It's So Hard for White People to Talk About Racism* by Robin DiAngelo
- *Caste: The Origins of Our Discontents* by Isabel Wilkerson
- *The Master's Tools Will Never Dismantle the Master's House* by Audre Lorde
- *Between the World and Me* by Ta-Nehisi Coates
- *Men Explain Things To Me* by Rebecca Solnit
- *Feminism Is For Everybody: Passionate Politics* by bell hooks
- *My Grandmother's Hands: Racialized Trauma and the Pathway to Mending Our Hearts and Bodies* by Resmaa Menakem
- *How the Word Is Passed: A Reckoning with the History of Slavery Across America* by Clint Smith

Books On Antiracist, Antibias Education for Teachers and School Leaders

- *We Want to Do More Than Survive: Abolitionist Teaching and the Pursuit of Educational Freedom* by Bettina L. Love
- *Culturally Responsive Teaching and the Brain* by Zaretta Hammond
- *Start Here, Start Now: A Guide to Antibias and Antiracist Work in Your School Community* by Liz Kleinrock
- *Textured Teaching: A Framework for Culturally Sustaining Practices* by Lorena Escoto Germán
- *Learning and Teaching While White: Antiracist Strategies for School Communities* by Jenna Chandler-Ward and Elizabeth Denevi
- *Coaching for Equity: Conversations that Change Practice* by Elena Aguilar
- *The Educator's Guide to LGBT+ Inclusion: A Practical Guide for K–12 Teachers, Administrators, and School Support Staff* by Kryss Shane
- *This Is Not a Test: A New Narrative on Race, Class, and Education* by José Luis Vilson
- *Other People's Children: Cultural Conflict in the Classroom* by Lisa Delpit

- *Pedagogy of the Oppressed* by Paulo Friere
- *Teaching to Transgress: Education as the Practice of Freedom* by bell hooks

Antiracist and Antibias Teaching Resources for English and Literacy Educators

- *Cultivating Genius: An Equity Framework for Culturally and Historically Responsive Literacy* by Gholdy Muhammad
- *The Anti-Racist Writing Workshop: How To Decolonize the Creative Classroom* by Felicia Rose Chavez
- *Literacy is Liberation: Working Toward Justice Through Culturally Relevant Teaching* by Kimberly N. Parker
- *Disrupt Texts in Your Classroom Educator Guide* (a free download) by #DisruptTexts cofounded by Tricia Ebarvia, Lorena Germán, Dr. Kimberly N. Parker, and Julia Torres (Penguin Classroom) and/or the disrupttexts.org website
- *Literature and the New Culture Wars: Triggers, Cancel Culture, and the Teacher's Dilemma* by Deborah Appleman
- *The Dark Fantastic: Race and the Imagination from Harry Potter to the Hunger Games* by Ebony Elizabeth Thomas
- *Liven Up Your Library: Design Engaging and Inclusive Programs for Tweens and Teens* by Valeria Tagoe and Julia Torres
- *Disfigured: On Fairy Tales, Disability, and Making Space* by Amanda Leduc

KEY TAKEAWAYS FOR EQUITY IN OUR CREATIVE WRITING CLASSROOMS

What are some key takeaways from the leading educators on culturally relevant teaching that will help us ensure that the creative writing we engage students in is a tool for empowerment and freedom for all of our students?

First, ABAR practices are good for everyone. If you read about culturally relevant or ABAR pedagogy, you'll probably find yourself thinking that these practices sound like what most of us view as simply good teaching, similar to practices that are labeled student-centered or whole-child. This alignment is good news—it means that in theory, most teachers want antiracist, antibias education in our schools.

An example of an ABAR practice is affirming the identities of our students; and this should easily resonate with every teacher who believes in teaching "the whole child." What's "new" or different about antiracist, antibias education is that it acknowledges that our system is set up with implicit biases we may take for granted, because we may not know anything else—and that we need to challenge these if we want to truly walk the walk of ABAR *or* whole-child practices that include everyone.

For example, many of the books traditionally selected as whole class novels in high school are by white, male, Christian, heterosexual authors. Unless we take the time to think about our students and our texts through an ABAR lens, we might assume we are affirming our students' identities simply because we like and care about them. But if students never meet characters they relate to in an English class, the implicit message is that their identities are not valued, at least not in the literary world, and likely not in our classrooms.

To be quite honest, that is exactly how I felt in most of my own middle and high school classes. I was a quiet but conscientious student, though outside of school I was not a particularly quiet person. The curriculum didn't elicit many personal connections for me (that was probably true for many students), and my teachers did not know me. I also happened to be a member of an ethnic and religious minority, one of a few or the only one in the room in most of my classes—though I wasn't conscious of the significance of this as an adolescent.

In her landmark article, "Mirrors, Windows, and Sliding Glass Doors," Dr. Rudine Simms Bishop wrote about the need for students to see their identities in their reading:

> Reading then, becomes a means of self-affirmation, and readers often seek their mirrors in books . . . when children cannot find themselves in the books they read, or when the images they see are distorted, negative, or laughable, they learn a powerful lesson about how they are devalued in the society of which they are a part. Our classrooms need to be places where all the children from all the cultures that make up . . . American society can find their mirrors. (Simms Bishop, 1990)

In Gholdy Muhammad's equity framework for culturally and historically responsive teaching, "identity" is the first of the five essential pursuits; it is a prerequisite or foundation for the others, which build from there: identity, skills, intellectualism, criticality, and joy. It's hard for me to even imagine what school would have been like if my teachers had taught with identity development as a primary pursuit, but I think it would have drawn me out of my protective shell (like I said, I wasn't quiet in other spaces) and excited my intellectual development—something I didn't experience until certain courses in college, and in my Master of Education program at Bank Street. I imagine that the impact on many of my peers, for a variety of different reasons, could have been transformative as well.

My teachers were operating in alignment with a traditional school system in the 1990s, and many schools are not so different today. But if we know better, we can certainly do better. Helping students know themselves and build their identities through their work in our classes is not an extra, SEL activity, but an integral part of what we need to do to meet our students' needs and "cultivate genius" (Muhammad, 2020). By prioritizing this element within our units and lessons, we can engage our students more deeply and help them flourish.

Vetting Texts and Curriculum Materials

When reviewing texts or other curriculum materials through an ABAR lens, think about whose voices are present and whose voices are silent. If a curriculum piece deals with injustice, this point is especially important. *To Kill A Mockingbird*, for example, is a popular book because of its layered writing and how it deals with themes of racial injustice. However, it is a book written by a white man, telling a story that centers around a Black man wrongly accused of rape. Whose voice is lifted up in this story? The white lawyer who sacrifices for justice. Atticus is a great character, but Black voices are pretty much missing, and that is problematic. Readers are learning about racial injustice in the Jim Crow South without Black voices. Black students may feel uncomfortable with this representation of Black people in a book that specifically deals with a theme of anti-Black racism. Non-Black students are getting a biased perspective that centers a "white savior" character, reinforcing an overused trope we already know well, rather than introducing other narratives that center Black and/or Brown voices on this same issue.

If we do choose to teach this popular book, it's crucial to supplement the study with Black writers on this topic or from the same time period, and to make sure our text choices throughout the year include a variety of diverse voices. This is the concept that drives the work of #DisruptTexts, a grassroots organization which advocates for and coordinates teacher collaboration around disrupting traditional teaching of classic texts with an ABAR lens. Students could also learn about the multiple debates happening over whether the book should be taught and weigh in to the discourse themselves. This is the central idea Deborah Appleman explores in *Literature and the New Culture Wars* (2022).

Teachers should also be intentional about not only including stories of Black people struggling against racism. Gholdy Muhammad emphasizes the pursuit of joy in our teaching. If all of the stories of Black characters represented in our curriculum are centered around suffering, we're not sending a message that Black joy belongs in our classroom.

Beyond vetting individual texts, audit your classroom book collection and the texts across your curriculum. The reading and the writing of our students are strongly connected, and it's essential that students meet wide representation of authors, characters, writing styles, and topics in the books they read. This includes authors and characters who are Black, Indigenous, Latino, Asian, from a variety of backgrounds, queer, gender nonconforming, immigrant, disabled, Muslim, Jewish, Hindu, poor, working class, etc. Check out the We Need Diverse Books website and Disrupt Texts website for help finding new books to build your library.

It's not just seeing Black or Brown faces on the covers of books, but the content and styles of the stories from diverse authors that let students know their own identities are welcome and belong in the literary community of your classroom. Not only does this influence students' relationships to reading, but it informs their perceptions of who can be a writer, who can be a character, which topics can be written about, and from whose perspectives.

It's also important that we as teachers read books by diverse authors so that our exposure to literature is not too narrow and we participate in the same broad literary world our students are coming to know. Reading a wide array of diverse authors equips us with many more reference points for viewing and encouraging our students' writing, and helps us shift away from unconscious biases we may hold about literature from our own upbringing and education.

→ **Exercise:** Decide on one action to take toward growing yourself as an antibias, antiracist educator, and write it down. For example, pick a book from the reading list and set a reading goal, or read articles written by two of the authors on the list. Take an inventory of the texts in your current curriculum and/or classroom library. Which perspectives are missing? Make a plan to include more diverse authors in your curriculum (check out disrupttexts.org and diversebooks.org for ideas).

ELEVATING STORYTELLING TRADITIONS

In the publishing world, there has been a tradition of white hegemony or a strong bias toward white, European, and American authors and characters. In the broader world of storytelling, however, this is not so—never has been and never will be. That is because humans are storytellers; our species does this universally, across culture, time period, and geography. Kind of an amazing fact! Elevating storytelling traditions in our classrooms is a relevant and meaningful way to show students that the world of stories is vast and that each of them, their families, and their ancestors have connections to valuable, interesting stories and storytelling traditions.

Very early in the year, I tell my students that we are "the storytelling animal," a term I got from Jonathan Gottschall, author of a book by the same title. I open up a discussion around the question, "Why do humans tell stories?" I record all of their responses on the board. They include things like for entertainment, to teach lessons, to pass knowledge from one generation to the next. I expand the discussion, asking, "What do you know about stories?" and see how much we can explore this topic. I make a circle in the center of the board with "stories" in it, and then make a web of ideas connected to that. Every year, the conversation goes in interesting directions, raising concepts and questions we can hold onto as we study stories across the year.

Next, I tell students a folk tale from my own cultural background. I do this from memory, because that honors the oral tradition, which is how stories were experienced until very recently in human history. I remind students of this as well: "Before there was television, movies, social media, *or even books*, people told one another stories." We use the folk tale I tell as a text to practice habits of response to reading, but I also continue the thread of oral storytelling in another way.

I ask students to interview adults in their families about stories they know from their cultures or any stories they remember from childhood. Students share the results with the class. Then I assign students to select a folk tale—a broad term I

Table 4.1: Folk Tale Storytelling: Note-Taking Protocol

Student	
Title	
Story origin	
Main characters	
Main conflict	
Magical elements (?)	
Purpose, message, or theme	
Connections to other stories (?)	

use to include fairy tales, myths, and legends—and learn to tell it from memory. Students are encouraged to find a folk tale from their own cultural background, but they are free to choose from anywhere. They may use the internet to research tales. They work on bullet point summaries and practice telling their stories to a partner. Exact words are not important; storytellers can adjust the story each time they tell it as long as they know the plot.

In the next phase, each student has a chance to tell their story to the whole class. The storytelling spreads out over a marking period, usually on Fridays. After each story, we record notes on the following categories in a table students draw in their notebooks.

This activity serves many purposes. It exposes students to a wonderful variety of stories from around the world. In many cases in my classroom, this activity affirms the value of stories that come from my students' families, cultural traditions, and the values they passed down from one generation to the next. Many of my ELL students share stories from their countries of origin, a chance for their experiences to hold direct value in our academic work. It helps all students develop their public speaking, and it gives us a chance to recognize students who already have strong storytelling or public speaking skills. We make connections among the stories, which helps to show the connectedness of human storytelling traditions across cultures and time periods. It provides a chance to practice identifying literary elements, as well as gain an under-standing of the values of different cultures through analyzing the themes of each story.

Oral storytelling has been particularly important for cultures that have endured slavery or colonization, because telling stories was one of few ways to record and transmit their history, since most of the history books were written down by the colonizers or slaveholding classes, and many other structures for transmitting knowledge were disrupted or destroyed. Enslaved African Americans were forbidden to learn to read or write (the penalty could be death), so oral story-telling was crucial to passing knowledge and lessons to one another and to younger generations. It was also a tradition that could be carried from West African griots when so much was lost. In an article entitled, "Why Telling Our Own Story Is So Powerful for Black Americans," writer Andrea Collier quotes the late Virginia Hamilton, African American novelist and author of *The People Could Fly: American Black Folk Tales*, as saying, "storytelling was the first opportunity for black folks [in the U.S.] to represent themselves as anything other than property." Collier writes, "Storytelling is our roots and wings."

Stories hold weight in all cultures, each in their distinct ways, and yet we are bound together by our common human drive to tell and experience stories. The idea of "regular" people reading and writing, especially books, is a new reality relative to the history of humankind. I think it's helpful for students to understand that storytelling is an ancient form, on which people of all cultures can lay claim. I want students to connect plots, themes, and archetypes from folklore with the stories people have written in books, much more recently. Every student, too, has a true connection to this ancient form, and they are contributing to these traditions with the stories they write themselves.

THE SHARE SPACE AND DEVELOPING OUR LITERARY COMMUNITY

Telling folk tales is often the first way we use the share space in my classroom in the beginning of the year. Later, it becomes a space for students to read their own fiction and poetry to the class, and occasionally other tasks, like speaking a poem by heart. Until very recently, the share space was a literal space in my classroom, distinct from the tables where students did their independent and small group work. Four benches created a U-shaped semi-circle we called the meeting area, and students moved there daily for class meetings, discussions, lessons, and shares. (This was like a middle school version of the rug areas common in elementary classrooms.)

Now, due to my extremely tight classroom, I'm not able to maintain the large meeting area with a spot for each student, but I still have benches in a "U" shape around a rug in the front. I have a large bean bag chair on the rug, and students move there voluntarily to be closer to the front, to work in a different space, or for small group discussions. Now, when my students share—whether it's their folk tale or their writing—they come to the front of the room and stand or sit on the "teacher stool." They have the floor, and I set a clear norm at the start of the year that the class gives their full attention to whomever is sharing.

In my early years teaching, I had a few classes that had so much trouble listening to each other that I created a format for note taking designed specifically to hold them accountable for listening to the speaker, using grades as leverage. I almost never use this exact format anymore, but it was a game-changer for me during those few years. It also was a stepping stone toward developing the notes protocols I now use. I'm describing it now in case it is useful to you in your context:

I created a sheet with a class list along the left column. Horizontally, I labeled each column with rubric categories for the share. I assigned each one point values, which added to ten points. The first category was always participation, 5 points. Next, audibility was worth one or two. Next, I would add categories specific to the assignment, such as conflict, descriptive language, figurative language, or expression (if we practiced reading with expression), or simply creativity. Each one had a point value, until I had a total of ten possible points.

I printed a copy of the rubric for each student with the class roster running down the left column. I instructed the students to fill out the sheet for each person who shared. We would go straight down (or up) the list to avoid disruptive discussions about who would read next. I told students that grades were ultimately my decision, and I maintained my own sheet with my grades for the students' readings, but that I would be checking their sheets for additional input. I expected them to be fair to one another.

Here was the kicker: If a student interrupted another student's reading, the interrupting student automatically lost a point off of their own presentation score. Each interruption would cost a point. For this group, the rubric sheets kept them focused. They made the expectations and consequences clear, immediate, and visible. They facilitated students feeling secure enough to read their work and ensured that everyone would be heard.

This meant we were suddenly able to focus on the highly imaginative writing that students were doing, rather than the constant low-level misbehavior and distractions from the work. Share days became the best days.

Now, I have adapted this practice to be less evaluative and more descriptive—partly in response to a former supervisor's feedback to me. She asked if there were other ways students could respond to the readers besides evaluating with numbers. I suddenly realized that I had held onto this practice, which made sense in its original context, but not so much now.

Students now record notes in their notebooks for each reader using categories I assign based on the specifics of the assignment, rather than assigning a number. We take the time to briefly discuss what we noticed in each student's writing before moving on. I still assign grades for the presentation and let students know the criteria. In the beginning of the year, I still tell students they will lose a point for any disruption to their classmates' reading. It's rare that I make such a deduction though.

The share space is a powerful forum for building connections among students across differences, as well as the chance to practice analyzing authors' choices and apply literary vocabulary to their observations. To maximize these many benefits, sharing creative writing regularly is essential.

English teachers tend to use sharing for the purpose of getting feedback to revise writing—which of course is valuable. That kind of sharing is something I do a lot with analytical writing, and earlier in the process for fiction writing. My approach with whole class creative writing shares at the end of a writing cycle is a bit different. The purpose is listening to the work, not revision—although sometimes students are inspired to revise their work after sharing. It's about exposure to classmates' creative writing, observing their craft choices, and appreciating the strengths in their work. It's about empathizing with classmates' characters and conflicts and making connections to other texts and the world, the way we do with most literature we read.

For the most part, my role is to coordinate and facilitate this experience for students. I create the context and space for students to write and share. The literature itself and the protocols we use for response do most of the teaching. Now and then I step in to seize a "teachable moment."

Share Space General Protocols

- Students have completed their stories, poems, or imaginative exercises. This doesn't always mean the piece has gone through more than one draft—that depends on the structure of the unit and the timing. I explain more of my approach on multiple drafts in Chapter 7.
- Students have a chance to practice reading their work to themselves or a partner. For longer stories, students select one scene to read. Students who strongly prefer it may ask a classmate to read for them.
- If possible, sit in a circle or create a space in the front of the room where the storyteller/reader sits and can be heard. For poetry readings, we have used a microphone, which is lots of fun.
- Set students up with a format for note-taking as they listen. I have done this with photocopied sheets with the class rosters and columns or in notebooks. The notes would include students' name, the title of their story or scene, and other categories of notetaking that reflect focus points of the assignment.
- One category is usually identifying a relevant craft choice, such as which setting did they choose to describe? Or what did they choose to change from the original story, or what conflict can you identify from this section?
- Another category is usually a highlight: what stood out to you? Or write down their most vivid language.
- See Chapter 2 for a detailed description of how the academic component of the share session works.

I like to keep the share space a place for listening, celebration, and observation rather than constructive feedback and workshopping. I model these kinds of responses myself and invite them from students. The note-taking protocols encourage these kinds of responses.

- Positive feedback should be specific: "I like how you showed his thoughts as the monster approached," rather than "Great story."

- Descriptive or analytical response: "The conflict is that she doesn't trust her friend. It begins to resolve when . . . "
- Constructive feedback is more appropriate during the drafting stage, and I generally do this in pairs, small groups, or through teacher conferencing.
- Suggestions can work here when they are generally encouraging and speak from the reader's experience. "I feel curious about . . . " or "When the characters said _____, it made me wonder . . . " or "I hope you write more about . . . in the future."
- Questions can work in the share space if they show interest in the story, rather than judgment, ask to clarify something the listener wants to understand better, and allow the writer the choice to answer or not. "Wait, did the main character actually time travel or was that a dream?" or "Where did you get the idea for this story?"

Another format I use for sharing is a gallery walk or reading party. In this format, students leave their finished piece on their desk. Next to it, they leave a "guest book," a folded piece of plain paper with their story title and name, where students can leave messages for the writer. Then students all stand and move to a different spot, sit down, and read. When they finish reading, they leave a specific affirmative comment or a question they have. Students continue moving and reading like musical chairs. I like to bring snacks on that day as well. Based on class input, I have also done this with names removed from the printed stories. The effect is a bit different, but it still works quite well.

The share space is about connecting with each other through our literary work, while at the same time building literary understandings through classmates' writing. It can seem like a lot of time to devote to the process when every student shares, but taking this time and including everyone captures students' attention, amplifies the full range of student voices, catapults understanding of literary elements, motivates students to try new things in their writing, and positively influences the climate of the class.

Voices in Our Classrooms We Might Not Hear

When I think about fighting for social justice as an educator, I've always felt that the work must begin in my own classroom, in the ways each of us in it—myself included—treat one another. I think about how the behaviors and values students practice in the classroom impact their lives beyond it and their pathways into adulthood. The classroom is the place where I have direct influence and responsibility, and if I don't start with conditions and relationships there, other attempts to engage students in social justice work can feel superficial or even hypocritical.

One way I assess the conditions of my classroom is to observe whose voices are present. How much of the time do I speak? How much of the time do students speak? Which students speak often? Sometimes? Who is silent? Just like in the broader society, the answers to these questions often are indicators of who holds power. If we want to model equality, we have to be willing to step back and observe, reflect, and make adjustments that allow more people the opportunity and confidence to make their voices heard.

In shifting the usual dynamics among students, imaginative writing and the share sessions have been indispensable. These processes change what "class participation" looks like and who feels comfortable doing it.

Typical class participation works well for people who like to think out loud, and process ideas verbally. Class discussions, whether student-driven or teacher-directed, are more challenging for students with introvert qualities. Introverts, while not a monolithic group, often need time to process their thinking internally, before feeling comfortable sharing. This may keep an introvert from participating orally in class. It becomes a disadvantage when we interpret this behavior as a lack of understanding or interest. The same can be true for other reasons (students who are learning English as a new language, for example).

By contrast, when students write stories or poems, they do the bulk of the work independently, sometimes sharing in pairs or small groups along the way. In my classroom, we usually share finished drafts with the whole class. Unlike in many other lesson formats, introverted students who prefer to process language internally are on equal footing with those who process verbally. And when we listen to their pieces, we hear a great deal of their personality, which quite often, the rest of the class has never heard before.

I remember when Ilana, an introverted student who generally kept her distance from her classmates, wrote a story from the perspective of an egg. The egg wanted to come out of its shell, but worried about the reality that once it did, it would no longer be an egg! The concept was so creative it caught everyone's attention, and the storytelling voice that emerged from it happened to be outrageously funny. It was a treat for everyone to hear. There was a remarkable parallel between the egg coming out of its shell—and becoming a chick—and Ilana revealing so much of her inner voice at once, as she read her story to the class.

A similar equalizing shift happens for many students who struggle with verbal participation in class activities, such as some English language learners and students with language delays. To be sure, there are many strategies for supporting diverse learners to participate in speaking activities in class. But writing creatively and independently, and then sharing with the community is one powerful way to bring all students into the forefront. The impact is both academic and social.

REDEFINING INTELLIGENCE THROUGH CREATIVE WORK, ELEVATING NEW VOICES

The intelligence I see emerging through students' creative writing differs somewhat from the kind of smarts students are typically required to express during a school day. Imaginative writing allows for more divergent thinking than most school tasks. Because there are infinite ways to approach a creative piece, and students make choices about what challenges they want to undertake in their own projects, I believe each student has an opportunity to be successful. Students are automatically the authorities over the stories they are telling, which is often not the case in other kinds of writing or academic tasks. There is some relief in this for students, and it also affects how they see one another.

As children move through school, they develop concepts of who they are as students based on their experiences and messages they receive from teachers, peers, family, and media. While educators influenced by Carol Dweck (2007) are trying to help students develop growth mindsets, to see intelligence as fluid, dynamic capacities, our culture in and out of schools has traditionally reinforced more fixed mindsets. Teachers and students alike often default to judging learners as either school-smart or not, and these identities are influenced by societal structures and inequities therein. That is a trap which makes everyone less likely to take risks and to bounce back from perceived failures. We have to consciously move away from fixed mindsets. Consciously changing our mindset is a metacognitive process, which is a little abstract for young people.

Another route to challenge our perceptions about what intelligence looks like and who has it is to switch up the nature of the tasks. Through live, direct counter-examples, we can disprove the validity of our preconceptions, making space for a more complex understanding of what makes someone smart.

Fiction writing allows students to draw on a number of the intelligences defined by Howard Gardner (2011) in his theory of multiple intelligences. The medium for story is usually language. So, all students must utilize verbal–linguistic intelligence. However, based on the choices students make in their writing, they express other forms of intelligence. Interpersonal intelligence is revealed in the way students imagine characters or play with readers' expectations; intrapersonal intelligence may inform their protagonist's perceptions of him or herself. Some students have expressed existential intelligence—a proposed addition to the official eight that Gardner has discussed—by creating literary pieces that engage in deep questions about life and its meaning. Some students utilize naturalist or even kinesthetic intelligence in their writing as well, if they select topics that allow them to channel those understandings. Musical intelligence can be utilized when students compose lines, and listen back for the rhythm. (Novelist Ottessa Moshfegh said in a 2018 *New Yorker* interview, "Studying music and playing music, I think, was the foundation for the way that I look at writing . . . the way that a voice can sound and the way that it leads the reader in a sort of virtual reality . . . ")

In imaginative writing, intelligence shakes out differently than how students are often expecting it to, defying images students have of themselves and stereotypes they have of their classmates. In diverse schools (which is really every school, but some more obviously than others) this point could not be more important.

In a classroom with students on both sides of the "achievement gap," which persists in dividing along socioeconomic and racial lines (Annie E. Casey Foundation, 2013, 2017), it's easy for students to quietly infer casuality: to draw the conclusion that intelligence and/or success in school are somehow based on these same racial and socioeconomic factors. Research shows that neither race nor socioeconomic status *creates* the disparity in academic achievement, but rather that the conditions of poverty and obstacles of racism pose substantial challenges for students to succeed academically. This doesn't mean students from low income families can't or don't succeed in school; it means that when they do, they overcome obstacles greater than those of their more privileged peers (International Education Studies, 2016). However, short of eliminating poverty, effective interventions to support students on this pathway have not been widely available. Instead, resources have been poured into more frequent, standardized measures of student achievement, and use of the data to pressure students, teachers, and school leaders to make choices that would help struggling students "do better," without additional resources or even autonomy to make these choices.

These narrow sources of data have reinforced fixed mindsets of intelligence. When I entered teaching in 2004, NCLB was just becoming a major influence. I was shocked to hear teachers and administrators refer to students as numbers: "She's a 3; he's a 1; she's a low 2." I learned that these comments were referring to the score on a four-point scale that the student received on the previous year's New York State ELA exam.

I would have to say that today, the influence of testing has actually grown. The systems around it are more complex, but they still measure and label students according to extraordinarily narrow criteria. It's almost dystopian, and I believe that students sense it.

When the power dynamics around intelligence change in the classroom, students feel it, too, and it can be very healing. Andrew came to seventh grade having scored a "Level 2," which is below proficiency in English Language Arts. He seemed to me to be quite capable as a student, though in class, he was sometimes more playful than focused, often looking for attention from his peers. He was not one to do his homework unless there was a phone call home about it. Andrew was African American, and it seemed to me he had learned to underperform in school, based on an unspoken, probably inaccurate fear that appearing "smart" would lower his social status. There is a body of research on the prevalence of peer pressure on Black boys to underachieve in school, based in part on underlying associations between achieving in school and "acting white," or giving up one's identity and communal solidarity (Ransaw & Green, 2016).

Still, Andrew seemed to enjoy learning when he could forget about how others saw him. That seemed to happen in his creative writing. When he read for the class, he revealed a keen ability to play with his audience's expectations. It was as if he took his preoccupation with what others thought of him and rechanneled it into his creative writing. We first saw this with a poem he wrote:

The Friend Who Comes and Goes

> I have a friend who comes for a little while each year.
> It's about the time of year for her to come around.
> Whenever there is heat
> she is never there
> but when it is cold
> there is a way for her.
> She is on her way, and I know this
> because she always calls the Fox Five News
> to let me know she's coming.
> Then I hear the silent
> but loud sound she makes.
> She blows and I feel a sharp
> cold breeze through the window
> then through my bones
> that lets me know she's here.
> I grab my coat and stumble outside.
> I see her crystal white hair sparkling.
> Then I jump right into her huge arms
> and I feel myself sinking into her.
> I call up Oliver and ask if he wants
> to come play with me and my friend,
> and he agrees.

> We meet at the park and
> we start throwing her around.
> But don't worry,
> she enjoys it.
> Kids always tell me how it's odd that I call the snow my friend
> but I smile and say
> I play with her
> and she only comes a little while a year
> so therefore I call her
> The friend who comes and goes.

My middle school students were in an uproar listening to this poem, their minds imagining it was about a mysterious girlfriend. But Andrew included enough clues to throw some confusion into that scenario as well. When the ending revealed it was about snow, there was more uproar and students immediately requested to hear it again. Andrew appeared to enjoy every second of the attention. He was able to express himself in a way that felt genuine in an academic context.

Andrew then developed this same skill of playing with the reader's experience in a short story, creating a number of effects, including dramatic irony. He took on a number of craft challenges, like writing realistic dialogue and balancing it with action, interior monologue, and figurative language all in service of a humorous opening scene. None of this is easy.

Here is Chapter 1 of his story. Note: After I received permission to use this work, students requested basic editing, so that's what I've done.

The Cup

Ahhhhhh I wake up like any normal day. I yawn with my mouth open extremely wide. I sit up and scratch my head then stand up. I feel a fresh breeze of air pass my room's window. I hear the neighbor's self lawn watering machine. Then I notice something. I have to peeee! I run down the hall trying my best not to use the bathroom on myself. I bum rush the door. Booooom!

Then my mom screams, "What the hell was that?"

"Nothing," I say while jumping around while trying to hold in my bladder. I bang on the door "Let me in," I yell.

"No you little twerp," my big sister says. I run to my parent room and tell them that Maya is taking so long in the bathroom again.

"5 more minutes," my mom says then rolls over.

Can you believe this? I'm here about to die and the person with authority is asking for five more minutes. This type of thing is common because my sister always spends 20 years in the bathroom trying to perfect her looks even though it makes her look even more ridiculous than she already is.

So I decide to take matters into my own hands. I run down the stairs and jump down from the midway part to the ground. I see a cup and take care of business. Ahhhhhhhhhhhh release all the stress. I walk back to my room happy as can be and get my clothes.

I open my drawer and get my socks and black shirt with the word "Sike" in big bold white letters. I get my jeans that have a little rip in them and grab my black and white sneakers. I put on my clothes then go to the bathroom. I'm prepared to karate kick the door to break it down. I run to bum rush the door then my sister opens it and I go flying like a plane into the bathroom. Then Maya starts cracking up and walks right out the bathroom.

I want to scream out so many curses at her. I feel like a volcano about to erupt but can't. I get up and brush my teeth. Then I take a deep breath and smell a wonderful smell. I continue to sniff and sniff like a bloodhound. I follow the smell all the way down the stairs to the kitchen. I see my mom, dad, and sister there and my mom's over the stove cooking my favorite food, bacon.

"Good Morning everyone," I say.

"Good Morning," everyone says but my sister. She just looked at me like I had 30 heads then went back to texting on her phone.

"I'm thirsty," my sister says.

She grabs the first cup she saw on the table and started gulping it down. Then she spits it all out. "EWWWW what was that!" she said.

She runs to the bathroom.

"Karma hahahahhaha," I say.

The five-chapter story continues. The main character goes out to play basketball with friends. Later, they see his sister in a troubling situation, and they help her. The last line of the story is, "And by the way, after what happened, I don't think I'll ever have to pee in a cup in my house again."

The story wasn't just entertaining. Andrew carefully built each moment, including an ending that connected to his beginning—I often teach students to do this later in the year, but I had not yet! Andrew was showing his smarts, and he seemed unafraid. His classmates enjoyed what he offered through his writing and were happy to see him shine. It's also worth noting that his writing reflected elements of the realistic fiction genre he always preferred during independent reading time.

Incidentally, Andrew moved up a level that year on the state ELA exam, scoring a proficient "Level 3."

I've heard that people who struggle with stuttering don't stutter when they sing. The language they are expressing is the same, but when they sing, the words are channeled through a different pathway in the brain, which bypasses the difficulty of the stutter. I believe creative writing allows many students to bypass internal conflicts they have around their school identities or their perception of their own intelligence to discover alternative pathways forward. In many cases, students' internal conflicts are direct manifestations of inequities in our society and an education system that puts children in the terrible position of doubting their own worth and potential. I've seen imaginative writing help students fight these obstacles.

EMPATHY ACROSS DIFFERENCES

I remember when Junie read her vignette to the class. This was a project in conjunction with our reading of Sandra Cisneros's novella, *The House On Mango Street*, which is told through a series of vignettes. Cisneros explains in an interview that many of the pieces contain autobiographical elements, while others reflect the experiences of others in her community growing up. I invited students to do the same in their own vignettes.

Girls/Girls/Boys

Everyone has had a crush before. When you first see someone you like, you observe their looks. You look at their eyes, their hair, the way they dress. All my life, the first thing I notice are the eyes of the boys that I liked. But one day, instead of noticing a boy's eyes, I saw these beautiful hazelnut eyes with long lashes that belonged to a girl. I started to panic and ask questions to myself. What did this mean? I depended on the Internet so I took many tests to see what I was.

Truth is that I don't completely know what I am and who I like. Even though I have accepted it, I still question it. I still have so many questions which may never be answered. I still need to live with the fear of coming out or my homophobic family finding out. If they do find out, I'd probably get kicked out. I don't have anyone to talk about these things. My mind is a deep, dark place that no one could understand. My mind is like an enigma, maybe more difficult to decode. My mind is a mess when I see the girl.

Maybe one day, I'll conquer all my fears. Whether it's coming out to my family or understanding my own mind or facing all this alone.

Meanwhile, I talk to the girl with the hazelnut eyes.

When Junie finished reading, the class erupted in cheers and applause. I actually discourage applause in these readings, but it was a moment filled with such warmth and affirmation, and I could not have stopped it if I tried. Our school has made significant effort to be a space where LGBTQ+ people feel safe and included in our community—it is more open and inclusive in this way than other schools I've known. At the same time, I knew that many of my students came from families where homosexuality is not accepted. Eighth-graders are struggling developmentally to decide what their values are and whether they align with those of their parents. Junie's strength in humanizing the struggle of a young person questioning her sexuality through her narrative elicited the powerful response of support and love, rather than separation, fear, and hatred.

> Taking others' perspectives, recognizing strengths in others, and demonstrating empathy and compassion" are aspects of social awareness highlighted in the CASEL Framework, which students develop through reading and hearing their classmates' stories.

CROSSING RACIAL, ECONOMIC, AND OTHER MAJOR DIVIDES

I remember students at a former school, who came from vastly different backgrounds within the same borough of Brooklyn—Black, white, Latino, Asian, and multiracial students from affluent, poor, middle, and working-class families. Because New York City neighborhoods are quite segregated, there was not a great deal of common experience and language to talk across these differences. I observed that students sought out classmates who felt familiar and generally did not take the initiative to get to know classmates who came from very different backgrounds from them. Over time, some of the divisions eroded, but I also remember hitting walls when I tried to encourage connection.

The most common wall showed up in the form of students expressing lack of interest in engaging with classmates from different backgrounds, beyond required group work in classes—in this case, socioeconomic status seemed to be a more prominent distinction than race, though the affluent students tended to be white, so race was always an issue. Students of all backgrounds were careful about what they said, avoiding judgmental comments, but many claimed firmly that, "We're just different; we don't like the same things."

This kind of separation is fueled by societal and cultural structures—and it perpetuates these same structures if we don't challenge it. In middle school, there may appear to be a cloak of equality over this quiet social "othering." Students of all backgrounds claimed that no group was better than another, just different. But considering the greater context, especially in adulthood, the separation becomes anything but equal. One group encounters job discrimination while the other doesn't. One group gets home loans with ease while the other doesn't. One group can afford a brush with the law and emerge without lasting damage; another group faces grave consequences for any small mistake, or even no mistake at all. One group lives in fear of detention and deportation, while another does not. One group lives in fear of violence, while another does not. The "othering" may feel innocent to children, but it feeds a dangerous pattern.

There are a number of angles that need work in order to fight the effects of segregation and create a truly integrated, democratic community in the classroom. Adults need to work themselves to develop awareness, dialogue and language around race, class, and gender. The more informed and conscious teachers are on these issues in our own lives and with each other, the more we can model critical engagement for and with our students. Dialogue around equity and the learning that emerges from it must be sustained by educators, as long as the conditions in which our students live are unequal—regardless of which side of it they are on.

Beyond self-reflection, we must revisit and question the curriculum and decisions regarding students, through a lens of equity: Does this choice or practice support or disrupt existing systems of oppression? We must be willing to make adjustments in our own work and call attention to the issues in our teaching communities in order to move in a direction of justice and inclusion. This is heavy work but nothing less is needed. We have a chance every day to do our part to deliver on the promise of democracy. My own learning is ongoing.

With that context in mind, a significant piece of my story as a teacher of diverse students has been the discovery that literature—reading, discussing, *and* writing it— is potent medicine for students to see beyond the barriers of race, class, and gender and the social cliques that so often mirror them.

Because reading and writing are explicitly connected in my classroom, it's significant that the literature students read and use as models for creative writing is literature that often engages in social issues. In the whole novels method I use, students drive the discussions of literary texts; encouraged by my facilitation, they learn to talk openly about the content of the books with their peers. The texts we read together by diverse authors and conversations about them are a part of the antidote to the "othering" frameworks students have picked up in their thirteen or so years on earth.

I believe this process helps students be more open to identifying and writing about social issues that matter to them. I don't encourage any particular content for students' creative writing, but the models we use help students see a wide range of experiences as relevant in literature.

When students share their writing, I can see the affects immediately. I remember Tyler shrieking with excitement during Claudia's reading of her creepy and extremely suspenseful monster story. Tyler and Claudia were not from similar backgrounds or social groups at all. Ordinarily, any interactions between these two were governed by an unspoken, seemingly mutual separation across race, class, and gender lines. But Tyler's shrieks are emblazoned in my memory as testament to the power of her storytelling in that moment, and his uninhibited appreciation thereof. The sentiment he expressed out loud seemed to be shared by most in the room. Claudia had nailed this story, and no one had seen it coming.

In the same class on a different assignment, we heard Sandra's "I Am From . . . " poem, an assignment I adapted from Linda Christensen's *Reading, Writing and Rising Up* (2000). In it, students interviewed an elder in their family or community about their culture and heritage and used it to write poems. There was a hushed awe in the room afterward, similar in intensity to Tyler's shrieks, but entirely different in character. Our minds had been expanded by the world she opened up through her poem, a world truly hidden from us throughout the school day.

If You Look At My Eyes

I am from the old valuable shoes she worked her entire life for,
and which we respect.
From one who has lived expecting us to change and standout from
other bulls.
I am from her.
The oldest generation.
You and I are from the third world, where money can kill justice.
Where once, the sun burned our soft, brown skin while hanging the
cloth on the same roof.
I am from your daughter who ran away.
I am from the house next to the river.
I am from the colorful Mexican folkloric dress.
Waving it back and forth, eagerly tapping the concrete with bright
colorful heels
begging for music to keep going.

Submerging into the melody of the old cassette played by humans.
If you look at my eyes . . .
my hands . . .
my hair . . .
my skin . . .
you will see where I am from.
Flip the pages back until you find my genes dancing around, enjoying
the ritual moves . . .
praising and chanting a forgotten god.
I am from the buckets of gold she carried on her shoulders hoping to
find an easier way home.
I am from wearing "Huaraches" and a embroidery manta vintage, sitting
on the dirt helping mama
putting the wood under "El Comal."
My grandma making "Salsa de Molcajete" and mixing "Nixtamal,"
a sacred meal.
I can tell this place will be here for life.
I can tell I am from the daydream I have during class.
I am from that place I see, when I see myself in the mirror.

We would never see Sandra, who had immigrated from Mexico with her mother four years before, the same way again. When we looked into her eyes, we would now see the place of this poem, her daydream, the music, her grandmother, and all of the finely tuned language she created to memorialize these parts of herself and her history.

Likewise, when Dominic read his poem, we understood him in a way his usual humor never allowed.

Miracle

I am from if you make it,
it's a miracle,
If you don't, you don't
I am from Summer
tournaments to big disappointments
(losing on your home court)
the work you put into it that goes to waste
I am from a split apart
family, not knowing which side to take
when my parents argue

I am from a neighborhood
where if you call the cops they
won't be there to help. Where
fighting is like a trademark
rather than a surprise
I am from that place
where a sunny day could
turn into a bloody day
where a family could be
destroyed in seconds
(thanksgiving)
I am from those parents
protecting us like a bird
protecting its eggs

Dominic explained things in this poem that are not easy to understand from the outside looking in. He humanized himself and gave his classmates a chance to learn. The border crossings that happen when we share "I Am From . . . " poems are particularly powerful and explicit, but these happen in more subtle ways every time we hear stories, real or imagined, from students whose experiences and worldviews are different from ours.

LEADING THROUGH DIFFICULT MOMENTS

An element of ABAR education is teaching students to ask questions about perspective and power within their learning. Adolescents are primed for this kind of critical thinking, because they look for inconsistencies and hypocrisies in the rules and adults in their lives. In ABAR teaching, we give students language to notice bias and stereotypes in texts and in life; to ask questions about who's telling a story and whose voices are left out, and to examine the impact of those facts. To implement this well, we need to be able to challenge negative biases that occasionally come up in student work.

During one read aloud session, Joseph read a vignette he'd written about a teenage boy who is looking for his first job. His uncle helps him get a job at a small grocery store working the cash register. Usually, I have a chance to read students' writing prior to the read aloud sessions, either during class while they write or outside of class, but not always. In this case, I had not worked with Joseph on this piece and didn't know what was coming.

It started with him learning to use a cash register and feeling bored and alone during lunch break with no one to talk to.

Then Joseph read, "When lunch break was over, I saw a Black man enter with a black coat and a beige book bag. He looked suspicious, so I kept my eyes on him." The room immediately felt tense. There were a few audible "Ooohhs" that expressed discomfort or disapproval. Not knowing where the story would go next, I decided to pause the reading to address what was happening.

"Joseph, I want to interrupt you for a moment to talk about what people are feeling in the room." Joseph nodded, looking a little embarrassed. "Does anyone want to make a comment? Let's also keep in mind that Joseph is the author here, not the character; so, let's focus comments on the story, not Joseph."

A Black male student raised his hand first. "Why does the guy need to be Black?" he asked. A number of classmates agreed.

"Yeah," said another student. "That's racial profiling." Joseph, by the way, is white-passing from a Latino background. He may not identify as white, but his light complexion means he's unlikely to have experienced racial profiling in the way that darker people regularly do.

"Can you explain what you mean by racial profiling?" I asked.

"He said the guy looked suspicious, because he was Black. That's what cops do when they stop Black people for no reason. It's racial profiling," the student said.

"I didn't say he looked suspicious because he was Black," Joseph responded. "I said he was Black. Then, I said he looked suspicious."

"Yeah, but he didn't mention the race of any other characters," the first student said. "Why did the character have to be Black?"

During this conversation, I quickly glanced at the rest of Joseph's vignette. It seemed conceivable that Joseph had woven a story that took a turn and did not ultimately reinforce the stereotype of Black males as criminals. However, the scene ended with the man putting bags of chips into his bag and walking out in plain view of the narrator, who was at a loss for how to respond. Stereotype fulfilled. The issue here was the racial element in the scene, and we needed to unpack that. The year was 2017.

"In the rest of Joseph's scene, this character ends up stealing from the store," I told the class. "Is that a situation that could actually happen in real life?"

"Yes," some students called out.

"Could it also happen if this character were white?" I asked.

"Yes," students answered again.

"Is it possible for a person of any race to steal? Do we all agree that happens in real life?" Everyone seemed to agree. "So why does it make us uncomfortable when, in this story, the character is Black?" I asked.

A Latina student responds. "Because the media always shows Black people doing bad stuff. They never show white people doing that. And then people discriminate. Black people get killed for doing nothing but so-called 'looking suspicious,'" she said, making quotation marks with her fingers. "Trayvon Martin, Michael Brown." There were some snaps of agreement from classmates.

"I grew up with mostly white people," I said. "As a teen, I knew a few girls who would steal from stores. They were white, and no one ever suspected them. Joseph, I think what's causing this reaction is that the way you introduced this character into the scene plays into unfair biases that our society already has against people of color, especially Black people, and they cause real harm. It's not that you cannot write this scene this way—you're the author and you have control. It's that we want to challenge racist stereotypes when we can, rather than adding to them. Your class-mates want you to rethink this decision." Students were familiar with the concept of stereotypes. It had come up in a number of texts we'd read, and in their social studies and advisory classes, so I was confident the message was not over their heads. The students who spoke had broken it down very well, in fact.

I thanked Joseph for being willing to hear our criticism and for taking it so well. He had stood in the hot seat and listened. I also thought the students did a good job of sticking to the topic and text, rather than attacking Joseph personally. It was less than ideal to have put him on the spot like that, but overall, it was a learning expe-rience for all of us. I know that we modeled having a difficult but respectful conver-sation about racism in relation to a fictional story. I believe that experience with this kind of communication prepares students to challenge similar stereotypes when they encounter them elsewhere in their lives.

As a teacher, it's not easy to lead through conflicts about topics that are so deeply important and often contentious. When I first realized the direction Joseph's vignette was taking, I wanted to run away and hide. I felt like a bad teacher for letting that situation arise. I could have read Joseph's work beforehand and had a private con-versation with him about this. Did my lack of preparation hurt Joseph? My Black students? Other students witnessing how the situation was handled? At the same time, teachers aren't perfect. No human is. We make mistakes and our obligation in each moment is to step up and do the best we can.

In that situation, the fact that I and my students had practice looking at racism, bias, and stereotypes was key to having a productive discussion that, I believe, bent toward justice. This is why antibias, antiracist education is so important—especially for teachers as leaders of classroom communities. We will likely never reach an end point, but through our experience and commitment, we get better at working out issues as a community.

That day, I had intended to have more students share, but our discussion of

Joseph's piece took us to the bell. I took a risk to address the issue right away, head-on. I did so imperfectly, but opening the floor for dialogue was worth it. That experience helps me feel more confident addressing stereotypes in student writing when they come up. It's never easy, but each time I feel less avoidant and more confident in the need to speak up for others' humanity and in my ability to do so.

The share space can be a place for students to practice a variety of aspects of self-awareness, as defined on the CASEL framework, including "examining prejudices and biases," "linking feelings, values, and thoughts," and "integrating personal and social identities." The CASEL Framework defines social awareness as: "**The abilities to understand the perspectives of and empathize with others, including those from diverse backgrounds, cultures, and contexts,**" with a subcategory of "**identifying diverse social norms, including unjust ones.**" We can facilitate learning opportunities among students if we have language in place in our classroom for understanding bias and injustice, through reading and discussion with an ABAR lens.

The literary world is a reflection of the human imagination, and of the specific people in a place and time. For growing young people, it's a place to deeply examine our current world and imagine a better one. For teachers, participating and leading in this world gives us tremendous power. It requires constant reflection on our own use of power and an investment in our own learning about educating for equity.

5

Designing Assignments That Teach Through Experience

WHEN I FIRST SHARED my idea for this book with my supervisor at the time, a supportive leader and former English teacher, she listened and then asked a good question: "I always saw my students enjoy the experience of writing stories," she said, "but how do you keep them from just going on and on and on, without really . . . getting anywhere?" I knew exactly what she was talking about, and you probably do too.

It's a little painful to admit, but sometimes student writing can be boring to read. While some students struggle with writing output, others seem to have internalized a message that the more you write, the better. And given the chance, they go for it. The ability to indulge in writing—to put on paper whatever comes to mind—is a wonderful tool . . . for the writer, that is. My private journals as an adolescent were exactly that way. They provided an invaluable outlet for me during a turbulent period; but they are mostly boring to go back and reread.

If we're writing with some notion that there will be a reader other than ourselves, and we're aware of the narrative craft of authors *we like*, then the work cannot simply be indulgent. Art requires a certain amount of freedom—the freedom to be honest and vulnerable, take risks, challenge norms, and break boundaries. At the same time, there is a great deal of discipline involved. Artists create using established, often ancient forms. Knowledge of these forms inform and expand an artist's domain.

Students need to build a repertoire of tools—craft techniques, plot structures and other literary elements that underlie great literature—and work to utilize them in service of telling their unique stories in their distinct ways. This process involves a nice balance of divergent and convergent thinking.

In this chapter, I'll share a few different ways that I teach students to write fiction. When I refer to teaching, I'm using an experiential approach. I'm rarely in front of the whole class delivering lessons. I design assignments that teach through experience and influence my students' processes along the way. With each assignment, I teach one or two more traditional lessons, which I share in Chapter 6.

In this chapter, we'll look at:

- How a cycle of inquiry looks in integrating imaginative writing into literature study
- Finding the right balance of freedom and limitation in creating assignments and setting students up for success
- Three ways to design fiction writing assignments connected to reading (a progression)
- How to teach the crucial element of plot
- Entering writing through dramatic play
- My small list of (extremely helpful) rules for students writing fiction

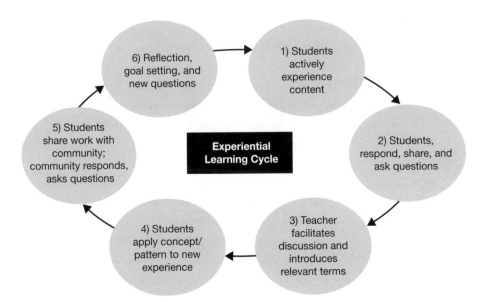

Figure 5.1: Experiential Learning Cycle

Table 5.1: Literature Learning Cycle with Four Integrated Roles

Learning Cycle	How it Looks with Integrated Four Roles
1) Students actively experience content	Students read a novel or other text—immersion in a story is a powerful direct experience. (Teachers prioritize students having their experience.)
2) Students respond, share, and ask questions	Students respond authentically as they read, noting and sharing reactions and observations. I direct students to track one literary element along with their open responses.
3) Teacher facilitates discussion and introduces relevant terms	Teacher facilitates open discussion. Points of interest/investigation emerge. Teacher introduces literary terms that help name student observations.
4) Students apply concept/pattern to new experience	Teacher coordinates an opportunity for students to try out an element they observed in the story in their own writing. Sometimes students cocreate assignments; other times teacher builds the task.
5) Students share work in classroom community; community responds, asks questions	Students share imaginative writing work in the classroom community; students respond, describe the work, ask questions.
6) Reflection, goal setting, and new questions	Students self-reflect on their writing: what worked, what needs work? What new questions arise? Students set goals and the cycle can repeat with new content.

EXPERIENTIAL LEARNING CYCLE

Experiential learning ideally follows a cycle of inquiry. There are many versions of a basic inquiry cycle, and these can be applied to any subject area. This is my variation, based initially on a "Learning Cycle," developed by Lawson, Abraham, and Renner for teaching science (1989). I've added to it to better reflect the reading–response–writing cycle in which students move through the four integrated roles of reader, member of literary community, critic, and finally writer of original literary pieces, outlined in Chapter 2.

The first three steps in the cycle center on student reading. In my class, we use the whole novels method, which I described in Chapter 2 and wrote about in *Whole Novels For the Whole Class: A Student-Centered Approach* (Sacks, 2014). In novel studies, the cycle takes place over a month or so. Reading cycles can be much shorter with short texts, and the entire cycle can take place over a few days. Both short and long-form fiction are useful and important. One great benefit of novel studies is that the longer form provides a more immersive reading experience. For students, there is more content to draw meaningfully from in discussions and writing, and there's a more robust shared experience and shared vocabulary for the class to connect back to as they build conceptual understandings across the year.

Designing fiction writing assignments is the major piece of teacher work in Step 4, which Lawson called concept application. The writing assignments we create provide an experience for students, connected to what comes before it and what comes after it. Those intentional connections expand the learning, helping students to pull lessons out of their experiences. Our assignment creation and guidance are key for students to get the most out of their writing experience.

LIMIT THE FOCUS TO LIBERATE THE IMAGINATION

As a young adult, I did almost no creative writing in school, but I wrote freely in my journals, in both narrative and poetry. I was a quietly dramatic adolescent, driven to express myself in what I saw as a cruel, hypocritical world. I viewed most of the writing I was asked to do in school as restrictive and inauthentic. In retrospect, this was a bit exaggerated, but not without truth.

One of my favorite teachers in high school, for example, told us straight up that in order to write successfully on the major gatekeeping tests, there was a formula to learn. A big part of it, he told us, was learning how to "B.S." Learn I did, but the outcomes were mixed. I aced my major tests, including a perfect score on the AP writing exam. And then . . . I had to unlearn almost all of it in college. It took me two years of muddling in mediocrity to discover how to write a quality paper that was both honest and academically rigorous. The trick was to write what I actually thought, not what I imagined the professor wanted to read; I learned to depart from some of the structures I had internalized and argue my points more freely and passionately.

My experience in creative writing was almost the opposite. When I began taking poetry writing workshop courses in college, I was looking for validation of the secret, self-taught creative writer I was. What I actually got was much better—the opportunity to expand my writing to new places, to learn new structures, and cama-raderie and encouragement along that journey.

As much as I valued the freedom I found in my private creative writing, it was the exercises in which the instructor strategically removed a few elements of freedom that helped me the most. Something as simple as an assignment to write a poem in the form of a letter ("Dear You-Are-In-Italy," mine began) would push me into a less familiar space, and that was exciting, personally and artistically.

Though the tasks presented some restrictions, the content and style were still mine, and I inevitably found there were plenty of options for authentic self-expression. In the letter-poem exercise, for example, if I didn't feel like writing to a person, I could write "Dear Fear" or "Dear Feet" or "Dear No One," adjusting the recipient to allow me to write the poem I wanted to write. The limitations stimulated less predictable responses from me. They took me out of tired patterns I had formed by myself—compelling me toward new directions, which were still uniquely my own.

Reading a sestina and learning how to write one, for example, which is a highly structured poetic form, was eye-opening and brought out something beautiful I could never have dreamed up without learning this form.

> **Tip:** Check out Elizabeth Bishop's beautiful and mysterious poem, "Sestina." Motivated poetry students, seventh grade and up, can read it and work on deciphering the pattern. Then you can teach them how to write one, by selecting six words, plugging them into the end of each line in the same line and stanza pattern Bishop uses. Students can also look up the steps on the internet and write their own. There are many resources to learn the pattern, and it generates some marvelous writing from students who are hungry for a challenge.

The key is to impose a right amount of structure that stimulates ideas, it must be accessible and open enough for creative decision-making—not too open as to overwhelm and not too restrictive as to shut down creative exploration.

Establishing Free-Writing

I start the year by establishing a practice of free-writing. This is the space where students can truly write whatever they want. With this practice, students learn not to feel intimidated by a blank page. We create a familiar, personal space for ourselves in our notebooks. The imposed limitation is that the free-writing we do in class is

Figure 5.2: My Old Journals

time-bound and in one consistent place. Some years, I have students create a Free-Writing Section in the back of the ELA composition notebooks they use for most of their work in class. Other years, I've asked students to bring in a journal of their choosing—there are so many attractive journals out there, but any notebook will do. Many students enjoy having a special journal, and they use it to write outside of class too. I share my own collection of journals, filled over the years, and a little bit of the story of how writing helped me as an adolescent.

Before we start, we brainstorm a menu of possibilities for free-writing together. I chart the ideas on the board and students write them in their free-writing journal space. These include writing what's on your mind, (a stream of consciousness vent or brain-dump), writing about a topic of interest, how your morning or weekend went, write a story or poem, continue a story from last time, create comics (must include words as well as pictures), write about places you'd like to go, music or games you're into, etc. Students drive this list.

Then we try it out. We typically start with seven minutes of free-writing in my middle school classes. The guidelines are that students must write until the time is up. They can pause to think, but cannot close their notebooks and declare themselves finished. They must imagine they are in a room of their own as they write and not speak to their peers. "Don't overthink free-writing! Just try something," I'll say.

They can switch topics or genres during the free-write if they want. They can write about not knowing what to write if they get stuck. I often write alongside students during this time, but I also circulate to see how it's going for students. At the end of seven minutes, we discuss how it went, what kinds of topics students chose, what challenges students encountered, what helped them move forward. Then, we may have time for sharing in pairs or small groups. It's important for the timing to feel very precise, because this balances the extreme freedom of this exercise.

We practice the routine regularly until it is a habit. We can build stamina by extending the amount of time gradually. Observing free-writing is a great way to get to know students as people and writers. There are always some students who take the opportunity to write stories, continuing each time until they have short novels. Throughout the year, I use free-writing sporadically, not daily—at the start of class, between units, and anytime I want to create some space for divergent thinking, especially when we've been writing in more constricted forms. (Check out Mary K. Tedrow's book, *Write, Think, Learn*, for a whole approach to developing students' freewriting and integrating it into an English course.)

Creating Assignments with Boundaries

With total freedom in an assignment like "write a story," most students struggle to find their footing. Some may write and write with no idea how to get where they want to go, while others have trouble putting a single word on the page. A key method for building students' creative writing is to limit the scope of their decision-making. The boundary becomes a grounding force, and it supports greater risk-taking and artistry in other areas.

Before we move forward into how to craft fiction-writing experiences, it's important to note how easy it is to overstep a healthy, supportive boundary and become overbearing in writing assignments for students. We have to be especially careful not to do so with creative writing, because we'll end up blocking our students' creative pathways and the exercise will lose its potency.

Once a middle school English teacher of mine assigned us to write a version of a cinquain, a five-line poem with specific syllabic structure. The poem had to be about the novel we just read, and for each line our words needed to be of specific parts of speech. For example, the first line was a noun, the second line was two adjectives, and so forth. It served as a grammar exercise that was also a test of our comprehension of the book. It was, perhaps, a clever challenge, but it was nothing like writing a poem.

This is an extreme yet true example of overstepping a supportive boundary. Doing so underestimates and thwarts creativity. Instead, we want to pick a direction to point students toward and then give them power over most other decisions.

There are two main directions focusing student writing: limiting content or limiting structure. To strike an ideal balance of divergent and convergent thinking, I advise limiting one or the other in a given assignment, rather than both.

Focusing Content

In focusing content, narrow down the topic students explore in their writing, but keep it loosely defined—"write about someone who makes a mistake," for example, or "write a poem celebrating where you come from."

Before writing, it's helpful to read several pieces, professional and/or student written, that fulfill the assignment in different ways. That practice also helps us avoid requesting a kind of writing that doesn't exist meaningfully somewhere in the world of literature (like the cinquain my teacher assigned). For example, I've seen assignments asking students to turn a fictional character's name into an acrostic poem that reflects the character's traits. This may be a fun puzzle for students and an exercise for the teacher to check reading comprehension. It's not a form that exists in the wider world of literature which spans geography and time. It is not, in my opinion, a means of developing students' creative voices as poets.

Limiting content can work well in a poetry assignment if you've already introduced students to free-verse poetry—non-rhyming; free use of line breaks, stanza breaks, and no prescription around syllables or rhythm. Some observation and experience with this form is adequate for students to try writing lines of poetry around any content.

In fiction, though, most students need help with structure to be successful, so limiting content can be tricky. When we teach or limit both structure and content, the requirements for the assignment start to pile up quickly, and can become too much for students at once. However, this can work when we're mimicking a text we've read and studied, so that students have a meaningful experience to draw from in which story structure and content are connected. For example, let's say we've read several folk tales that involve a character disguising themselves and then their true identity being revealed at the end. Here, the content and structure are connected and students write their own variations of a story with this specific motif. Or students can borrow content from a novel they've read and invent scenes involving characters from the novel—I call this playing in the world of the novel. More on both of these kinds of assignments later in this chapter.

Focusing Structure

When limiting structure, we can do so, not by randomly making decisions for students, but by teaching real literary forms, especially those that we've seen in our current reading. We always start with reading (or viewing or listening to) existing works that utilize these forms. We focus our observations on a specific pattern or element, and then students borrow these elements for their own work.

Reading, observing, and then borrowing forms works equally well in fiction and poetry, but in poetry the forms are so much shorter that they can be viewed and studied on a single page. This doesn't mean they're easy to write well, but the scope of a poetic form is smaller and easier to grasp, at least enough to get started. In general, reading lots of poetry tends to help us produce poetry.

Fiction is so much larger that even when students read a ton and are inspired to write their own fiction, they still have difficulty executing an idea. This becomes more of an issue as students get older. The stories that young children read are short, so they can often mimic a basic story structure more organically. Older students who are accustomed to long-form novels tend to have more complex ambitious ideas, and they need guidance in a number of areas, especially structure. Later in this chapter I will cover several ways to guide students in story structure.

Begin With Exercises

Starting small may seem obvious, but because fiction writing isn't often taught in an ongoing, recursive way, it's common for students to be assigned to write a full story in a standalone fiction writing unit without much practice. To write a full story, many skills, ideas, and choices need to come together. We can help students build these skills through shorter exercises throughout a school year. Later, students can integrate them into full stories. The exercises have benefits on their own, even if we never get to full stories. They build students' critical reading, their understanding of author's craft, as well as their writing voices, style, confidence, and our classroom communities. (It's not as if these skills only serve to prepare students for a later project of writing a full story.) Creating assignments that are regularly connected to literature work and are both accessible and challenging to students is key to integrating the fourth role into the ELA classroom.

THREE WAYS TO DESIGN ASSIGNMENTS

These are the three major ways I design fiction writing assignments for my students. There is overlap among them, but the distinctions are helpful in that they identify where the assignment begins, both for me as I plan them and for students as they work on them. They determine the primary tools students will have to guide their writing. **These three types also represent a progression from most accessible to most complex for students.** All of these are connected to the reading we do together in class, in which students are readers, members of a reading community, literary critics, and, in these assignments, authors of literary pieces (the fourth role).

Scene Writing: Playing in the World of the Story

Playing in the world of the story is, in my opinion, the best way to have students begin to write fiction. They work on just a scene, not a full story, and they use a story or novel we have read and discussed as a class as the foundation for creative exploration.

First, what is a scene? For students, it's helpful to define this. A scene is a part of a story that is told in what feels to the reader like "real time." Usually, a scene takes place in one location, and there are no jumps forward in time or backward. A typical scene in a novel involves one or more characters talking or doing something in one setting. In a movie, a scene would break or end with a cut to a different location and/ or time. A scene of a family eating breakfast together ends with a cut to the main character at school. Viewers infer what happens between—the character somehow got to school—but the writer hasn't detailed this transition. Writers do this same thing with words.

To illustrate, if time permits, show a clip of a movie scene and have students identify when a scene ends and another begins. (Avoid opening sequences with lots of cuts.) Then have students identify beginnings and endings of scenes in the book you've just read.

How do we play in the world of the story? Students imagine scenes that try out an idea related to the novel. They change something in the novel, and imagine how that would unfold in a specific moment. Here are the types of tasks that generally come up in this assignment:

- Alter a scene: Imagine the character makes X choice instead of Y choice; imagine the character did not win the game, or the character did not miss the phone call, for example.
- Add a scene: Add scene that shows what happened in between scenes (off screen) or develops a minor character's life beyond what's in the book; sometimes students have invented therapy scenes for troubled characters.
- Add a character: Imagine a friend, a sibling, a teacher, a monster, etc. into the book. Write or rewrite a scene with that character.
- Extend the story: Imagine what might happen next, after the real ending of the story, or write the beginning of a sequel.
- Kill a character: Write a character's death scene. This is really for fun, and a popular choice. If you include it, be prepared for many students to choose it!

• Change point of view: Rewrite a scene from a different character's point of view.

These exercises can stem from students' responses, criticisms, and musings about a story. I often create assignments based on students' comments in our whole novel discussions. For example, a criticism: "I didn't like how X character was lying to her friends," could lead to a question of "What if she had told the truth from the start?" which could lead to an exercise of writing that scene. Or, "I liked X character. I wish we got to know him more," can lead to imagining what X character's life is like, and writing a scene that features X character. Students often have unmet expectations for endings of books. When a student shares, "I expected X and Y characters to get together in the end! I was so mad at the author for leaving it like this!" there's a great opportunity for the student to write the scene they wished had happened or simply extend the story to include the scene a reader felt was missing.

Creating assignment choices from students' responses to novels shows them that their voices matter and gives them decision-making power. Students can cocreate assignments with us, which lead to interesting options. If we start our menu of options with an example such as rewriting a scene from a different character's point of view, students can usually help generate assignment choices from there. Try to connect the assignment to a "what if?" question, such as "what if the X scene was told from Y character's perspective?"

When students play in the world of the story and then reflect on the impact of their choices and/or classmates' choices, they get firsthand experience which helps them understand Common Core Standard RL.3 for 11th and 12th Grade: "Analyze the impact of the author's choices regarding how to develop and relate elements of a story or drama (e.g., where a story is set, how the action is ordered, how the characters are introduced and developed)."

Providing choice in these assignments, via a menu of options, is important for two reasons. First, there are several built-in limitations to this assignment for students. Students are already working with the materials of another author's story. We've also limited the writing to one scene (though I really don't object if students want to write more). Rather than limit the scope of the writing even more, I find that offering the choice of what to change in their scene is motivating and reserves enough space for student creativity.

Secondly, when students make their own decisions about what to change, we can utilize the variety of scenes to expand everyone's learning later when students share with the class—Step 5 in the Inquiry Cycle. Students' own reflections on why they chose to write their scene and the impact this scene would have on the rest of the story become a rich opportunity for critical thinking, and students can similarly observe the choices of their classmates and their corresponding impact. (See Chapter 2 for detail on this activity.)

At the same time, for younger students it may work well to narrow down the assignment choices, and have everyone do one type of scene. For example, all students could rewrite a scene they select from a different character's point of view. I personally find this a bit less exciting, but it allows the teacher to break down the process more for students, which is helpful in some contexts.

Step 1: Choose a scene.
Step 2: Brainstorm characters other than the main character who could tell this scene from their perspective.
Step 3: Choose a character to narrate your scene.
Step 4: Open your book to the scene. How does it begin? How could you begin your scene, now that your character is telling the story?
Step 5: Begin writing.

I also find that this particular assignment—changing point of view of a scene—is often simplest for students who are struggling to get started. This is a go-to process for me when I have a student who is stuck making a choice once we've introduced the assignment. For students who have selected a different choice, but struggle getting started, having them open their book and look at how any chapter begins, helps them get into the mode of narrative writing. They can copy the general structure of an opening sentence to a chapter get started.

I like to involve students in scene-writing in the world of a story twice, usually in the first half of the year. The first story is often a folk tale, and the second story is usually a novel.

→ **Exercise:** If you're a literacy coach or department leader, this kind of scene writing is a great exercise to try with teachers using a short story or folk tale. Teachers should help cocreate the prompts, have time to write (this can be as little as 10 minutes for adults), then share, discuss, and reflect. It brings a joyful energy to the team and demonstrates how this assignment connects powerfully to reading as well as our life experiences. Have teachers approach the assignment authentically as a reader and writer, taking their "teacher hats" off. At the end of the session, have them put their "teacher hats" back on and debrief the experience to apply it to their teaching practice.

Assignments That Start with One Literary Element

Another way into fiction writing is by focusing on one literary element. In each novel study, I select an element that is especially strong in the author's writing. We observe how the author develops this element, and then we use it as a starting place for creative writing. In assignments like this these, students create their own characters, conflicts, settings, etc., rather than borrowing them from another story. I take an active role in determining the format of the assignment, but I do this after students have investigated examples of the element in an author's work. Students construct an understanding of the element through activities related to their reading. Then we transition to students applying a concept or pattern to their own fiction writing.

In the progression toward more complex assignments and full stories, these are exercises in which students create their own fictional content "from scratch," but they don't yet need to deal with the task of developing a plot. Although plot is a literary element, I handle it differently.

There are many ways into writing through the lens of a literary element. These are examples of assignments I've created over the years that grow out of work we do reading literature. These assignments can often be copied or translated to other texts. However, as you read these, you will probably have ideas related to the books your students read with you. I encourage you to follow those leads and create assignments that flow from your students' reading.

As you develop assignments, remember to strive for the "just-right" balance of focus and freedom. Try out your own assignments. Make sure there's enough room for students to surprise you with what they come up with; if you notice that many students are writing similar pieces, that's a sign you've probably gone too far in prescribing the assignment. If you present the assignment and you don't have about half of the class excited to get started without any help, you may need to adjust the requirements to offer more guidance to ground students or fewer guidelines to free students.

Setting: This activity works when a novel or short story has a richly developed setting.

> Reading Investigation: Students can hunt for language that describes this setting. Remind students that everything they picture in their minds has been put there through the author's words. In a novel study, I might have students track

descriptions and changes in setting on their sticky note annotations. In a short story, I would have students highlight and then share out those sentences.

- Students identify language in the text that describes setting. This work can begin independently or in pairs or groups.
- Ask, what does the author take the time to describe? Share as class and chart their responses so that they become a reference for all.
- Students might notice that authors "zoom in" to specific areas or items in a setting: an old desk, the sky, the movement of people in a hospital waiting room.
- Authors include sounds, as well as sights, and sometimes smells or tastes.
- Authors may describe what a place makes the narrator think, feel, or remember.
- Authors may use figurative language to make their description more vivid or meaningful.
- Ask, why might the author take the time to describe this aspect of the setting? What does this add to the story?
- If there is time, and setting is a major focus of the novel study, students can work in pairs or small groups on a "mini-project" on chart paper to copy quotes from the text which describe the setting and then draw, paint, or sculpt what they imagine.

Transition to Writing: Students think of a setting, real or imaginary, to describe in detail as if they were an author and this was a section of their novel or short story.

- Students should not just write as if they're listing off the specs of the setting, but "zoom in" to describe specific areas or items in detail and to make readers picture the place as if they were there.
- All of the observations students made in relation to reading now become guideposts for writing.
- As students write, they will probably notice that it's difficult to write *just* a setting. Other story elements will want to creep in! This is because the literary elements of a story are connected and impact one another.
- It's okay if students begin to introduce some other story elements, such as a character/narrator with a point of view and possibly a conflict, as long as the main focus of the exercise is setting. Most students will be relieved not to have to craft a plot, but this teaser may spark their imaginations, and that's a good thing.
- A fun twist: Tell students not to clearly name their setting. When they share with the class or in small groups, classmates can guess the setting the student chose to write.

- Length is usually one page, but can be more. Illustrations encouraged.

Character/Point of View: This assignment works when a novel includes multiple characters' perspectives, whether that is through an omniscient third-person narrator or a multiple first-person narrators.

Reading Investigation: This assignment came out of reading the book *Bronx Masquerade* by Nikki Grimes. The book is told from multiple narrators: Each character is a member of a ninth-grade English class involved in studying poetry of the Harlem Renaissance. This book is especially nice to use alongside a poetry unit. In the book, each classmate narrates a few chapters from their point of view. Some of their stories stand on their own and some intertwine with other characters. After students have read and discussed the book, we look at the format of a chapter and the way the author develops characters through first-person monologues. The chapters begin with the name of the character and then the character starts talking on the page. Students observe the kinds of things these characters bring up that help us get to know them and identify with them—their interests, conflicts, insecurities, how they view others and how others view them. Then we hear a poem this character has written and read at "Open Mic Friday." We note that one character, who is the MC or host of Open Mic Fridays, seems to have more frequent short chapters, in which he comments and reacts to other characters' poems.

Transition to Writing: Students create their own character and write a monologue from the point of view of their character. They stick with the realistic fiction genre, and if you're also studying poetry, they can include a poem "written by" their character. The character can resemble the student themselves, or be totally different, or a combination of real and imagined details. The chapters can then be put together to create a "book" called [Insert name of school or neighborhood/town] *Masquerade*. Another example of a book like that which can be used in a similar way is *Seedfolks* by Paul Fleischman and to some degree other multi-narrational books like *Wonder* by R. J. Palacio.

Theme: This assignment can work well with any book in which students are focusing on identifying themes; it works especially well with texts that are told as a series of vignettes.

Reading Investigation: As students read *The House on Mango Street* by Sandra Cisneros, they identify and track themes in their sticky notes. Similar themes pop up in chapters about different topics. At this stage, we are identifying topical themes like identity, home, or sexism, rather than thematic messages. This work of tracking themes can be fruitful in any literary text, but the writing assignment works especially well with books that are written as a collection of vignettes, such as *The House On Mango Street, Brown Girl Dreaming* by Jacqueline Woodson, and *The Dreamer* by Pam Muñoz Ryan. In these cases, it's important to take the time to examine what a vignette is.

- To explore how theme is operating, have students work together to select three vignettes (or scenes in a more traditional novel) that seem important to the book, and then look for a common theme among them; or simply select three vignettes that share a common theme.
- Discuss: what made you identify this theme in each of these places?
- What do these vignettes have in common?
- What's different in each one, especially when it comes to this theme?
- Do the three vignettes, in the order they appear in the book, show a progression or a change?
- Finally, what does the author seem to be showing about this theme?
- Students share back what they found. This can also be a path toward writing thematic essays. I usually give an in-class essay writing assignment at the end of a novel study.

Transition to Writing: Students will write a collection of three vignettes that build on a common theme. This is best for eighth grade or older (but could work as a challenge in seventh grade), because of the abstract thinking needed to put it together. I ask students to imagine they are writing their own version of *The House On Mango Street*, adapting it to a setting they know well and creating their own characters and conflicts.

- I have students select a theme that was present in the book, which slightly limits their range of choice.
- Once students select a theme, they can map out ideas for three vignettes—or snapshots that involve characters, setting, and possibly hints of conflict. Each vignette should be told by the same narrator, but can focus on different topics, characters, places, experiences. Students should note how each vignette touches on their chosen theme.
- Students can reread vignettes from the book to get ideas about what kinds of topics might work and how to begin a vignette.
- If you're connecting this to a more traditional, plot-driven novel, then the assignment can be, imagine you are writing a novel. Write three scenes, or moments that could appear in this novel that share a common theme.

- This allows students to explore a narrative voice, and to create a piece that coheres through a thematic thread, without worrying about a full story.

Conflict: This works with any novel or story of any genre in which students will analyze conflicts.

Reading Investigation: In any novel with rich, layered conflicts, students can learn to analyze them using this simple process.
- Identify a conflict happening in the story.
- Focus on the character having the conflict. If there's more than one, pick the character you want to focus on. (You can always return later to look at the conflict from another character's point of view.)
- What does this character want or need in this situation?
- Who or what is getting in the way? Is the obstacle another character, the character's own self, the society, or an element of the natural world?
- Categorize the conflict: character vs. character; character vs. self; character vs. society; or character vs. nature.
- Many conflicts can be categorized more than one way, depending on what you say is "getting in the way" of the character's want or need. The same conflict can also be looked at from different points of view.
- As students read on, note what changes as a result of the conflict. Conflicts aren't always resolved but they always lead to some kind of change.
- Students work on this process in their sticky notes as they read and also in small groups to look more in depth at one conflict's various layers.

Transition to Writing: Once students are versed in this process in their reading, they can use it to generate an idea and a structure for an original short story. They need the following elements: (1) a character who wants or needs something, (2) someone or something who gets in the way, and (3) some kind of change. This assignment is the closest we get to a full story without studying plot. The format we use above to analyze conflict becomes the structure for a multi-scene story. Each scene is approximately one page. Students who want to write longer pieces are allowed but this is the baseline format.

Scene 1: Show what your character wants or needs.
Scene 2: Who or what gets in the way? (If you showed this in Chapter 1, you can make this obstacle intensify in some way, through action or confrontation.)
Scene 3: What changes? Conflict could resolve or there could simply be change between the character and the obstacle.

I encourage students to add more than one layer to the conflict—a conflict with another character also reveals a conflict with the self, or a conflict with society leads to a conflict with a character—just like they see happening in the novel. In this assignment, students can draw from their previous experiences imagining and writing setting and a character's point of view.

Designing Whole Story Assignments

The third kind of fiction writing assignment is built around a classic plot or story type. In this case, we study a specific plot archetype, ideally through multiple stories that exemplify it. Then we work together to determine the pattern or requirements of this plot. We use that to create an outline of the major scenes in this type of story. Students plan and then write full stories. This is a much bigger undertaking than the previous two kinds of assignments, and it helps if students have experience in the first two categories, which helps build their narrative writing chops for this challenge. Before looking at specific examples of these assignments, let's take a closer look at the role of plot in fiction writing.

HANDLING THE CRUCIAL AND OVERWHELMING ELEMENT OF PLOT

Ernest Hemingway famously said, "The hard part about [writing] a novel is to finish it," and the prolific and influential writer, Neil Gaiman, says his number one advice for aspiring writers is to "finish things." Besides the obvious hard work and perseverance it takes to write whole stories, knowing how to handle plot is probably the most crucial factor in being able to finish, and finish well. If there is one big secret to writing fiction, in fact, that secret is plot.

I learned about plot in graduate school, in Madeleine Ray's Children's Literature course, which was part of my masters in teaching at Bank Street College. Somehow, this had been missing from both the fiction writing workshops and the literature courses I took as an undergraduate English major at Brown University. (Perhaps that was why I gravitated more to poetry, even though some of my poetry professors advised me to write fiction . . .) And of course, it was also missing from my primary and secondary schooling as well. For some reason, which I have not discovered, educators tend not to teach plot structures, and we should.

When I did learn the secret about plots, I chuckled to myself, remembering how much I'd struggled as a child. In elementary school, I would read novels and watch epic films, which inspired grand ideas for stories I wanted to write. In my mind, they'd be cinematic, filled with large casts of characters. One such story took place on a ship leaving from Ireland. The main character's name was Lavinia. I wrote down elaborate plans for who was who, where they were going, who they would meet. And I wrote an opening scene. I thought it was awesome. I even recall telling my parents about it. Yet, somehow, I never got past that opening scene. This thing was simply too big to handle, and I had no clue how to proceed.

I was not alone in my struggle to write a complete story. Most of my students tell me they, too, have had exciting ideas for stories. They think they are off to a great start, but they lose steam quickly. Or, they persevere, but they find that the story keeps going and going, and they can't figure out how it could ever end. This common struggle is all because of missing foundational knowledge of plots.

The big secret, it turns out, is that there are no new plots. There are a small number of basic plots that get told and retold and combined in new ways. In graduate school, Madeleine Ray lent me a copy of Christopher Booker's *The Seven Basic Plots: Why We Tell Stories* (2006). This was connected to a method Madeleine developed called "Polyplots," which involves students in improvisation and writing through archetypal story plots. I'll outline this method later in this chapter. In his huge book, Booker makes the argument for the universality of seven specific story archetypes—which are at least 5000 years old and appear in all story forms, from folk tales to novels, to films, theater, comic books, detective shows, and soap operas. Booker also explores why these story patterns endure. Each one plays a role in the human psyche, reflecting and influencing human experience.

Booker isn't the only researcher, historian, or scholar to talk about story archetypes. Joseph Campbell, author of *The Hero With a Thousand Faces*, for example, studied human storytelling across cultures and time and uncovered plot archetypes as well. Much of his focus was the hero's journey archetype, which he believed could be literally or metaphorically applied to any story. The concept of three or six or seven basic plots, though, isn't new, but Booker's work is focused and comprehensive, and truly unlocks doors for fiction writers.

Roxanna Elden, for example, is a teacher and author, who used the seven plots to move past a stuck place while writing in her first novel, which includes storylines and points of view of multiple characters. Elden's first book is nonfiction, called *See Me After Class: Advice for Teachers By Teachers*, and like me, she wrote articles and blogs about teaching. For her second book, though, she wrote a novel about teachers called *Adequate Yearly Progress*. I learned a little about her writing process in a newsletter series she created, offering up the best writing tips she learned over the years attending the Miami Writer's Institute. In one of the letters, she explained, "This was the class where I first learned that you don't need an original plot to write a good story . . . " Then she explained that the teacher introduced her to Christopher Booker's *Seven Basic Plots*. (Elden shares her summaries as well as resources for teachers to use with students around each plot on her website, roxannaelden.com.) Elden then described the breakthrough she had after reading about these plot patterns.

> As a writer attempting a novel with several different points of view, this infor-
> mation [the seven plots] came along at the perfect time. I'd been working on the
> novel I'd started for over a year now and had become fully obsessed: I worked
> during my lunch periods at school, emailed ideas to myself between classes . . .
>
> After learning about the seven basic plots, however, I stopped writing.
> Instead, I went back into outline mode, lining up the storylines of each char-
> acter with the plot they best fit into. This allowed me to see what might be
> missing, fill it in, and make sure the storylines were moving forward at a
> steady clip.
>
> This also helped me do something that had been even more of a challenge:
> Fans of ensemble stories like *The Wire* or *Orange Is the New Black* (or my all-
> time favorite movie, *Crash*) have probably admired the way the storylines of
> different characters impact one another.
>
> Lining the character outlines up next to one another forced me to answer
> the question of exactly what characters X and Z were doing while the camera
> was focused on character Y, and how the actions of each of these characters
> might impact the others down the line. (Elden, 2018)

Roxanna's example of applying knowledge of the plots to her multi-perspective novel is complex, fitting for a professional author, and probably not something to bring directly to most students. But it's a wonderful window into how an understanding of plot helps a writer take an exciting idea and deliver it.

Introducing Students to Plot Archetypes

Madeleine said all the plots could be found in the ancient folk tales and myths. The human tradition of oral storytelling exists in every culture and precedes written story forms. Before there were novels, plays, movies, or shows to binge-watch, there was storytelling. The plots, which originate in ancient times, are foundational to the cre-ation of new stories. By educating students about these plots, we can provide them with an amazing tool they can use in both their reading and writing.

How do we do it?

First off, don't hand students a list of the seven plots with an outline for each, or present them on slides—and call it a day. That would be akin to hand-ing students a list of the ancient civilizations with their locations, dates, and few facts about each, to teach ancient history. For students to make sense of these as archetypes and utilize them in their own writing, they need substantial experience with each one.

I also discourage creating a unit specifically on the seven plots, unless it's for very experienced upper high school or college level readers. In those cases, students might have enough prior experience with each plot that they could possibly bring all seven frameworks into their working memories in a short amount of time (like Roxanna Elden did).

So how *should* we utilize the powerful tool of plot archetypes as teachers?

In K–12 education, students should learn the plots slowly over years, the way they might learn about various ancient civilizations for a few months at a time in social studies. This doesn't mean they are not constantly exposed to stories that develop other plot archetypes through their independent reading and viewing. In one year, I suggest students explicitly study one or two plots.

At Bank Street College, I learned to prioritize depth of learning over breadth of learning. Going deeper into fewer topics creates more opportunities for critical thinking, time to develop personal connection to the content, and time for the learning to stick, rather than being introduced and quickly forgotten. Simply, students understand better and retain more from in-depth studies than they do in broad surveys.

I also learned to employ a constructivist approach, which means that whenever possible, I give students experiences that put them in a position to actively construct their own knowledge. This is what the Experiential Learning Cycle process facilitates. Instead of "teaching from definitions" as Madeleine calls it—telling students what's what, and then having them practice it—we try to design experiences and help students develop definitions and conceptual understandings through their own observations, questions, and discussions.

This is a value system and framework for teaching, not an absolute rule. I avoid starting directly with definitions, so that students have more opportunities for discovery and critical thinking. Exploration of academic content can be a form of play for older children: This helps their cognitive development, their sense of efficacy, and their readiness for complex problem solving in the adult world later.

In this context, introducing students to a plot archetype is fairly simple. We coordinate students to be able to do the following, focusing on one plot type at a time:

1. Get to know a few stories that offer differing adaptations of a similar plot.
2. Notice a pattern.
3. Examine the differences between the iterations, and the impact of those differences.
4. Determine the main elements of that story type.
5. Play with that story type in creative writing.

Plot patterns become an outline and grounding framework for creating original stories. This really does work—for students and adults alike.

THE POLY-PLOTS METHOD: USING DRAMATIC PLAY TO GENERATE IMAGINATIVE WRITING

How do we put this process into practice in our classrooms? The possibilities are many, and you may already be imagining a number of ways. I'll start by sharing the most dynamic method I know. It's called Poly-Plots, and it was invented by my mentor, the inimitable Madeleine Ray.

Poly-plots allows students to go deep into a particular plot type, and it makes the connection between reading and writing three-dimensional. It is also a different format for playing in the world of the story. Madeleine taught this to me during my first year of full-time teaching, and I tried it out with my seventh-grade students in East Harlem that spring.

Poly-plots begins with a folk tale. Taking Madeleine's recommendation, I began that year by telling from memory the story of "Ashputtle." Ashputtle is the Grimm's version of what later became Cinderella. It's an important story because versions of it exist in so many cultures around the world, and it is a representation of the story archetype, "Rags to Riches," which is one of Booker's seven plots. Cinderella-type stories are a particular variation of rags to riches, in that they begin with a loss—generally the loss of a parent figure—causing the protagonist to lose their security and identity, and then fight to regain it. The Grimm version is exciting for students, because they recognize the story, but it is shockingly gory, compared to the more widely known Perault version, which inspired the famous Disney movie. For example, in "Ashputtle," the stepsisters literally cut off their toes at the urging of their stepmother, to fit into the prince's shoe.

After telling the folk tale, I asked students for a few of their favorite scenes or those they thought were most important. With a few scenes selected, we begin what Madeleine calls a **play-through**. In a play-through, students volunteer to embody a character and dramatize the selected scene.

Folk tales are built on plot and theme, but they don't include a lot of dialogue and character development. In this way, they provide a rich opportunity for students (and professional writers) to invent using the bones of the story and their own imaginations. Play-throughs create a three-dimensional process for writing and revising, and they are also great fun for people of all ages.

In order to support play-through as a creative space to try out ideas, rather than perform and evaluate one another's acting skills, we use the following rules.

Rules For Play-Through

1. We use the language of "playing," or dramatizing, not performing.
2. No applause—this can be challenging, because sometimes we want to show appreciation, but applause quickly becomes evaluative. The play-through that gets big applause will be a rush for everyone, but then it will deter many students from participating.
3. Any student can play any character, regardless of gender.
4. No props—just pretend.
5. Play with that story type in creative writing.
6. Teacher gives signal to begin and end the play-through. I always say, "One, two, ready, begin" and later "And . . . scene."
7. After each play through, we pause for reflection. The guiding questions are, "What worked? What didn't work so well? What could we try next?"

In the toe-cutting scene, one boy volunteers to play the stepmother and a girl plays the stepsister. When the "mother" says, "Cut off your toe!" the stepsister shouts back. "How could you ask me to do that?!" "Do it!" the stepmother hisses. Stepsister pretends to cut off her toe, while laughing hysterically.

"And . . . scene." Everyone is laughing, and I have to remind several students not to applaud.

Revision Through Improvisation

"Okay, so what worked well in this scene?" I ask.

"It was funny," someone says.

"What else?"

"The way they argued," someone else says. "It's like how a mother and daughter really sound sometimes."

"Can anyone remember the words they used in the argument?" I ask.

A few students offer the actual lines the two said. I write them down on the board, under a heading, Dialogue To Remember. (These days, I'd have students record these notes in their notebooks.)

"What didn't work so well? What could we try next?" I ask. At first no one responds. I wait.

"Well, she was laughing while she cut her toe off," one student finally says.

"What about that?" I probe.

"You wouldn't be laughing if you cut your toe," he says.

"Great. What would you be doing?"

"Screaming! Crying!"

"Cursing!" students offer.

Then, I remind students that the scene is happening in a side room, while the prince is waiting in the entryway of the house. "Why does the stepmother bring her daughter into a side room?" Students remember that this is being done secretly so the prince won't know. We discuss that the argument and screams would need to be done quietly, not shouting, so as not to draw suspicion from the prince.

Two other students try it now in lower voices, and the agony of the toe cutting comes through much more dramatically this way. There are some giggles when the stepmother orders the daughter to cut off her toe, but this time the students quickly restrain themselves.

As the dialogue continues, the stepmother adds something new: "You've always been my favorite daughter; come on, now cut off your toe so you can be queen!"

This line adds new dimension to the relationship between these characters, which is not in the original story. And as I've seen countless students play through this and other scenes, there are always new variations that come from the opportunity to improvise.

We are really engaging in a three-dimensional process of writing and revising. I might ask, "Now that the stepmother has revealed that she favors one of her daughters, what else might change in the story to show this? In other words, how might we hint at this earlier in the story to lead up to this moment?" Students will think critically about this, and come up with a number of places this dynamic could be implied. For example, when the two sisters are getting ready for the ball, the stepmother could treat them differently.

We can continue with playthroughs as long as students can maintain attention. I find this varies significantly depending on the group. It can be just ten minutes, or it could go on for thirty. If the group can sustain attention, the results of a longer session are worthwhile. Either way, the playthrough process can be revisited for several days. This is not something I do for each creative writing piece, but rather once in a year in the context of studying a story archetype. Often we use poly-plots in connection with a novel with a similar plot structure, and leading toward imaginative writing that borrows elements from this plot as well.

Here are some ways to get students to try out new ideas:

- Extend a scene: Pose a challenge that would require an extension of the scene. In the above scenario, what if the daughter pushes back instead agreeing to her mother's requests?
- Change the mood or tone: What if this scene were a little bit scary, instead of

being a little bit funny? Or what if the stepmother speaks in a sugary sweet tone as she's telling her daughter to cut off her toe?

- Add a character: Maybe there is a butler who walks in unknowingly to the toe-cutting scene. A character can be added to any scene, and students can creatively improvise possibilities for how the interactions would unfold.
- Students can suggest what-if's themselves once they see how the process works.

Play For Older Children

When young children play pretend (often "house" or "family"), they are not just having fun, but processing their experiences with others and constructing understanding of their world. Early childhood educators understand that play is actually the "work" of childhood. When students play with blocks, they are working on visual-spatial skills, for example. When they play games together, they are working on turn taking, communication, and more.

In play, children don't need to be aware that they are working on a skill in order to be building it. When they work on developmentally appropriate skills, they feel happy, because they are experiencing the positive side of their current stage in cognitive development, as Piaget named them: "initiative" rather than "guilt" in ages three to five and "industriousness" rather than "inferiority" in ages five to twelve.

For older students ages twelve to eighteen, the issue of adolescence is identity. Play or improvisation is something they are now doing in life in ways that have a more tangible effect—for example, what will happen if I don't study for this test? What will happen if I tell a friend how I really feel? The issues can be heavy, and teens often don't feel comfortable sharing with adults. Playing with blocks is not going to feed their need for identity development, but playing in a story world can.

I remember my seventh-graders that first year in East Harlem. After the toe-cutting scene, someone suggested we play through the opening scene, which is the death of Ashputtle's mother. There is not much detail in the text recorded by the Brothers Grimm. It begins, "A rich man's wife fell ill, and on her deathbed, she calls her only daughter to her side. 'My dear girl, be good and say your prayers, and I shall look down upon you from heaven for as long as you shall live.' And with that, she died" (Grimm Brothers, 2011).

The tone of the class during the toe-cutting scene had been pretty boisterous, though we made some progress in creating suspense. Overall, students had found the process fun and hilarious. Now, two boys volunteered to play the death scene. One lay down on a bench in the meeting area of the classroom, playing the dying mother.

The other kneeled beside him, hands clasped in a prayer-like position. They began with dialogue similar to what was in the story I told. The boy playing Ashputtle pretended to be teary, and this elicited a few quiet giggles, but quickly the tone turned very serious and sad.

This was nineteen years ago, and I cannot remember much of what they said, except, "Please, mother, don't go!" What I'll never forget, though, was that this scene went on . . . and on. It could have ten minutes or more. I usually cut off scenes after about two minutes, but I could not bring myself to do so. We were all absorbed in what they were creating.

And then it occurred to me that the boy who was playing Ashputtle's mother, Caden, had lost his father the summer before that school year began. He had been an emotional wreck most of the year, acting out in all kinds of ways. Seeing him and his classmate enact a child's tragic loss of a parent was cathartic. For Caden to embody the dying mother, rather than the child, may have allowed him to be more creative than playing the child would have.

Dramatic play created an opportunity for these two students to zoom in on an aspect of the story that was meaningful to their identity development—especially for Caden, but for his classmate by association as well. The events we bear witness to are a part of our development as well.

We don't usually think of Cinderella as being a story about losing a parent. More often we think of the rags to riches storyline, the jealousy of the stepsisters, the wickedness of the stepmother. One of the wonderful things about a folk tale is the canvas it provides for young people to invent in the spaces that matter to them, without the overwhelming task of making basic plot decisions. The poly-plots method is the most effective way I know for getting started with this work.

Transition To Writing

Writing is much easier when we write from experience. The play-through process provides three-dimensional experience for students with a specific plot and its characters. Once students have explored the story through dramatic play, they can transition comfortably to writing. How you do that depends a bit on the direction you want to take the work and how much time you have for it. There is a lot of room for teachers to be inventive here. The ideas below progress in complexity, so if there is time, these can be implemented in this sequence.

Script Writing: Augment the play-through process by integrating student script writing. Have students work independently, in pairs, or in small groups, to write versions of a scene from the story. The task could be creating new variations of the scene the group has been playing through, or each group could focus on a scene of their choice from anywhere in the story. They write the dialogue in script format, and then they, or other students can perform it. The chance to think and write allows for a new level of creativity, and students will feel that power. It's a wonderful way to demonstrate how useful the tool of writing is. This is especially helpful for ENL students, who benefit from writing words they've already heard spoken, and later seeing words they've written acted out loud.

"Small Writing": This is an exercise developed by Madeleine Ray at Bank Street College, and it helps students make the transition from drama to narrative. The task is basically to pick a very small moment of the story, one without dialogue, and write through it in narrative form. The activity begins with a silent dramatic exercise. Madeleine picks a moment—typically this is the stepsister getting ready for the ball. The group picks one action, such as putting lipstick on in the mirror, which is always very rich for this activity.

We sit in a circle, and each of us takes a turn pretending to be the stepsister putting on the lipstick. This takes about five seconds each. Everyone else simply watches. The variety of postures and facial expressions is surprising, and illuminates the choices a writer can make in developing this character and this moment. After this exercise, everyone turns to the page and writes a version of the moment. Writers choose the narrative voice and genre. It can be an interior monologue from the point of view of the stepsister or a third-person narrative description or even a poem. Writers have developed sympathetic, misunderstood stepsister characters and villainous ones. It's always surprising the variety of quality writing students (and adults) produce through this exercise. Small writing can be used to lead into longer pieces or just be an exercise in writing craft and seeing possibilities within any small moment.

Narrative Scene Writing: Students are generally comfortable writing in script form after the play through process. It's a bigger leap to write a scene in a narrative form, because the decisions involve more than just dialogue. And writing dialogue in narrative form requires some additional technique. Focusing on a scene from a folk tale that involves conversation between characters is a great occasion to teach some of these skills. It's also fine to start by thrusting students into the situation with a little bit of modeling: "Let's try writing a scene together between Ashputtle and her stepmother," and projecting it visually for them to follow. Then students select a scene (same one or different) and write their own short narratives. You can take note of what kind of help students need and what lessons might be helpful to them for later. I'll go into some of the main needs that come up in the next chapter.

DESIGNING ASSIGNMENTS FOR WHOLE STORIES USING PLOT ARCHETYPES

Studying one plot structure in depth and utilizing it to write whole stories is ideal, because students develop a sense of expertise with the story type. That's satisfying in itself, it also means they bring the understanding to new story experiences.

Once students know a folk tale, they can write their own versions of it. Folk tales don't include much dialogue, description, or character development, so there is a lot of opportunity for students to be creative. Retelling or reimagining a folk tale seems to be such a natural mode of storytelling that it is possible to assign this writing task to students without a ton of pre-work. However, going through the stages above from play-through to script writing to small writing to scene writing prepares for students to bring more to the table when they write their original stories.

> When students study classic plot structures, they develop their understanding of reading standard RL.8.9: "Analyze how a modern work of fiction draws on themes, patterns of events, or character types from myths, traditional stories, or religious works such as the Bible, including describing how the material is rendered new." They develop their writing toward W.3: "Write narratives to develop real or imagined experiences or events using effective technique, relevant descriptive details, and well-structured event sequences" and subpoint. a. "Engage and orient the reader by establishing a context and point of view and introducing a narrator and/or characters; organize an event sequence that unfolds naturally and logically."

Realistically, I can do a poly-plots-to-story-writing cycle about once per school year. There are other ways to get to know a story plot and begin writing.

The key is to expose students to multiple versions of the plot. For Ashputtle (Cinderella), this is easy to do because there are so many versions from around the world, and they are readily available on the internet and at the library. I put older students in groups and have them read a version together aloud in a "station." Then they discuss and take notes on what the story includes—how it's similar to other versions, and what is different about it.

I've had them take notes in the following categories:

- Ashputtle character
- Antagonist(s)

- Helper character(s)
- Major event (festival, marriage, competition, etc.)
- Disguises
- Consequences
- Magic

Then the groups switch stations and focus on a different story. We spend a few days looking at the different versions of the tale. Then we come together and create a master outline of "What to Include in an Ashputtle-Type Story." This becomes an outline and brainstorming tool for students and a map for their writing, which takes the most difficult decision-making off their plates, freeing them up to experiment within the structure.

For example, students have asked, how could I make an Ashputtle-type story with a male protagonist? Or, what if I make one of the stepsisters an ally to Ashputtle? Or what if I really develop the father character? What if I took the romance out of the story completely, and made the culminating event that my character wants to take part in a math competition, rather than a ball? Yes, yes, and yes. My students have come up with stories for all of these ideas and more.

Here is the assignment sheet I created with a ninth-grade English class after going through this process. The list of scenes is based on what the students generated from their reading investigation. For younger grades, the format would be a little bit simpler.

ELA 9 WRITING PROJECT 2: ASHPUTTLE-TYPE STORY

Your Task: Write an original version of a story using the archetypal "Ashputtle" story plot.

Your Scenes should have the following:

◊ **Dialogue** between characters

◊ **Description of actions** and body language of characters

◊ **Interior monologue**—shows the characters' thoughts

Due Date: Thursday, October 23rd, at the beginning of class.

Length: Each scene should be 1–2 pages. Type if possible. Double-spaced, 12-point font.

Style: You must write in prose. These are not scripts, so you must punctuate your dialogue using quotation marks. Make sure to use paragraphs.

Point of View: You may write in the first person (in your protagonist's voice) or in the third person, using an outside narrator. Once you make your choice, stick with it.

Elements: Setting is entirely your choice—realistic today, ancient, fantastical, futuristic, etc. Main character may be of any gender. Character can be human or non-human. There must be a helper character or symbolic item, often with a magical element.

Scenes:

◊ Loss of a loved one

◊ Introduction of evil character(s)/antagonist(s), often in the form of family or step-family member(s)

◊ Protagonist is treated unfairly; loses place in the world; hard times

◊ Introduction of helper character or symbolic item

◊ News of special event/opportunity

◊ Protagonist blocked from opportunity by antagonist

◊ Protagonist receives help from helper

◊ Special event

◊ Protagonist is recognized for who he/she really is

◊ Protagonist is rewarded/antagonist is punished

Freedom: You have the freedom to change the order of scenes, add or subtract scenes. Make sure the story has elements of the traditional plot, but feel free to play with details and structure. Remember many of the "Ashputtle" stories we have read their own twists.

This process can be applied to any basic story structure, such as journey stories, detective stories, trickster tales, tragedies, etc. Using an inquiry approach, the formula is to read and/or view several versions of the story type, determine the essential elements of the pattern together, and then plan and write an original story utilizing the pattern.

We don't need to stick to folk tales, either, though different versions of the same folk tale is a wonderful way to make the initial point that plots are blueprints for stories. Novels and plays work with classic plots as well, often mixing more than one at a time. Picture books and movies are also great resources for introducing students to more variations of a specific plot. Picture books are especially helpful, because the plots are short and they can be reread to study.

I've paired "Ashputtle" with the novel *The Skin I'm In* by Sharon G. Flake and the novella *The Jacob Ladder* by Gerald Hausman and Uton Hinds. In each one, there is a loss of a parent (not always through death), an antagonist who is close to the family, a conflict involving the protagonist not having the right clothes, a helper character who intervenes, and the main character finding their own power and prevailing, though in the novels the endings are less straightforward.

Table 5.2: Finding the Journey Pattern

Stage	*Where the Wild Things Are*	*Sylvester and the Magic Pebble*
Exposition: Where does the story begin? Who is there? What are they doing?		
Initial Conflict: What problem comes up first for the main character?		
Rising Action (and other conflicts): What else happens; what other conflicts come up?		
Climax: What happens in the final moment, the turning point when the central conflict begins to resolve?		
Falling Action/Resolution: How do the conflict(s) resolve?		
Denouement: What happens (or is suggested) at the very end of the story?		
Themes we notice:		

My students have studied journey stories using a novel, *The Ear, the Eye and the Arm*, by Nancy Farmer, along with classic picture books, *Where the Wild Things Are* by Maurice Sendak and *Sylvester and the Magic Pebble* by William Steig, and revisiting a film we'd watched earlier the year as part of a different study called *Smoke Signals*, which also follows a journey structure. Students can also brainstorm movies and books they know that seem to follow a similar pattern.

In each of these cases, we read/view each story individually first for its own sake over a reasonable period of time. Students have a chance to respond and discuss before we analyze the journey or the Cinderella structures within them. Students work together in small groups to find connections between the stories. Then we come together to determine the key pieces of the plot.

With the journey study, we also watch an interview with Joseph Campbell talking about the hero's journey. Bringing in articles or bitesize pieces of literary theory about the plot archetype can be very helpful and a welcome challenge for adolescents at this point—but this should supplement students' own thinking, not replace it. Therefore, don't bring in theory right away. First give students a chance to make connections and think critically across texts themselves.

Journey Story Sequence

Here is a sequence I use for reading, studying, and then writing journey stories.

1. Usually, students are reading a novel as a class that follows a journey structure. We have also divided into groups with each group reading a different journey novel. During the reading portion of the study, students engage in the following steps.
2. Read Maurice Sendak's *Where the Wild Things Are* aloud to the class.
3. Students work in groups to reread and take notes on the story using a template I provide asking for identification of basic elements, such as character, conflict, and reactions. Share what we noticed with the whole class. Chart these as a reference.
4. Work in groups to create a graph of the "intensity" of the story—main events on the x-axis and intensity rating on the y-axis. Gallery walk to compare graphs. Select a graph that looks most like a classic "plot mountain" to introduce general plot terms: exposition, introduce conflict, rising action, climax, falling action/ resolution of conflict, and denouement.
5. Read William Steig's *Sylvester and the Magic Pebble* aloud to the class.
6. Students work in groups with copies of the book to create a Journey diagram in the shape of a circle—main events in sequence around the circle. Create color coded seasons. (The story takes place over a year with each season visible in illustrations.) Create a code for the location of Sylvester, the main character.
7. Come together to share observations.

8. Work in pairs to look for patterns between the two texts. I provide a graphic organizer to guide the process.
9. From here we create a general outline of a journey story in the shape of a circle, which shows that the story begins and ends in the same place.
10. I create an assignment sheet for students to begin planning and writing their own journey stories.

JOURNEY STORY WRITING PROJECT GUIDELINES

Assignment: Write a fictional story that follows the basic plot structure of the hero's journey. Use descriptive detail and dialogue throughout the story.

Length: Five scenes. Each scene should be approximately two pages handwritten or one page typed.

Due: First draft due Friday end of class.

Remember . . . there are four types of conflicts you may use throughout your story.

Monday	Tuesday	Wednesday	Thursday	Friday
Scene 1: **At home**	**Scene 2:** **Journey Begins**	**Scene 3:** **Adventure Challenge #1**	**Scene 4:** **Adventure Challenge #2**	**Scene 5:** **Return Home**
Exposition	**Conflict**	**Rising Action**	**Climax**	**Resolution**
Introduce your main character and his/her life at home. *Describe setting. Use dialogue between characters. There may be hints of conflict.*	A conflict occurs, causing the main character to leave home and begin a journey (even if he/she doesn't know it will be a journey). *Balance dialogue and description of setting with action.*	While away from home, character encounters a new challenge in a new setting. *Describe new setting, and possible new characters . . . what conflicts arise here?*	Character encounters final challenge— rising intensity leads to climax of story. *Remember to include dialogue. Character may do something heroic . . .*	Character returns home. Character has changed, become more mature since beginning of story. Remember to include description. Does home even look the same now?

☐ Character vs. character

☐ Character vs. society

☐ Character vs. himself

☐ Character vs. nature

Your story may be a **realistic** journey, or it may include elements of **fantasy/sci-fi.**

This general process can be applied to other kinds of stories, and not just to look at classic plot structures. We can, for example, base a story outline on a theme, such as power. This story outline comes out of our reading of George Orwell's *Animal Farm* and prior viewing of the film *Swing Kids* about a group of German youth living during World War II. As part of this unit, we studied the terms oppressor, victim, bystander, resistor, and martyr, as well as the concept of an allegory.

POWER STORY PLAN: *ANIMAL FARM* CREATIVE PROJECT

Assignment: Write an original story that involves power as a theme. Use descriptive detail and dialogue throughout.

Challenge (optional): Make the story an allegory and use anthropomorphism to reveal a particular reality and point of view.

Length: 4–5 scenes, approximately 1–2 pages handwritten each, or one page typed, double-spaced, in 12-point font (at least four pages in total).

Suggested Plot Outline:

Scene 1	Scene 2	Scene 3	Scene 4	Scene 5
Background, setting established	Power struggle begins	Adventure/ Challenge; resisting oppressive power structure	Turning point/ climax	Outcome of confrontation; transformation
Exposition	**Conflict**	**Rising Action**	**Climax**	**Resolution**
Introduce main character(s) and setting. *Describe setting. Use dialogue between characters. There may be hints of conflict or oppressive structures or characters. You may set your reader up to expect something . . .*	Conflict occurs; main character encounters problem(s) related to power/ oppressive conditions. *Balance dialogue, setting description, with action*	Character encounters increased challenge; must make choice about how to respond—resist, follow, become oppressor? *What new characters or conditions could arise here?*	Character confronts final challenge— rising intensity leads to climax of story. Heroic act? Big realization? Tragedy? *What do you want your reader to feel here? Think about climactic moments in books/ movies . . .*	Characters experience outcome of confrontation; transformation (for better or for worse) has occurred. *What does setting look like now? What message can you send about power? (Think of the final description of the pigs and humans in Animal Farm.)*

A FEW HELPFUL PRO-TIPS FOR STORY WRITERS (AND THEIR TEACHERS)

One more thing before I close out this chapter! Although I give students license to create their own content, over the years I have developed a few rules to help eliminate some of the most unproductive issues (and frankly, annoying) I see when students work on full stories. Deciding that these could be rules has been liberating for this teacher! They ensure, from the start, that I will be able to focus my feedback for students on more substantive aspects of their writing. I add these rules to the end of assignment sheets and go over them when introducing the task.

You can't kill your protagonist. This can be a big letdown for some students, but I find that this particular choice is almost always made because the student is struggling to figure out how to end their story. The answer to that problem should include character development, and I want to help students with that. Killing off the main character brings the story to an abrupt end and almost always serves to avoid character development and the resolution of conflicts introduced throughout the story. (Plus, it's depressing!) Some students try to fight me on this rule. I push them to explain to me how they will include character development if their main character dies. Usually, they cannot tell me and admit they need help thinking it through. That in itself is a productive conversation.

Don't end with your character waking up and "it was all a dream." Similar to killing the main character, this ending is almost always used to avoid the work of resolving conflicts and developing characters. It's also a very unsatisfying ending for readers. Students usually nod knowingly when I state this rule and rarely argue against it.

Don't use classmates' names for characters in your story. This is designed to avoid a very middle-school situation, in which I have the feeling a student is making fun of another student inside of their story. Sometimes this is playful and not mean spirited, but these dynamics are distracting to the creative process and the sense of safety in the room. I tell students to do what real authors do: if you are basing a character on a real person, disguise them enough that it's not obvious. This tends to keep creative channels open for the writer as well.

Don't borrow characters from television, movies, or social media. Create original characters! Similar to the rule above, students can draw inspiration from characters in other stories, or from celebrities, but they should disguise and adapt them for their own work. Every once in a while, I give special permission for a student to have a celebrity or cartoon character make an appearance in their story, but this is the rare exception. I maintain this rule, because in the past, when students would try this, I found the writing to be much less creative or compelling to read. I sensed that students would get caught up essentially retelling pieces of movies or series they enjoyed, but I didn't have enough pop culture mastery to really know what I was reading. I actually believe fan fiction is an exciting, worthwhile form of writing for anyone drawn to do it. It's pretty much what we're doing when we "play in the world of the stories" we read. I can imagine doing a fan fiction project with students, though I've never tried it. That said, when we write full stories, I want students to channel all that they enjoy as readers and have tried out in their other writing exercises—and produce something totally original.

Avoid writing characters you don't understand well. This is not a rule, but a strong caution. This tends to come up when students design a story around a middle-aged protagonist. Even though kids do know the adults in their lives, they don't have a lot of insight into an adult's point of view. For the most part, students show little interest in writing (or reading) about adult characters. When this happens, I've found, it is almost always because the student wants to imitate a movie, television series, or even a video game they like. The genre tends to be action and/or suspense. These media influences aren't a problem on their own, but the student will be more creative and successful if they can create a younger protagonist. I ask students in this situation to think carefully about the genre they're inspired by—which aspects do they like best about it and how can they incorporate those into their story, featuring a younger character with more relatable conflicts. If the student is very attached to their plan, I won't continue to fight them on it. Students can see for themselves, and learn from the experience. Sometimes after trying out their idea, the student decides it's too difficult and takes my advice after all.

6

Deciding What to Teach Directly: Style and Mechanics

THE EXPERIENCE OF PUZZLING, struggling, or dancing through fiction writing pieces, in connection with literature study, teaches students a great deal. However, when we see the work students produce, there are clear needs as well as interesting opportunities for further teaching. I've developed a general sequence of skills I teach intentionally along the way. These skill points help students accomplish the visions they have for their stories and to develop their authorial styles.

The wonderful thing about teaching skills in fiction writing—when we've identified the right skills at the right time—is how much they improve students' writing overall. Writing narrative fiction develops their ability to write sentences that sound good, for example, and their audience awareness as they write. Both of these are difficult to teach without a strong occasion that provokes students to want to work on them. Story writing provides such conditions. The repetition in this curricular approach allows us to teach just one or two skills at a time, building slowly across a year with plenty of reiterative practice.

In this chapter, I'll share:

- A framework for deciding what to teach and when
- An inquiry approach to lesson planning
- The paragraph and other useful organizational tools
- A collection of essential lessons for fiction writing
- The link between audience awareness and writing mechanics
- A yearlong progression of technical skills in fiction writing

INSTRUCT SPARINGLY

With so many demands on ELA teachers, prioritizing our objectives and use of time is an art form all its own. One of the ways I make space for ample reading and writing time during literature study cycles is by cutting down on what would traditionally be seen as instructional time. You could almost say I'm stingy with my formal instruction. Experience, I believe, is more potent for student learning than traditional teacher-led instruction from the front of the class. There are many students who don't learn very well from teacher talk. I recall paying almost minimal attention to my teachers' lessons in middle school. Instead, I'd read the instructions later on the worksheet they handed out and work from there. That amounted to a lot of time spent zoning out and bored, or engaging in "off task" behaviors like writing notes to friends or reading for pleasure (ha-ha).

I think there is an unspoken pressure teachers feel to fill up a certain amount of class time with instructional talk, because this is part of a traditional definition of what teaching looks like. Sometimes the pressure is built into a required lesson plan format, and other times it's simply a norm. I think that there's a corresponding understanding for students about what teaching is and how school is done. Many students learn to gauge how necessary it is to pay attention and participate in teacher-driven lessons, seeking the line that separates acceptable minimum engagement from getting completely lost.

There are strategies for shifting the line so that students are more engaged in teacher-driven instruction. Some strategies help the teacher to make this part of the lesson more interesting, and others hold students more "accountable" for their attention, making it more difficult to get away with zoning out.

Although these strategies are useful when teacher talk is necessary, my preferred strategy for maximizing student attention and learning is talking less, and getting students involved in *doing* meaningful work—whether that be reading, writing, sharing, discussing, researching, dramatizing, or otherwise collaborating—most of the time.

Whole class lessons are not a daily routine in my classroom. Students learn that when I lead one, it's going to be important—immediately relevant to their work and, hopefully, interesting at the same time. The rest of the time, I work to *influence* my students' learning in many other ways—the design of curricular experiences, the framing of those experiences for students, and frequent conversations with the class and individual students—in which I am both a speaker and a listener.

If I'm providing ample time for both reading and writing in class, and moving through books and writing projects at a decent pace, there is less time for teacher-led whole class instruction. I believe this is a worthwhile tradeoff in a school day with limited time and with students who struggle to sustain attention on teacher talk and who learn more by doing.

CATEGORIES FOR INSTRUCTION AND GENERAL LESSON STRUCTURE

In an entire novel study, there are just a few objectives I formally instruct on, from the front of the class, with a carefully planned, interactive mini-lesson. Within a creative writing piece connected to a novel study, I generally teach into two or three objectives. (Other skills from previous units are reinforced through the new experience.) The instructional focus points tend to be in these three categories:

1. **Instructional Focus Point: Planning/Structure**
   For bigger projects, one lesson will need to be around the planning of the story. This process builds on elements we've discussed as readers of the novel, and is guided by the assignment sheet I provide.
   a. Assignment Sheet: Creating the assignment is often a collaborative process with students, but for larger pieces, I still take the step to write up a formal sheet with all the details and expectations for the work. This is useful for other adults who work with our students, including parents, and for students who may have been absent. I introduce the assignment by handing out this sheet and having students read directions—as a whole class or students reading first themselves. Then, I take clarifying questions and note anything that needs emphasis.
   b. Collaborative Example: Students benefit from seeing an example of how to transition from reading a particular story type or element to writing it. I sometimes show examples from previous students, but more often I model the decision-making that goes into planning the story. Rather than straightforward teacher modeling, I solicit student input in a collaborative task: "Help me get started planning my story," I might say. "What's my first step?" Students refer back to the directions sheet and offer suggestions to me. I combine their ideas and my ideas, making decisions about my story. I record my planning, using the same materials and format they will use. This gives me a chance to call attention to something that I know will be important for them, or offer a challenge. For a shorter piece that doesn't need an outline, I would have students help me get an idea and start writing. I wouldn't write a whole assignment, just enough for them to get a feel for the sound of it and the kinds of decisions they'll need to make.

c. <u>Writing/Work Time</u>: Next, students have time to get started with their own work. Usually, by the time we get to writing full stories that need outlining, students have enough experience writing fiction not to struggle so much getting started. Earlier in the year, it's important to show an example of how to get started writing in narrative form. Otherwise, some students will struggle to put anything on paper; others will begin, "Hello my name is _____, and I'm writing a story about _____. My character is named _____." A quick example goes a long way. Shorter scene writing assignments help students learn to jump into the story.

2. Instructional Focus Point: Narrative Craft

In most projects, I pick a craft element to teach and emphasize. I try to select this element based on an area of strength of the novel, something we've been observing as readers. But I also prioritize a progression of skills across the year, starting with more basic tools and then getting more complex. Craft elements include descriptive language, dialogue, interior monologue, writing action, character development, foreshadowing, beginnings, endings, figurative language, and symbolism.

Here's a typical structure I would use for an interactive craft lesson. This can be adapted in many different ways. The key here is that the interactive process is more "sticky" than just offering students the definition and some examples, and telling students to try it. This way, students are more active. They are learning how to look back to the novel for examples of how this element looks and sounds, which is something they can repeat any time with any text.

a. <u>Student Investigation</u>: For a craft lesson, I give students a task for investigating the element in the book. If the element is interior monologue, I would ask students to find places where we hear a character's thoughts and record those in their notebooks or mark them with sticky notes.

b. <u>Share, Term Introduction, Discussion</u>: We come back together for students to share the examples they found. I type these, projecting for students to see. All students should have a copy of the text, so we can turn to the page and read together, but it's helpful to have examples in a central location as a reference. Have students copy down one or two shared examples in their notebooks. Then I would introduce the term—in this case, interior monologue—to name the craft element. (This step is only needed if the term is new.) Next, I ask, what do we notice about how the author writes characters' interior monologue? Note key observations.

c. <u>Collaborative Example</u>: Next, I have students help me try it in my story, so they can see how this looks. Or I can ask a student if they would volunteer to have the class try adding some interior monologue to their story. Students apply it to their own.

d. <u>Writing Time</u>: Students work on their own stories with the task of adding interior monologue. Follow up at the end of class or in the middle of the writing session by having a few students share out a section of their story that includes interior monologue. Depending on the timing of the previous steps and length of period, this part may happen the following day.

3. **Instructional Focus Point: Mechanics**

In each piece, I introduce one mechanical skill relevant to narrative writing. Earlier in the year, I focus more on mechanical skills than craft. Once I've taught some of the most pressing items, I can focus more on craft elements. The most urgent mechanical skills for fiction writing are paragraphing, punctuating dialogue, formatting on Google Docs or MS Word, and titling. Close behind these for my middle school students are comma usage, sentence combining, consistent verb tense, and varying sentence length. These items are very important for fiction writing, but fall under the more general umbrella of writing mechanics. Mechanical needs also depend on your group of students and their grade level. For example, in earlier grades, capitalization might be an urgent need. In upper high school, students might be working on using more sophisticated conventions.

To teach mechanical skills, I follow a similar structure as outlined above. Students investigate the item in the novel to observe how the pros do it.

a. <u>Student Investigation</u>: Give students task of finding examples of the element, in use in the novel. What do you notice about how the author punctuates dialogue? What rules do they seem to be using? Students take a stab at inferring the rules based on their observations. This works best in pairs.

b. <u>Share, Clarify Rules</u>: Students share what they found. We work together to clarify the rules and try them out. Students copy down the official, teacher-approved guidelines and I also post them as a reference.

c. <u>Practice</u>: With mechanics, I follow up with practice exercises, which I like to create using anonymous examples from students' writing (often from another class) that the class can work to correct or improve. The practice can be woven into the work over several days with short exercises at the start of class.

d. <u>Writing Time</u>: Finally, students apply this mechanics lesson to their own writing. This usually means going back to review what they've written so far and making edits. This is great using a computer, but if students are hand writing their drafts, it may be best to just ask students to apply the rule moving forward. They can edit their earlier sections in a second draft (if there is one).

These three categories make for about two or three instructional points per project. In the whole novels method, students are usually working on creative writing while half of the class is discussing the novel. In this case, it's best if two of these lessons— the structural one always, and either the mechanical or the craft lesson— can happen in the last few days of the reading period, before discussions begin. If there is a third lesson, it can happen after a day or two of discussions and writing, pausing the discussions. Teachers with double blocks are fortunate not to have to fit everything into one period a day. Overall, the idea is to push on just a few levers in each unit, and allow time for students to integrate the learning through experience. Students get to practice these same skills again in their future writing pieces.

Different Than I Do, We Do, You Do

The lesson structure I find most effective is different than the popular "I do, we do, you do." Beginning with "I do," means starting with a teacher demonstration, then a teacher-guided "we do" exercise, and finally, students practice on their own. This is a "gradual release of responsibility" approach.

In an experiential learning model, we flip this and begin with "You do," meaning students begin with an active experience, such as investigating, exploring, critically observing, or trying to solve a problem with whatever tools are available. This pushes students to (1) find out what they can do on their own and (2) identify challenges or questions for which they need additional help. Then, the class can come together with the teacher to share what they figured out and ask questions. The teacher can present the tools, terms, or processes students need to move forward, and students are more invested in receiving the lesson.

Philadelphia-based instructional coach David Ginsburg, who has blogged as Coach G on Education Week, wrote about the problems of the more typical teacher-led approach:

> I Do, We Do, You Do didn't work for me as a student because it conditioned me to rely on teachers for information and modeling rather than develop self-reliance. The repercussions of this were evident when college professors assigned case studies, and I felt paralyzed. It was even worse in the workplace when my boss assigned projects and provided little or no direction. (Ginsburg, 2015)

Ginsburg goes on to discuss how, as an instructional coach, he sees approximately two-thirds of a class zoning out frequently during the "I do" and "We do" stages of this kind of lesson. He advocates for starting with "You do", where students (often in groups) can discover their own ways of doing things, not just learn the one way the teacher presents. He explains, "The gauge of students' readiness for a learning task isn't whether they'll complete it correctly, but whether they have the prior knowledge and/or skills to attempt it at the level of productive struggle." Then the teacher can help to create order from the multiple findings of the students, answer their questions, and help the students improve their processes.

Reinforce With Worksheets: Practice and Assess

When teaching technical skills of narrative writing, I believe the context should be students writing their own authentic pieces. That said, with mechanics students need some repetitive practice to solidify their understanding and build automaticity in their application of the skill. I teach a skill like punctuating dialogue in the context of students applying it in their own writing. Since this skill involves a number of extremely precise rules, I reinforce it with practice worksheets that work on the skill with simple examples that are separate from their own work. However, I may use examples from students' work or from a story they know (removing the punctuation) to keep the context meaningful.

For technical skills, it's helpful to create a quiz or formal assessment of students' learning, in addition to the goal of them using it in their writing pieces. Since I don't give frequent quizzes and tests, students tend to feel motivated by the challenge of proving they know how to apply the skill.

THE PARAGRAPH AND OTHER USEFUL ORGANIZATIONAL TOOLS IN NARRATIVE

If you have the pleasure to assign a fiction writing piece to students and the majority of the class turns it in with proper formatting, paragraphing, and dialogue punctuated correctly, without you teaching these skills, find the teachers who worked with your students before you and give them some props. In my experience at several different New York City public schools, most students don't have basic knowledge of how to organize narrative writing. It seems most of their writing experience has been in expository formats in which the paragraph structures are prescribed within the assignment, or simple narratives that follow a version of a first, next, then, last sequence.

Students are used to seeing the way fiction writing looks on the page, but only a handful of students seem to connect this with how their own writing should look on their own without guidance. For several years, I would open students' Google documents, and many of them looked something like this, often for many pages without a single break:

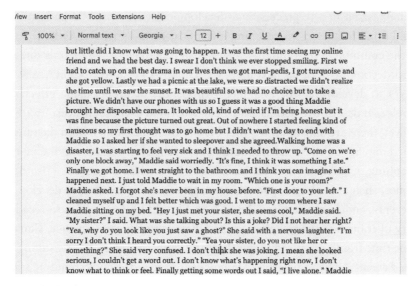

Figure 6.1: Block of Story Text

Even if the content was blowing me away, the process of reading through it was extremely frustrating—doing this many times with a full load of students becomes almost intolerable. Sometimes I would start chopping the text up myself, creating paragraph breaks to make it more readable. But I knew this was no solution.

Sometimes I would teach paragraphing haphazardly, saying something along the lines of, "Hey class, remember to divide your writing into paragraphs . . . " Some students would voice confusion. "Paragraphs in a story?" because the word "paragraph" made them think of formal writing done in response to a text-based question. I would add something like, "Yes, every time something changes, like time or place—just look in your book and you'll see what I mean." Believe it or not, that reminder turned on a light for some students, who went back and tried it with decent success. For most students, this brief mention didn't accomplish much.

I also tried going around helping individual students who were the most extreme non-paragraphers in the room. I left many a reminder comment in Google Docs too. It was tedious work. I could never get to everyone who needed it, and often my guidance didn't seem to stick.

It took me some missed opportunities to realize that paragraphing was, possibly, the first thing I needed to teach students in fiction writing, once students had begun to get their ideas onto paper. And I needed to teach it with the full commitment I brought to teaching anything I believed was important. Looking back, maybe it took me so long to realize this, because when to start or end a paragraph in fiction was never emphasized in any professional development experience I'd had on teaching writing. I don't recall anyone teaching it to me as a young person, either.

In the common core standards for English Language Arts, there is one writing standard devoted to writing narrative, CCSS.ELA-LITERACY.CCRA.W3: "Write narratives to develop real or imagined experiences or events using effective technique, relevant descriptive details, and well-structured event sequences." Within each grade level, there are substandards that break down the skills within narrative writing. The language in these substandards approaches but misses specific mention of paragraphing. CCSS.ELA-LITERACY.W.8.3.B for example reads, "Use narrative techniques, such as dialogue, **pacing**, description, and reflection, to develop experiences, events, and/or characters." And CCSS.ELA-LITERACY.W.8.3.C reads, "Use a variety of **transition words, phrases, and clauses to convey sequence, signal shifts from one time frame or setting to another,** and show the relationships among experiences and events." The same general language is used in the corresponding standards at other grade levels.

In the common standards, paragraphing isn't named as a narrative technique. It isn't a transition word, phrase or clause, though it certainly supports transitions. I can't help but joke that the authors of the standards must not have spent much time working on fiction with middle school students or they might have mentioned this especially glaring need.

Having spent some time learning how to teach the paragraph in fiction, and seeing what it does for my students' writing, I have to say, I love it. Paragraphing takes an unappealing block of text and turns it into expressive prose. It's like giving a piece of writing a makeover! Students enjoy the difference too. "Wow, this looks like a real book now!" I've heard many times.

The great mystery novelist Stephen King, in his wonderful book *On Writing: A Memoir of the Craft*, advises writers to pay attention to paragraphs: "I would argue that the paragraph, not the sentence, is the basic unit of writing." King notes that we tend to judge whether a book will be easy or hard to read based on how the paragraphs look on the page. The easier books have short paragraphs with lots of white space and dialogue, and that's what modern readers (our students, ahem) are looking for. "Paragraphs are almost always as important for how they look as for what they say; they are maps of intent," King says.

Paragraphs signal shifts and changes to readers. They create a visual rhythm that supports readers as they process the meaning of the text. Learning to use the paragraph as a tool to tell a story helps students develop their writing style. It gets them away from depending on formulas for the paragraphing of a writing piece. Nonfiction writing in the professional world does not follow a formula and generally uses a mix of expository and narrative styles, such as in a book like this. Paragraphing is key to writing an engaging website bio, a readable article, or a persuasive email, and none of these rely on formulas prescribing the boundaries of each paragraph.

Essential Lesson: Paragraphing in Fiction

Objective: Students will learn basic guidelines for transitioning from one paragraph to the next in narrative writing as a tool to signal change or to emphasize a moment to readers.

Context: Students have begun to write fictional scenes/stories in connection with a novel we've just finished reading.

Hook:
- Project two images: one is a block of text that takes up a full page and includes zero paragraph breaks, and the other is a page out of a typically structured YA fiction book (written in prose, not poetry or as a screenplay). Make sure the second one includes some dialogue.
- Ask students what they notice about each one. The idea is not for them to read the words on the pages, but to look at how they present visually.
- Ask students which book they think they would prefer to read and why.
- Summarize: "When we see a page of text with no paragraph breaks, it's hard to read it. It's harder to pay attention and it may even hurt our eyes. So paragraphs in fiction exist and they are very important!"

Investigation:
- Students use the novel they are reading (or just finished) as a resource. Open to a page and look at the paragraph breaks. Work in pairs or table groups to try to figure out why the author starts a new paragraph when they do. There is more than one answer, so look for three to five different kinds of situations in which the author starts a new paragraph. Make a list together.

Share/Create Guidelines:
- After about ten minutes, bring the class back together to share what they found.

- If students give a specific example, like on Page 9, the author starts a new paragraph when . . . have the class all turn to Page 9 to see for themselves.
- Create a list of guidelines for starting a new paragraph. Consolidate items that are very similar. The list probably includes some version of these items:
  - When a new character speaks (only one speaker per paragraph, but this requires a separate lesson, so don't dwell on it now)
  - When a different character thinks or moves
  - When the topic or focus changes
  - When time changes (forward or backward)
  - When the location changes
  - To emphasize a line or moment (one sentence paragraphs!)
  - When the paragraph would be too long. (Even making a break somewhat arbitrarily is better than a paragraph that takes up half a page.)
- Students are usually surprised when they realize that paragraphs in fiction can be very short! The usual four to six sentence measurement doesn't apply here.
- It's also important to note that there isn't one correct way to break paragraphs in fiction. There are places where it's very much needed, but there are other times when the author gets to use their judgment or feeling about where a break should be.

Collaborative Example:
- I project a typed block of text—a student's work from another class or a previous year, so that it's anonymous, but recognizable as student work.
- "Let's add paragraph breaks to this student's story." Review the guidelines. "When you notice a good place to start a new paragraph, raise your hand."
- It's really important to remind students that there isn't one right way to do this.
- When a student suggests a paragraph break, have them refer back to the guidelines to explain why they are suggesting it.
- Ask students, now that I know where I want to make the break, how do I do it with the computer? Students can tell me to put the cursor right before the first letter of the sentence and then press Enter and Tab.
- Teach and remind students to use the tab button! Otherwise, many students will press enter until they see the line indenting. Also note that most programs will start to automatically indent paragraphs once tab has been used.
- Go through the first half a page or so, creating paragraph breaks with the students.

- Show at least one an example of more than one way to break the paragraph. "Wherever you break the paragraph, you are giving the next sentence visual emphasis. How does it feel when we break here? What if we break here instead?"
- Soon enough you will have almost a full page of beautiful looking prose, and students will remark on the difference.

Writing Time:
- Now it's time for students to apply the guidelines to their own writing. This is much easier when students are typing. If students have handwritten their drafts, have them put a slash mark or the paragraph symbol to indicate a paragraph break.
- Once students have edited the paragraphing on their work so far, they can continue writing, this time paying special attention to their paragraphs.
- I remind students—if you are not sure where to break the paragraph, review the guidelines. If you're still not sure, ask a classmate. Or you can just break it up anyway when it gets too long. The break will help you see your writing better, and you can always go back and change it.
- Circulate to help students and compliment them on their professional-looking fiction writing!

Other Organizational Tools

In addition to paragraphing, there are a few other ways to visually organize a narrative, worth highlighting for students. We can begin by asking students to look in a novel and notice how the author divided the text beyond paragraphs. Chapters are the most obvious tool. As readers, we appreciate chapters, because they break up the long book into more manageable chunks. Chapter titles can help us anticipate what will come in the chapter, either literally by telling us what the chapter is about (e.g., "The Party") or by making us curious (e.g., "Things that Lock"). Some books have chapter titles and some don't. I ask students to title chapters when they write multiscene stories, because it helps them become aware of their own structure and it makes their story easier and more fun to read.

In between chapter and paragraph breaks is the scene break. This is more significant than a simple paragraph break, yet not as big as the end of a chapter. Authors sometimes signal scene breaks with an extra space or two between paragraphs: This usually means time passes or that we are moving to a different location or point of view. Students often notice these breaks in the lesson above when they search for paragraph breaks in a text. Some authors signal more major breaks within chapters with three asterisks. (The technical term for the symbol is *dinkus*, so depending on your sense of humor, you can decide whether to share that with students).

These visual scene breaks are not required but they are helpful for students who write longer pieces. Teaching them to everyone helps build awareness of the kinds of shifts that happen in stories. It helps solve a common problem for students just beginning to write stories—how do we move forward in time without telling every little thing that happens? We can use transitional phrases, like "The next morning . . . " and/or we can use scene breaks.

We can teach these tools using a process similar to the one we used to teach paragraphing—students investigate, share back, and we clarify the rules around scene breaks. If, in the paragraphing lesson, a student asked about the extra line spaces between some paragraphs, I can use that as a hook for the new lesson: "I noticed that some paragraphs have blank lines between them. Did anyone else notice this? Let's go back to the text and look for examples like that. When you find one, read around it and try to figure out why the author put extra spaces between those particular paragraphs." Then we share what we found and create guidelines for using the double line space—a scene break, where time, location, and/or point of view changes.

As with the paragraph break, there is not one right way to apply this tool. It is up to each author when and whether to use it, but students should understand that it helps readers take a pause when reading and know that a change in the narrative is happening.

Essential Lesson: Punctuating Dialogue

Once students have a grasp of how to use paragraphs in fiction, the second most urgent mechanical need is for students to learn to punctuate dialogue. Dialogue between characters is one of the most engaging aspects of fiction to read; it brings their characters to life and students get excited about writing it as well. However, the punctuation and paragraphing of dialogue is complicated, and most students don't come to me already knowing how to do it. In the beginning of the year, without instruction, students try various approaches: some write dialogue in script form; some avoid direct dialogue ("and then he told me that . . . and then I said that . . . "); some use quotation marks without paragraphing; some use paragraphing without quotation marks.

Because it takes time and practice to teach the rules of dialogue, I don't like to do this in the very first fiction writing assignment, because I want students to focus more on content, and feel a sense of freedom as they write. I teach them paragraphing first, and I informally remind students to use quotation marks around the words characters speak. I know they won't get this quite right yet, but I'm pointing them in that direction. By our second or third assignment, confusion around the rules is getting in students' way, and they have enough experience writing fiction that spending time on these rules won't distract them too much from their imaginative work.

Objective: Students will learn basic rules for punctuating and formatting dialogue in narrative fiction.

Context: Students have begun to write fictional scenes/stories in connection with a novel we've just finished reading.

Hook:
- Project pictures of a few examples of writing that include dialogue between characters but don't punctuate or format properly. These should not have names or be from students in the class. Ideally, use student examples from a previous year with no name, or create your own if you don't have these handy.
- Ask students what they notice about the examples. Have them jot down thoughts before sharing.
- Give students a chance to share briefly. Do not get into the rules for punctuating dialogue yet. We are just trying to help students visualize the need for clarification of these rules.

Investigation:
- "Many of you are noticing the rules for writing dialogue in fiction and some of you have been working on using them in your writing. How many students have felt confused about how to do it at one point or another? I understand! There are quite a few rules to learn, and it's time we worked on this together."
- Work with a partner or table group. Open your novel and reread a section that has a lot of dialogue between characters. Try to write a list of the rules you see.
- Give students 5–10 minutes for this task.

Share/Create Guidelines:
- Bring students back together to share what they found. Ask them to start by sharing the most important rules they found.
- You can record them exactly as students share them as a brainstorm, and

then create an Official Rules List that revises those items to be more clear and accurate.

- An alternative is to revise as you go, taking student items one at a time, and saying, "Yes! Good idea. I'm going to write it down this way . . . " and then record the applicable rule in clear language.
- Students copy down the official rules into their notebooks. The official rules should come out something like this:
  1. Put quotation marks around the words a character speaks aloud.
  2. Start a new paragraph when the speaker switches (one speaker per paragraph).
  3. You must have a punctuation mark inside the end quotation mark. It can be an exclamation point, question mark, or period—if the sentence continues after that, use a comma instead of a period before the end quotation mark, and then continue the sentence.
     - Example: "Follow me."
     - Example: "Good morning," said the reporter.
     - Example: "Where are you going?" I asked.
  4. Name the speaker, enough so that it's always clear who is speaking.
  5. Always capitalize the first letter of a quotation, even if it's not the beginning of a sentence.
     - Example: She announced, "The yellow team has won!"
  6. Put a comma before a quotation, when it is not the beginning of the sentence. (See example in #5.)

Collaborative Example/Practice:
- Next, have students help you try out the rules.
- Ask a volunteer to give you an idea for two characters who can have a conversation. Each character needs a name.
- Ask another volunteer to give you a topic for that conversation.
- Then ask for a volunteer to decide what the first character will say.
- Ask a student to tell you exactly how to write it, including indentations and every punctuation mark needed.
- Ask students, "Is this correct? Are you sure?" Refer back to the rules often to clarify why it is correct or why it needs a change.
- Students should copy down the dialogue as you write it.
- Practice going back and forth between the two characters, sometimes naming the speaker before and sometimes after the quotation marks.
- Try adding a sentence of description in the middle of it. Clarify that you do not need to go to a new paragraph, because no one is speaking. If

the same speaker continues after the description, no need to start a new paragraph either.

- You may now have students practice formatting a brief made-up dialogue exercise to apply the skill or you can have them go to their own stories and try it out.

Writing Time:

- When students go back to work on dialogue in their own writing, it will take some time for them to get the hang of it. The process is infinitely easier on the computer, because mistakes can be fixed in paragraphing and indentations without having to rewrite the whole thing.
- If students are working by hand, have them apply the rules to the next section they write. They can fix what they've already written in their next draft.
- I like to check in briefly with each individual student and see how they're doing. The rules are listed in order of importance, so when a student is struggling, I focus on the most relevant or two on the list, not all of them at once.
- By the next session, I identify a few peer helpers—students who are applying the rules well in their own work without help—who can help other students.
- I provide a check list for students to use for reviewing the punctuation and formatting of their dialogue, before they turn in their assignments.

DEVELOPING AUDIENCE AWARENESS THROUGH WRITING MECHANICS

Learning the skill of punctuating and formatting dialogue (as well as paragraphing) helps students build awareness of their audience on a practical level. Students notice how much easier their writing is to read now that it is properly formatted "like a real book." This is an organic way to get students thinking about how their writing looks and reads to others. Go a little deeper into the finer points of these rules and that path continues.

For example, when we work on the rule of naming the speaker, we have to put ourselves in the shoes of our readers. If two characters are having a back-and-forth dialogue, we name the speaker the first few times they each speak. At some point "said Ryan" and "said Elisa" become redundant, and we can drop them—but only as long as the reader is able to visualize the back-and-forth clearly in their mind's eye. I ask students, "Have you ever been into reading a book and suddenly you're confused about which character is speaking? You have to go back and reread from the last time the narrator named the speaker to try to figure it out, right?" Everyone has experienced this.

As writers, we want to avoid that problem, because it interrupts the "dream" of fiction, as John Gardner famously described it, which must be "vivid and continuous." The author's job, he explains, is to maintain that dream and avoid any mistake or incongruity that might distract the reader from the story (Gardner, 1991). We can make this mistake by not naming the speaker enough, but if we name the speaker too many times in a dialogue, that too can become distracting. We have to actually listen to our work as if we were a reader and not the author . . . and that is one way of developing awareness of audience.

Similarly, when we teach students to vary their word choices and use words other than "said" when we name the speaker—replied, asked, exclaimed, shouted, whispered, and so forth—students can easily over-do it with these verbs. Using "said" every time can become tedious, which can be distracting, and using a different verb every time can also become a distraction. We have to find the correct balance that allows the reader to read through the dialogue without much noticing the word choices. We find this by listening to our own work.

A social studies teacher I know recently lamented that students are passing in writing without reading it over to check for simple errors. He has told them to do so, but most students don't take the advice. I have experienced the same problem many times. The best way to get students to correct their own work is to read it aloud to them. This is something we can have students do for each other in pairs. The second-best way is to get them to read their work themselves, imagining they are an outside reader. That is a habit that needs to be practiced.

I notice that students seem to find the question of how to make their fictional dialogue *sound good* an inviting context for reviewing their own writing. I believe that developing audience awareness in fiction writing works well, because students have lots of real experience as readers of fiction, and they can learn to put themselves in their readers' shoes. They know more or less how fiction should sound. It's more difficult with a social studies essay or a science lab report, because these aren't genres students are very accustomed to reading; but I do believe that once we acquire the general habit of listening to our own writing as if we were a reader, we can apply the same process to other kinds of writing. It's part of learning and maturation to be able to apply a skill to increasingly challenging contexts.

Sentence Length and Rhythm

Once we start to focus on fiction writing at the word level and get students thinking about what sounds good to readers, sentence structure and length is a good topic to explore; motivation tends to be high. The combination of teaching writing mechanics in the context of imaginative writing provides a great balance of divergent and convergent thinking.

To be able to write longer sentences well, students need to know basic strategies for sentence combining. There are many resources and different methods for teaching sentence combining. Lately, I have been using Quill.org as a resource for catching students up on grammar and mechanics, because the online program differentiates based on student needs. I like to come up with exercises on my own, but a good grammar workbook can be very helpful. These days lesson plans and materials abound online, both free and paid, for lessons on writing complex sentences.

Whichever resources we select for teaching sentence structure, we can augment our instruction by using student sentences from their stories to practice the strategies. I take the time to review how to use a comma followed by a conjunction to link two sentences (clauses) for all students. For example:

We wanted to go to the fair. The fair was canceled due to rain.

This can be combined with a comma and the conjunction "but." The point for students is that the comma is necessary and it always goes *before* the conjunction.

We wanted to go to the fair, but it was canceled due to rain. I read it like this: "We wanted to go to the fair—COMMA—but it was canceled due to rain." Many students put the comma after the conjunction. Hearing it read aloud with punctuation can help them remember correctly.

There is so much to teach in grammar (and I love grammar!), but this simple clarification can be done successfully without needing to go into too many other grammar concepts when time is limited. My students tend to write run-on sentences and struggle with where to place commas. The lesson is as much about how to combine sentences as it is about how to break up run-ons. We practice with student examples.

I instruct students not to go beyond three clauses. For example, this three-clause sentence is acceptable:

We wanted to go to the fair, and we got everything ready the night before, but it was canceled due to rain.

But a four-clause sentence would generally be too long:

We wanted to go to the fair, and we got everything ready the night before, but it was canceled due to rain, and Jennie was heartbroken.

We read it out loud. How could we break this up? If we keep three clauses together, then one can be on its own. After a long sentence, a short sentence like this one seems to get special emphasis. For example:

We wanted to go to the fair, and we got everything ready the night before, but it was canceled due to rain. Jenny was heartbroken.

Jenny was heartbroken could even be a one sentence paragraph!

Look at it another way:

We wanted to go to the fair. We got everything ready the night before, but it was canceled due to rain, and Jennie was heartbroken.

In this case, the short sentence, *We wanted to go to the fair*, gets the emphasis. The sentence that follows seems to reflect the falling apart of the plans. Authors listen to how their sentences sound and make decisions based on what sounds better and how the decision impacts the meaning or tone.

This leads into a lesson on varying sentence length. We can follow the general lesson format I've used in this chapter, starting with an investigation into the length of sentences on a specific page photocopied from a book. Students can color code long, medium, and short sentences and look for patterns. Some writers tend toward shorter sentences and others tend toward longer ones. All writers vary sentence length and pay attention to the rhythm of their words. A short sentence among longer sentences creates emphasis, calling the reader's attention by breaking the rhythm created in the longer sentences.

I have students practice using commas and conjunctions properly in their writing. I have them revise a piece of writing to vary sentence length. Later in the year, I teach the semicolon. This opens up a new kind of rhythm. It's not the hard stop of a period, but it creates a pause; by contrast, the comma with conjunction helps the sentence keep going without much of a pause. The semicolon is beloved by students who like writing long sentences—or make the mistake of comma splicing. Can't decide how to break it up? Try the semicolon!

In these lessons, students are working on a number of Common Core Language Standards, including CCL 6.3: "Use knowledge of language and its conventions when writing, speaking, reading, or listening. a. Vary sentence patterns for meaning, reader/listener interest, and style." and CCL 8.2. "Demonstrate command of the conventions of standard English capitalization, punctuation, and spelling when writing. a. Use punctuation (comma, ellipsis, dash) to indicate a pause or break."

Alongside these language standards, a note on range and content use of student language reads, "To be college and career ready in language, students must have firm control over the conventions of standard English.

At the same time, they must come to appreciate that language is as at least as much a matter of craft as of rules and be able to choose words, syntax, and punctuation to express themselves and achieve particular functions and rhetorical effects." This is the kind of sensibility we are developing when students learn to hear their work as a reader would.

Beyond these lessons, students can learn a lot from mimicking the structure of specific sentences from acclaimed authors. There are many excellent resources for delving into this practice. The basic steps for sentence imitation work are to first get students to notice great sentences in their reading. You can stay in this stage for a while—the more students can look closely and appreciate the way an author puts words together, the better. Students can work in pairs to choose great sentences and write them on sentence strips. I post these around the room with the title "Language We Like." Next, we can show students how to imitate a sentence, borrowing the author's exact sentence structure, but substituting our own words and content. Then students choose sentences they like, and try adapting them for their own stories. This practice helps students jump into longer, more sophisticated sentence structures without needing to teach all of the grammar behind them. This is like learning to sing a melody and putting your own words to it, without knowing all of the music theory behind it. In this way, students learn new ways of creating rhythm in their narrative. Sentence work is fun and can become a thread that develops across the year.

HOW STUDENTS DEVELOP STYLE: COLLECTING WRITER'S CRAFT TECHNIQUES

For students to develop their writing craft, first they should be reading a lot. We tend to mimic what we read. You've heard the idea that children learn by watching what we as adults do, more than from what we tell them. I think there is a similar truth in writing. The same is true in learning a second language. Taking a course is useful, but it's not a given that we will emerge with real speaking skills. Living where the language is spoken, on the other hand, is a faster path to fluency. Our instruction is important and needed; I just want to emphasize that the best context for our lessons is one in which students are immersed in reading and writing experiences. It's also important for students to hear literature read aloud, because this provides models for how strong narrative style literally sounds—these auditory reference points inform how students hear their own writing.

Beyond immersion, we can purposefully strengthen the connections students make between their reading and writing of fiction. We do this first through investigating specific elements in novels and then designing writing assignments that explicitly build on those elements. I also have students listen to writers talk about their writing processes in interviews, and then "collect" writing craft techniques from each author we read.

Students keep a Writer's Craft section in their notebooks. It's a simple log that includes the book title, author, and a space to record favorite writing techniques of that author. We do this together as a class at the end of a novel study. Just before this, we have discussed the novel over several few days and we have watched or listened to the author talk about their writing in an interview or presentation (there are many available on the internet, and occasionally we have the privilege of actually meeting or video calling with the author).

As we wrap up the study, I ask students to open to this section of their notebooks and log the title and author's name. I ask, "What elements or writing techniques do we want to remember from this author? What do they do really well?" I like this question, because students can answer it even when they do not personally love a book. They can recognize and appreciate the strengths of an author, distinct from their overall personal response to the work.

I give students about five minutes to think and write on their own, and then we share. I chart students' responses, and I encourage students to add the items to their own lists, if they agree with them. Returning to this section of the book with each novel study helps students see the repertoire they are building, and the similarities and differences in the styles and strengths of different authors.

TEACHING CRAFT LESSONS: NARRATIVE, DIALOGUE, INTERIOR MONOLOGUE, DESCRIPTION, PACING, AND ENDINGS

Along with the urgent lessons of paragraphing and formatting dialogue, I try to introduce one **craft lesson** into each writing piece. These depend on the elements that are strongest in the literature we're reading, and the techniques students seem to need. There are many concepts and techniques that can be taught when they come up in our reading. For example, the idea of a "composite character" (based on a combination of various real people) comes up when we listen to Sandra Cisneros talk about writing *The House on Mango Street*. We note this in our Writer's Craft section and students can hold onto the idea to use in the future if they want.

However, the main writer's craft tools which students need to be able to build an intelligible, compelling story are narration, dialogue, interior monologue, and description. There are many interesting lessons available to teach these. I'm sharing my general approach to each one below. I focus on just one of these in a writing piece, adding to our menu of techniques with each new assignment.

Narration

Students need to establish the voice telling the story, whether this is a first-, third-, or possibly second-person narrator. This voice is in charge of telling readers everything, including the next three elements; but at core, narration tells us what's happening, what are characters doing, and any other information we need to know, like backstory.

A folk tale consists almost exclusively of narration and provides a good example how narration sounds. In a folk tale, there is minimal dialogue, interior monologue, and description. We basically get a simple narrative telling us what characters do and what happens.

- Teaching the concept of narration is not usually a full lesson in my class, but more of a quick talking point and collaborative modelling as we get started with an assignment.
- Some students need to see how to start writing narrative, especially when they are so used to writing essays and reports. Otherwise, I see some stories begin, "My character is named _____, and she lives _____. Her conflict is that . . . " etc.
- Show students directly how to jump into a narrative story with a collaborative example.
  - Here's an example my students and I worked on during a remote session after creating outlines for conflict stories. I took these notes during our conversation. I then made the Google Doc available as a resource for students.

HOW TO GET STARTED WITH FICTION

Character: Millie

Conflict: Character wants to go out and spend time with friends, BUT parents are concerned about COVID-19 and forbid it.

◊ Put character in a place.

◊ Have them **doing, thinking, or saying something.**

Place: in bed, getting a text message from a friend.

◊ How it sounds in first person:

I rolled over to grab my phone. It was buzzing . . . . It was probably Julia. She liked to wake me up on the weekends.

◊ How it sounds in third person:

Millie rolled over to grab her phone. It was buzzing . . . . It was probably Julia. She liked to wake Millie up on the weekends.

OR start with dialogue. (Reminder: Indent each time speaker switches. Enter, then tab.)

"Hey, you up yet?" Julia texted.

"Uhhhhhh," I responded. I could hear dishes clattering in the kitchen. It sounded like everyone else was already up in my house. "I guess I am."

"What are you doing today?" Julia wrote.

"Nothing much," I said.

Dialogue

Teaching the punctuation and formatting, is an early "must." Beyond that, I find that students are able to get started writing dialogue in their own stories without much help. Nonetheless, here are some ways to help students practice and be more creative. It never hurts!

- Practice with exercises. Assign tasks like, "Write a dialogue between a child and parent arguing about cell phone use." Or, provide the beginning of a dialogue and have students continue it, then share out to see how students took it in different directions.
- Create a game. Put cards with general characters in a box: "student," "Crossing guard," "teacher," "singer," "wizard," etc. Have students pull two cards and create a dialogue between them.
- Dramatize variations on scenes from a known folk tale or class novel using the Poly-plots method described in Chapter 5. This is described in the section on "play-throughs." Then have students write dialogue based on the improvised scenes.

- Have students collect interesting real-life dialogue by listening discreetly to people talk and jotting down lines. This can be a homework assignment for a few days, so that students come to class with 5–10 lines they heard and wrote down in their notebooks. You can have them dramatize the dialogue they recorded with a partner. Students choose a line or two from their notes to incorporate into their story.

Interior Monologue

Students enjoy writing interior monologue in the context of a focused point-of-view exercise related to a story we've read. For example, students write a journal entry from a minor character's point of view during a key moment in the novel. When writing their own stories, though, only some students include their protagonist's thoughts in their narratives, having internalized how this sounds from all the reading they've done. A lesson on interior monologue helps the majority of students utilize this craft tool.

Investigation: Have students find examples from the novel of the author showing a character's thoughts. You can also have students look in other novels to get a variety of styles.

Share/Respond: Students read out the examples they found. After hearing many examples, ask students what they notice about them. How is this helpful to us as we read? (For example, some students might find a long stretch of interior monologue. Others may find a sentence of interior monologue in the middle of an action or dialogue.)

Term Introduction/Guidelines:
- Introduce the term "interior monologue." Define the words "interior" and "monologue" (from Greek, *monologos*, meaning speaking to oneself; mono means one, and logos means to speak). These are the character's "inside thoughts to themselves."
- Looking back at the examples, how does the author show characters having interior monologue?
- The answer is essentially that the narrator tells these thoughts as part of narration. Usually, there are no special symbols—no quotation marks needed. Occasionally writers use italics to differentiate characters' thoughts from the narrator's voice, but this isn't necessary.

- The thoughts are interspersed with other kinds of storytelling, like dialogue, action, and description. There are long sections of interior monologue and sections as short as one sentence.

Collaborative Example:
- Have students help you write an example. You can make up a scenario, use a story you've already started, or have a student volunteer their story for the class to try it out.
- Show how the interior monologue might be short—interrupted quickly by something else like dialogue or action—or it could be long.
- Depending on your goals, you can extend the lesson to show how a third-person narrator might stay mostly in the protagonist's thoughts, but could show thoughts of another character. This is a good moment to introduce or reinforce the concept of limited versus omniscient narrator.

Writing Time: Have students practice adding interior monologue into their story. Share with a partner. Have a few students share with the whole class. (I like to encourage students to "Nominate your partner to share!" instead of taking volunteers.)

Description

Description is a basic concept for students to understand, but it requires conscious practice for them to get a feel for it and apply it in their writing. Authors can take the time to describe settings, objects, characters' appearances, and movements. When authors use description, the story slows down. Too much can sometimes feel boring, but too little means we may not have enough detail to visualize the story as it's happening. We may also get bored of constant action without moments that slow down, create contrast, and help us process.

Once again, I begin with students investigating an author's use of description in a text. I usually do a short assignment early in the year on description of setting as a prologue to *The House On Mango Street* using an excerpt from Ray Bradbury's *The Martian Chronicles*. I described this lesson in Chapter 5, as an example of an assignment focused on setting. But the same concept can be extended to look at description more broadly in a recent novel and for students to apply it to a longer writing piece.

Hook: What's the difference between a book and a movie of the same story? Students can chat with a partner, and then share out ideas. A key point is that in novels, unlike in movies, graphic novels, and other visual media forms, authors must create pictures in our minds entirely with words. It's a lot of work!

Investigation: Pick a section of the book and have students look for description of any kind within it. For each example, students record what is being described. Consider printing copies of the pages so students can use a highlighter and annotate on the page.

Share: Students read aloud examples of description they found and what they identify as the subject of the descriptive language. Record the subjects to create a list of the kinds of things authors take the time to describe. A variation of this would be to circle the most vivid words the author uses.

Discuss: Why do authors take the time to describe these pieces of the story? Description includes **sensory details**—what does it look like, feel like, sound like, smell like? Note that authors usually don't run through all of those senses at one time.

Collaborative Example: Let's look at my story. What could I take the time to describe? Or, work with a partner. Look at each other's stories. Circle places you think your partner could add description. Add a comment if you have an idea of sensory details the writer can include—e.g., the sounds of birds in the trees.

Writing Time: Students work on adding descriptive language to their stories. Circulate to see what students are working on. Read a few student examples out to the class.

Extensions/Variations: Focus just on imagery—visual description. Focus on figurative language as a mode of descriptive writing in a story (not just in poetry). Collect figurative language in a novel—practice analyzing what two things are being compared in this figurative language? What does this comparison show or highlight in the story right now?

Lesson Plan: Keeping the Pace with Narration, Dialogue, Interior Monologue, and Description

This is a more advanced lesson for when students already have a grasp of narration, dialogue, interior monologue, and description. It brings these craft techniques together to create a well-paced narrative.

Investigation: Photocopy a page from a popular novel that has all of the craft elements. Create a color code for each kind of narration: dialogue, interior monologue, description, and narration (default, but tends to be action). Students work together in pairs to color code each kind of narration.

Share: What did you notice as you tried to color code? Students should notice that the author switches between these modes often. Why do you think the author does this? Which modes make the story move quickly? (Usually dialogue and narration of action.) Which modes make the story slow down? (Usually description and interior monologue.) We tend to like when a story moves quickly, but we need to be able to picture what's happening, and hearing a character's thoughts makes the story more interesting.

Collaborative Modeling: Help me try out switching between these modes with a section of my story. OR ask for a student to volunteer their story for us to work on. (This works well when students are writing on Google Docs, and I can project a students document and add to it.) Take student suggestions of which mode to start with, what to try next, and after that. Show that there isn't one correct way to do this. Try it more than one way; move things around. Discuss how these choices affect the pacing, our feeling as readers of how the story moves.

Writing Time: Students try alternating between narration, dialogue, interior monologue, and description in a section of their own writing, either writing new material or revising a section they already drafted.

> In these craft lessons, students are working toward Common Core Writing Standard 3b: "Use narrative techniques, such as dialogue, pacing, description, and reflection, to develop experiences, events, and/or characters." When students investigate these techniques in texts and become readers of their own and their classmates' work, they are also working on Common Core standards for Reading Literature 8.3: "Analyze how particular lines of dialogue or incidents in a story or drama propel the action, reveal aspects of a character, or provoke a decision."

Lesson: Connecting Beginnings and Endings to Craft a Satisfying Story Ending

This is another lesson for later in the year when students are writing endings of full stories, or have completed a first draft and are now revising. It helps them write a satisfying ending by understanding how beginnings and endings are connected. A prerequisite for the lesson is that students have an idea for how their character changes over the course of the story. In this lesson, students look closely at the opening lines or opening scene and the closing lines or closing scene in books they've read this year. We model it together with a picture book first, and then students work in groups on assigned texts they've already read. It works with almost any novel or film, but some have more clearly connected beginnings and endings than others. This lesson usually takes two periods.

Objective: To be able to craft a satisfying ending to a journey story that reveals a character's transformation.

Aim: to explore strategies writers use to create satisfying endings using stories we've read together this year and then apply the lesson in revisions to their own stories.

Common Core Standards Addressed

- W3. Write narratives to develop real or imagined experiences or events using effective technique, relevant descriptive details, and well-structured event sequences.
  - W3.b. Use narrative techniques, such as dialogue, pacing, description, and reflection, to develop experiences, events, and/or characters.
- R5. Analyze the structure of texts, including how specific sentences, paragraphs, and larger portions of the text (e.g., a section, chapter, scene, or stanza) relate to each other and the whole.
- SL1. Engage effectively in a range of collaborative discussions (one-on-one, in groups, and teacher-led) with diverse partners on Grade 8 topics, texts, and issues, building on others' ideas and expressing their own clearly.

Part I: Critical Reading

Hook: What makes a satisfying ending to a story? Discuss with your table group. Identify two or more components that make satisfying endings. Students share results of table talk. Record notes. Summarize main ideas that students bring up. This might sound like, "As many of you said, a satisfying ending needs to have some kind of change. We don't like cliff hangers very much. The conflict needs to resolve, but not too neatly, or it sometimes feels fake."

Introduce Investigation: One classic symbol for story is, instead of a mountain, a circle. Draw a circle that starts on the left center. It represents the character's journey. Sometimes there is a physical journey, and sometimes the journey is more emotional or metaphorical. In the circle, the ending is connected to the beginning, right? In stories, satisfying endings are often connected to beginnings. There is some major similarity . . . but, something major has also changed.

In your groups, you'll be assigned to a story we've read this year. You'll review and discuss:

1. Look carefully at the beginning of the story. Take notes together on imagery and other details.
2. Look carefully at the ending of the story. Take notes together on imagery and other details.
3. How is the ending of the book/story connected to its beginning? What is similar? What is different? What has changed? Sometimes we see opposites, e.g., fire imagery in the opening lines; water imagery in the closing scene. This is true in the film *Smoke Signals*, which we watch when we read *The Absolutely True Diary of a Part-Time Indian*. It's more common than we realize, though, in films and books.
4. What does this connection, between beginning and ending, show or represent about the main character? How has the character changed? How does the ending connect to that change?

Collaborative Example: Quickly try the task together with *Where the Wild Things Are* by Maurice Sendak, or *Sylvester and the Magic Pebble* by William Steig, or another picture book with clear beginning and ending connection. It's best if students have already read the story, so all we're doing is reviewing the first and last pages.

1. In the first pages of *Where the Wild Things Are*, Max is making mischief and he's sent to bed with no supper.
2. In the last pages, he returns home and finds supper waiting for him.
3. The connection is that the supper was denied him in the beginning. He takes a journey and we forget about the dinner and his mother. In the end, the dinner is there. Dinner is a concept in beginning and end but in opposite ways.
4. Max learns a lesson. After being too wild in the house, he leaves home and becomes king of the wild things, he starts to miss home "where he was loved best of all." Finding dinner that his mother has left him is a symbol of her love for him, and now he appreciates it. He is done being a "wild thing."

Group Investigation: Students work in groups with copies of one of the books we read as a class this year. Together, they discuss and answer the previous questions. The books represent varying levels of challenge in relation to this activity, and I assign them with that in mind. I spend time with each group as they work. If groups finish quickly, I'll ask for textual evidence, which will lead to a closer examination of word choice.

Share: Groups share examples. Students take notes on each example presented. Discuss any patterns that emerge.

Part II: Writing

Application: This would usually take place the following day. Now that we've seen how many authors connect their ending to their beginning, think about your own story.
- How has your character changed at the end of your story? How was your character in the beginning?
- What can you add to your ending, and/or your beginning, to make them connected?
- What will be different? How does this difference highlight your character's transformation?

Collaborative Example:
- "Let's say in my story, my main character starts out shy. In the first scene she is walking to school. The crossing guard says 'Good Morning' to her, but she keeps walking with her head down. As the story goes on, my character develops more confidence as she confronts her obstacles. I want to show at the end of the story that my character has more confidence. How can I do that by connecting my beginning and ending?"
- Students can brainstorm ideas with the person next to them. Then share. One possibility is to have the student walking to school in the final scene, similar to the first scene. She sees the crossing guard, but this time she says "Hello." This way my ending mirrors my beginning, but with one big difference: my character has more confidence. Students may come up with other, better ideas, but this is something to use if needed.
- Write the last few sentences of the story using students' suggestions.
- Note if your beginning doesn't have some detail or imagery to connect to,

you can go back and ADD such a detail to your beginning, and then write a connected ending.

Independent Work: Use a graphic organizer to plan your own story. It's fine to invent places to show the character's change. (7)

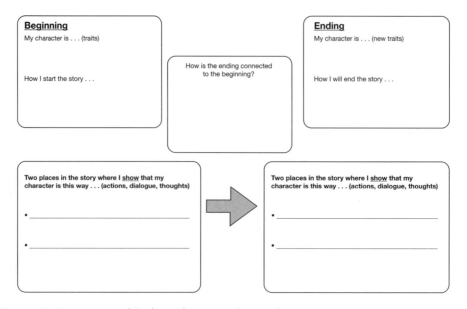

Figure 6.2: Beginning and Ending Character Change Planning Page

Share: Students share their plans for revision with a partner. Then, a few students share with the whole class.

Writing Time: Students work on writing their ending and/or revising other parts of the story to reflect their character's growth and to craft an ending that mirrors the beginning while also showing change. I ask students to highlight the parts of the beginning and the ending that are connected.

PROGRESSION OF SKILLS IN FICTION WRITING

There is no correct order for these skills and I do not teach all of these in a year. An ideal scenario is a two-year trajectory, in which the basic skills are taught in the first year, and students have the opportunity learn more complex skills and revisit elements from the previous year more in the second year.

- What is a scene?
- Narration: How does narration sound? (Check out sentences that open scenes. How is narration of a story different than the voice we use when writing an essay?)
- Paragraphing in fiction
- Titling stories and chapters; using scene breaks
- How to move forward in time (or backward)
- Punctuating and formatting dialogue
- When to use "said" or another word
- Descriptive writing—setting
- Using figurative language in narrative (best if students already have knowledge of figurative language in poetry)
- Interior monologue
- Writing action
- Describing characters
- Character development
- Sentence combining with commas and semicolons
- Plot: borrowing from classic plots to create an outline
- Pacing: moving between the four main storytelling voices—narration (includes action and backstory), dialogue, interior monologue, and description
- Varying sentence length and structure for better rhythm
- Characterization through physical description, actions, words, and interior monologue
- Beginnings and endings—connecting the two to show change

→ **Exercise:** Think about your teaching context. What possibilities are there for working with colleagues to spread the skills of fiction writing across two or three years? Which skills would you like to teach in the first year?

These technical skills are listed loosely in an order that prioritizes those that are most pressing for students to be able to get started writing. As students get their bearings, we can introduce other elements of craft.

7

Organizing and Assessing Imaginative Writing Instruction in a Standards-Based ELA Classroom

You might be thinking, *Yes, I would love to increase the creative writing my students do, but the idea of fitting it into my curriculum hurts my brain!* A mix of factors probably causes you to hesitate around major changes: an annual curriculum map you've already created, successful units you've worked on and carefully revised to meet certain necessary criteria, external pressures in general, as well a level of comfort with your pacing and materials that would be costly to disrupt. By costly, I mean the time, organization, and possibly politics (if you need approval or buy-in from others) needed to make changes. If so, I have reassuring news for you. I don't think you have to restructure everything (unless you want to) to increase creative writing in your classroom enough to see some real benefits. I, too, have a robust curriculum map with literature and writing units aligned to state standards. Most years, none of my units are devoted specifically to fiction writing—and that's actually how I like it.

In this chapter, we'll look at:

- How to carve out time for creative writing within a literature program
- The benefits of developing a long view of learning and differentiating along the way
- Encouraging the long view in students through celebration and self-assessment
- Managing grading, feedback, and goal setting
- Students building identities as writers across the year—and beyond
- Our students and the future of storytelling

MAKING TIME AMONG MANY COMPETING DEMANDS

People who've known me a long time are probably not surprised to find out I'm writing a book advocating for creative writing in K–12 education. Since I was little, I've loved writing poetry and stories. I took every creative writing course in college I could and even briefly considered trying to be a professional poet. Creative writing was also one of my ways into teaching. The first "class" I ever taught was a poetry workshop at the Fox Point Boys and Girls Club in Providence as part of an independent study at Brown. And come to think of it, some of the teaching work that I've received the best feedback on from students, colleagues, and supervisors have been around creative writing.

And yet, somehow, the idea for this book snuck up on me. I never imagined writing a book on this topic. I didn't even see myself as a teacher particularly focused on creative writing until very recently. Instead, I've put most of my attention on learning how to foster authentic reading through literature study, using the whole novels method, which I first learned about in my graduate program at Bank Street College from Madeleine Ray. I spent so much time and energy building the whole novels method and advocating for it, when it was neither popular to teach whole class novels nor to give students significant time to read independently in class. The quest to make a student-centered approach to whole class novels successful and practical led me to write my first book *Whole Novels For the Whole Class: A Student-Centered Approach* (Sacks, 2014).

That didn't mean I wasn't doing plenty of writing with my students, but the dialogue I was having with educators around the world, which constantly pushed my thinking and awareness, was mostly around novel studies. I wasn't talking as much about writing—and to some degree, I wasn't thinking as much about it either. A question that teachers sometimes asked me was, *With all this reading work, do you do enough writing with students?*

That question prompted me to reflect more on my writing instruction and become more purposeful in my choices. One of the perpetual challenges is this: I want to be in a novel study or independent reading cycle all of the time. Many of my students come to me without an active habit of reading. Once I've helped them build it, I never want them to drop it. I've learned that if I want students to practice reading at home, I have to be willing to invest precious time and demonstrate its value in class. For many years, however, I've taught in middle schools that don't have daily double English Language Arts periods or specially designated independent reading periods as some schools do. So, I've had to solve the puzzle of maintaining daily reading time, while carving out space for in-depth writing as well. Some years, I've had just forty-five minutes a day, and other years I've been fortunate to have a double period or two added to the week.

Over time, by necessity, I've found the solution I can live with. It's nothing earth-shattering, but it works on a practical level, and it helps foster meaningful connections between reading and writing:

> **In conjunction with each novel we read together, students work on one creative writing piece and one essay.**

In a novel study, we begin creative writing during the reading process, and continue alongside the discussion sessions; we work on essays after students have finished reading *and* discussing the book. We generally do about five whole novel studies in a year, with independent reading cycles in between each one. Students are always reading something, and I devote a *minimum* of ten minutes per day to reading time. I also have two additional units focused on writing—one on analytical paragraph and essay writing and one on journalistic writing. These include reading shorter texts, but the focus is on writing techniques. I integrate poetry in moments throughout the year and lead one intensive poetry unit that includes both reading and writing.

On that note, the benefits of creative writing I've argued for in this book apply to all imaginative writing forms: fiction, poetry, playwriting, etc. My pedagogical focus for this book is fiction writing however as a component of novel study. Novels are a cornerstone of most English Language Arts programs and occupy a significant amount of curricular real estate.

There are several great benefits of including fiction writing in each novel study, rather than trying to tackle it in a standalone unit (or not at all). I've discussed each of these in earlier chapters:

- **Repetition:** Students benefit from repeated practice writing fictional narratives across the year, developing their craft and an awareness of it.
- **Rich Context:** Each novel provides students a unique chance to learn from its author, borrowing elements of his or her storytelling style, and applying them in their own writing pieces.
- **Connection:** I design assignments that connect a literary focus of our reading—a story element or specific plot pattern—with students' creative writing during that novel study. These connections help frame the assignments; and students gain a stronger understanding of the function of an element in literature through firsthand experience as both reader and writer.
- **Joy:** The creative writing work brings a spark to the classroom and to partic-

ular students, truly brightening up the school day. Students come to associate that joy with the process of reading and studying literature.

DOORWAYS INTO CREATIVE WRITING THROUGH NOVEL STUDIES

In whole novel studies, there are several entry points I use for engaging students in writing imaginative pieces. These doorways can be created within any literature unit, but I will illustrate them here within the whole novels method to share an accurate picture of what's worked for me. Here is the layout of a whole novel study. Then I will go into detail on the creative writing opportunities.

Prologue (0–4 days)

The prologue is designed to engage students in an *experience* that will be helpful during the novel study. I don't always include a prologue, but when I do, here are the kinds of things we do:

- Watch a film or read a short text that will build background knowledge on a historical time period or foreign setting featured in the novel.
- A written, theatrical, or visual exercise to build interest and experience with a theme or other literary element that will be prominent in the novel.
- Read a shorter text/picture book/folk tale that has structural or other key similarities to the novel, in order to build prior experience with the form that students can then bring to their reading of the longer form.

Reading Period (2–3 weeks)

Students read the novel according to a schedule I provide. They are generally required to annotate the text with their responses using sticky notes. They have time to read during class and must finish whatever is left to meet the daily minimum for homework. During class, students might read independently, with audio, with a partner, in a small group, and/or with teacher support. Occasionally, we read sections aloud together as a whole class.

In this method, we don't hold formal discussions until students have read the "whole novel." My goal during the reading period is to help students access the text, and experience it with some independence and well as in community with classmates. Here are some of the activities other than reading we do during this time.

- Group mini-projects, visualizing and analyzing a literary element in the text such as character mapping
- Scene dramatizations
- Imaginative writing within the world of the text, such as writing letters to characters or a poem or diary entry from the point of view of a character
- Creative writing piece mimicking style or structure of the novel, using original content and characters

Discussion Sessions/Creative Writing (6 days)

When the due date for completing the book arrives, we begin student-centered discussions of the whole novel. I divide the class into half groups for the discussions. While I meet with one group, the members of the other group work independently on their creative writing pieces. (Sometimes I have a co-teacher who can support students as they write.) Each group meets three times for whole novel discussion sessions.

Sometimes, the creative assignment builds on writing we began during the reading period. It is almost always based on a concept we've been observing in the novel. I spend at least a day prior to discussions introducing the assignment, helping students generate ideas, and get started writing. That way, they are better able to be productive without my help during the discussion periods. Here are a few of the assignments that happen at this entry point.

- Scene writing within the world of the novel: killing off a character from the novel, adding a character, rewriting a scene from a different point of view, to name a few
- Writing original short stories, built around a literary element we observed in the novel—stories developed around an original conflict, using an outline that mirrors the process we used to analyze conflicts in the novel
- Writing original stories using a plot pattern we observed in the book— a "journey story" for example, or a collection of vignettes on a common theme

Students work on these writing pieces during class while they are not in the discussion group and continue at home as needed. We may add a period of two of whole class writing after or in between discussion sessions.

Collecting Craft Elements (1 day)

After we have discussed the book, I like to ask students to record in a special section of their notebooks the writer's craft elements that are most notable and memorable about this author. (Some students have read additional books by the same author, which I try to make available for students who read ahead of schedule.) "What does this author do really well? What might we want to remember and try in our own writing?" Students brainstorm about this independently, and then we share to create a longer collaborative list that everyone copies down. On this day I like to show a video of an interview with the author talking about the book and/or their writing process. We discuss and add anything new to the list based on the interview.

Essay Writing (2–3 days)

Based on the content of the student-driven discussions, I craft essay questions that allow students to write formal arguments around ideas they've explored in discussions. I give students a period to select a question—or propose their own—and plan. Then they have about one period to write. We usually do not go through revision cycles with these pieces; instead, we review a few example essays from classmates, and then students reflect on the successes and weaknesses in their own work, talking through this with a partner. I ask students to set goals for the next literary essay they write.

Celebration/Share (2–3 days)

We wrap up the unit with students sharing and celebrating their creative writing. I have a few formats for this, but the most popular one is for students to read their pieces aloud. For longer pieces, students select an excerpt. I often incorporate a note-taking process for listeners which differs based on the details of the assignment. In Chapter 2, I described one example of this.

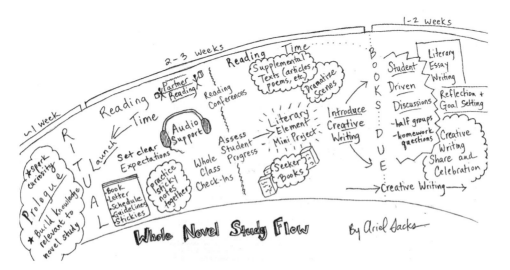

Figure 7.1: Whole Novel Study Diagram

There are many ways to adapt this basic outline to include more time for writing and instruction around writing. If you have double English periods, you can lengthen the writing time for both the essays and creative pieces, offering more instruction and support.

One major adaptation I make is in our final novel study. We write much longer stories, so students need more time and support. We discuss the novel as a whole class (instead of in half-groups), and then I introduce the story-writing project. We stretch the writing over two or three weeks, and I'm able to incorporate more instruction, conferencing, and multiple drafts into the time. I substitute the literary essay for an end-of-year reflection on their reading and writing.

Another variation is to make the prologue into a mini-study of its own. In one unit, we spend about two weeks reading, dramatizing, and analyzing different versions of Cinderella-type folk tales from around the world using the Poly-plots method described in Chapter 5. We then determine the characteristics of this story type. We begin reading a novel that loosely falls into this category (I've used *The Skin I'm In* by Sharon Flake in seventh grade and *Speak* by Laurie Halse Anderson in ninth), and students draft their longer stories alongside the reading.

To be clear, we do at least one creative piece per novel study. There are several possible entry points—creative writing could be a part of the prologue, could begin during the reading period, and always happens toward the end of the novel study, as we move into discussions. Here are a few examples to show options. We do not do all of these in one study. (Most of these have been detailed in the earlier chapters.)

Entry Points Through Prologue

- Before we begin *Animal Farm*, in which power is a major theme, I have students work in small groups to create silent dramatizations of a situation that involves power. They present the scenes, and we discuss briefly what we notice about how power was depicted. Then, students have the choice to either journal about one or more of the scenes, or write a poem connecting to the theme of power and/or something they saw in the dramatizations. This process can help students generate ideas for stories later, around a theme of power.
- Before we begin reading *The House On Mango Street*, in which setting will be a major focus, I read aloud the first few pages of Ray Bradbury's *The Martian Chronicles*, which is a vivid description of the book's imaginative setting on Mars. Students highlight lines that describe the setting. Then they pick a real or imaginary setting to describe as vividly as they can in writing. They write in class and we end the day with a share. Some students build on these pieces later when they write original stories.

Entry Points During Reading Period

- While we are reading *Animal Farm*, students write a poem from the point of view of a character. These are just wonderful fun.
- While we are reading *The House On Mango Street*, students pick a vignette from the novel to mimic using content from their lives. I model this first. For example, "My Name," focusing on their name or "The House on _____ Street," about their own home. Students usually use these in their final writing pieces, which are a collection of vignettes around a common theme.

Final Creative Writing Pieces

- For a shorter project, students can write a single scene in which they've changed an element: They may add a character, kill off a character, change the point of view, change the setting, or write the beginning of a sequel to the novel.
- While reading *The Absolutely True Diary of a Part-Time Indian*, we use a particular process for analyzing conflicts in the book. Then, students apply this process to imagine a conflict and plan a story around it. They write while they are not in discussion groups.
- While reading various novels in small groups that follow a journey structure, we study the hero's journey, using the novels, some excerpts from Joseph Campbell's theory of the hero's journey, as well as picture books. Toward the end of the reading, we create an outline format together and students use it to plan original journey stories.

DEVELOPING A LONG VIEW OF LEARNING AND DIFFERENTIATING ALONG THE WAY

A key way that I manage the overwhelming curriculum demands of ELA is to take a long view of my students' learning. This means internalizing that learning takes time, and learners have their own unique trajectories. Even if we've carefully fit every important skill and concept into a curriculum map, there is no assurance that students will learn these items on our timeline. Some skills are acquired gradually. Some of what we teach will not show up for certain students as significant until years later. Some times we see no evidence of learning at all with a particular student, despite our efforts—and then one day we witness a sudden breakthrough. The student seems to goes from zero to "aha" all at once.

We could conclude in such a moment that our previous efforts hadn't worked, and that whatever we did that day worked. And we might be right. We could also conclude that everything leading up to this moment played its part, and the student was finally ready to connect it all in the current context. We usually never know for sure, and that's one of the wonders of teaching. There are mysteries and occasional miracles. This doesn't negate the value of careful pedagogy; it means that our teaching lens should allow for these gray areas, rather than try to shut them out or pretend they aren't there. Understanding this can be liberating as well as productive.

Each learner is different, and it's frustrating for everyone when we expect students to progress in lock step. In a lock-step model, we almost always leave students behind when we move on; we hold other students back when we wait.

The concept of differentiation has encouraged teachers to adjust our teaching based on the variety of learners in the room. This is an important strategy, but it has pitfalls. It's common to end up with tracked groups within a class, each working at different levels or on different skills. While useful at times, these groups can also end up reinforcing existing differences among students rather than helping to balance them in an equitable way. We should adjust our lessons and activities to meet the needs of our diverse learners, but that doesn't mean we can always differentiate our way into a neat lock-step progression. Something more is needed in order to help each of our unique learners to thrive.

Taking a long view of my students' learning is a shift that's helped me become more effective and compassionate at managing the realities that (1) learning complex skills takes time, and (2) every learner does it differently. **I emphasize certain skills in each unit, but I see this as just one piece of what is happening for students in any given moment.** Students are practicing many skills when they write creatively, or read a novel, or write an essay, or have a discussion, and students will have multiple opportunities across the year to practice *all* of these skills.

It's relieving to know that we will cycle through the major endeavors of English Language Arts many times together and students will make progress at each turn. I have influence, but I know they won't all progress on the same skill, the same amount, or in the same order. I highlight certain pieces in each stage, while allowing for a variety of pathways. This longer view means that I'm less wedded to my short-term objectives and more trusting that students learn with time and practice. "Playing a long game" takes a lot of the judgment and anxiety out of the experience for students and me. Students are freer to take risks, which is essential to complex, creative, higher order tasks.

Supporting this long view, I envision ELA curriculum as having threads that run through it concurrently, as in a weaving. Not all threads are visible at once in a given moment, but they are all there, and each will come to the fore soon enough if we keep creating opportunities for students to take on the roles of each one. Fiction writing is one of those major threads, carrying with it a number of distinct skills; discussing literature and argument writing are two other major threads, among many. The major threads connect to and feed one another, a benefit of having them run concurrently in cycles, rather than separating them into standalone units of study.

This visualization of threads is, perhaps, a homespun version of standards-based assessment, in which students are assessed in their progress across the year on each standard, rather than in relation to the specific requirements of each assignment. Ideally, charting progress on standards actually replaces grades. In my case, my mental model is farther toward that ideal than my actual grading practices reflect. I'm moving in that direction, but I'm not there yet. My school and community are very accustomed to traditional number grades, so I work within that system. Nonetheless, my attitude has changed as I'm focused on my students' progress over time, rather than dwelling on their performance on a single assignment.

When we limit our focus to evaluating just a few current objectives, we may focus more on what a student didn't do well—this makes some sense, because we're looking for what we need to teach. However, we may miss that the same student showed great improvement in a skill we taught in the last imaginative writing assignment. This is often true for students who start out a little "behind" the curve or who take longer to learn a particular skill. Students, too, are accustomed to paying attention to what they did wrong in school. I see this mindset weighing heavily and preventing some students from wanting to try their best—what's the point if I never get it right anyway?

When we train our brains to look for areas of growth, whatever they may be, we focus on the positive in each student, and this can illuminate a pathway for more growth. Students often grow more by extending their learning in an area of strength than directly focusing on an area of weakness. This can depend on the student and how much they are already assimilating into their working memory to fulfill the assignment at their current level. If the student has limited bandwidth for taking on a new challenge, making a suggestion that helps a student build on their strength can be more productive. In this way, we're supporting individual students to learn at their zone of proximal development—where students are most able and motivated to learn.

In ELA, we have the benefit of practicing the same skills cyclically. For example, in the first fiction assignment of the year, J came up with a great idea for her scene and wrote it out in narrative form. I taught paragraphing, but she struggled to implement the technique. In the second assignment, J came up with another great idea and she is developing a creative voice. In this assignment, I taught students how to format dialogue. J is now struggling with this; however, she applied the paragraphing techniques we focused on in the first assignment successfully!

If my view is narrow and short-term, then J failed to learn paragraphing in Assignment #1 and failed to learn dialogue in Assignment #2. If I take a broader and longer view, I can see that she is making great progress, and that she may just need more time or repetition to acquire a new technical skill in writing.

In an individual conference with J, I could focus on her strong ideas and offer some questions to help her develop them further. I could also take the paragraphing that she has now begun to implement, and reinforce how dialogue uses paragraphing in a particular way. I wouldn't go into every formatting point for dialogue, but focus just on paragraphing in dialogue (one speaker per paragraph), because this builds on her recent success.

J's scenario is fairly common, and I see many variations of her trajectory in students over the year. With a clear idea of where we want students to go over the year, we can shift our lens to a strengths-based, differentiated approach. This can keep us feeling more positive and attuned to students' progress; and we can help students to do so as well.

ENCOURAGE THE LONG VIEW IN STUDENTS THROUGH SELF-ASSESSMENT, FEEDBACK, AND GOAL SETTING

When we guide students to develop a long view of their learning, they can become partners with us in seeing their own pathways forward. In relation to creative writing, I take a mostly narrative approach, encouraging students to build awareness of their progress—both strengths and areas for growth—set goals for future work, and articulate those through discussion and writing. Here are a few ways I help students see their progression across the year.

Community Feedback

Through these community practices, students learn to notice the craft techniques of writers they read—and to take that a step further, to notice how one writer (whether professional or student) might shine in certain techniques more than others. This helps them apply the same critical lens and vocabulary to their own writing.

- After we finish reading and discussing a novel together, we practice identifying strengths of the author's writing—sticky note annotations and other activities during the reading support this. Students keep a list of craft strengths for each book in a designated section of their ELA notebook.

- When a student reads their own creative piece aloud in a share session, the other students record the elements and/or lines that stand out to them in their classmates' pieces in their notebooks, and we briefly discuss after each reading. Students have specific instructions for their notes during these readings; I adapt the instructions based on the objectives of the assignment. (See Chapters 2 and 5 for more on this.)

- In an alternative format for sharing, students leave their writing pieces on their desks and circulate around the room to read classmates' work. They comment on each piece they read with sticky notes or in a "guest book" we can set up beside each writing piece. We identify strengths of the work— specific comments on what's working well; *sometimes* we identify questions or areas for development. It's important to have practiced this kind of commenting in the share space in a previous assignment, then briefly practice the kind of feedback we want to see in this activity—before turning students "loose" in the gallery walk. I participate in the gallery walk as a reader, but I also keep an eye on the comments students are leaving and give reminders if needed. This can also be done with names removed from the stories. Students receive their peer feedback at the end of the activity.

Written Self-Reflections

The chance to reflect on their writing at the end of the unit guides students to apply the discerning lens they're developing to their own work. This is often in the format of a journal entry in their ELA notebook. In it, I ask questions about the choices they made and their process. Here are some of the prompts I typically use.

1. What choices did you make to create this piece? Why did you make these choices?
2. What worked well in this piece?
3. What still needs work? What might you add or change if you had more time?
4. What was most interesting about this assignment?
5. What was most challenging?

Those questions condition students to be descriptive as well as evaluative. Depending on time, I augment this process by having students discuss it with a writing partner, or shorten it to just two or three questions.

Self-reflections can be combined with one or both of the next two items: individual feedback sheets and goal setting.

Individual Feedback Sheets (Rubrics)

For each major fiction writing assignment, I create a feedback sheet. The sheet can be used as a grading rubric, a tool for self-evaluation, or both. On it, I write a list of the specs of the assignment, the skills we've focused on, and a point value for each, usually totaling ten points. It's more of a checklist than a full rubric. **With each new assignment, one or two new skills are added, but the old ones remain, so long as they are relevant to the assignment.** This is how I can visually show students that we're building skills of fiction writing with each piece we work on.

For example, our first novel study in eighth grade is often *The House On Mango Street*. Students write a collection of vignettes. The feedback sheet looks like this.

VARIATIONS ON A THEME VIGNETTES PROJECT

Feedback Sheet

Name_____

3 vignettes (each 1 full-page handwritten, shorter if typed) _____ / 3

Creative, fitting title for project and for each vignette_____ /2

Vivid, descriptive language throughout _____ /2

Figurative language in at least 1 vignette _____ /1

Vignettes connected thematically to one another _____/1

Vignettes are divided into paragraphs _____/1

Total _____ /10

Warm feedback:

Cool feedback:

The next novel study has often been *The Absolutely True Diary of a Part-Time Indian*. Students write stories around a conflict they create. The feedback sheet looks like this:

CONFLICT STORY PROJECT

Feedback Sheet

Name_____

3 pages typed, double-spaced; includes title _____ / 3

Clear central conflict _____/1

Rich dialogue develops conflict and characters _____/2

Clear change as a result of conflict developing _____/1

Vivid, descriptive language _____ /1

Appropriate paragraphing _____ /1

Dialogue is punctuated correctly _____ /1

Total _____ /10

Warm feedback:

Cool feedback:

The specifics of the assignment have changed, so a number of items reflect that. The skill of "vivid, descriptive language," which we emphasized in the vignettes project remains on the feedback sheet for the conflict story. We didn't do any additional lessons around it, but students have the opportunity to practice that aspect of their craft again in this new context. In the first project, we worked on paragraphing, and in the conflict story, we added dialogue. Some students included dialogue in the first assignment, but we hadn't worked on that yet, so I didn't include it in the grading. Moving forward, these skills remain relevant. Students get the chance to practice them again, and they are included in the feedback sheets in all subsequent fiction-writing pieces.

Managing Grading

I use feedback sheets in most of the major creative writing pieces, but not all. The time it takes can be overwhelming. Sometimes, too, I think, it's not productive to scrutinize student work too much. Smaller assignments are often ungraded, or just recorded for completion. Occasionally, I decide to drop the itemized feedback sheet for a larger assignment simply to maintain a kind of balance between evaluating the work and describing the work and appreciating the progress. In those cases, we just do a share, followed by reflections and goal setting. That can be just as powerful as a detailed checklist or rubric. It's also worth noting that I've heard teachers express hesitation around assigning longer writing pieces because of the amount of time these take to respond to and grade. I understand this sentiment, but I think the solution is to grade less—as long as the work load is reasonable for students—rather than avoiding writing for this reason.

Furthermore, it's good for students if some writing is not evaluated, so that students don't come to associate their feelings around evaluation too closely with the feeling of writing. Most of the writing adults do is not formally evaluated, though it has an impact. We need students to learn to assess the impact of their writing without it necessarily being measured by the teacher.

Goal Setting

Goal setting is invaluable in helping students see the threads of connection between the various writing pieces they do and orient themselves toward growth. It's simple, and it doesn't take a lot of time.

- I ask students to write down two goals for their next fiction-writing piece along with their reflections or their feedback sheets (if applicable).
- Students add a note about how they could work toward each goal.

The first time we do this, I frame it with a talking point about specificity. "We don't want a vague goal like 'Do better,' or 'Punctuation.' Why?" I ask. Students can usually say why that wouldn't help them very much. It's hard to know what to do differently with so little detail on the issue. Do better on what? How? Which punctuation skill do you want to work on?" I ask students to offer an example of a specific goal or two. Then, we quickly brainstorm ideas as to how someone could work toward that goal. I walk around and check in with students as they do this. I allow them to share goals with classmates, and then volunteers share out to the whole class. After going through this process once, goal setting goes much more quickly, and remains a powerful practice. (We use a similar process with essay writing, by the way.)

When the next writing piece comes up, students review their previous goals. Some students take the goals to heart more than others. I encourage them, but I'm not going to have a fit if a student doesn't pick up exactly on both of these goals. I provide tools and support, but I'm not a micromanager.

Like anything else, goal setting is a skill. I introduce it, knowing that it will take time for some students to come around to utilizing it. If a student makes progress in a different area, I'm not going to respond with an admonishment about not progressing on a specific goal. The student will often bring it up in the reflection, which is much better than me playing enforcer.

Writing Portfolios

Students' writing pieces, reflections, feedback sheets and goals all go into their writing portfolios. At the end of the year, based on a model I learned from Penny Kittle in *Write Beside Them* (2008), students reflect on their year of writing and then present about it to students and teachers in our school community. One component of the portfolio process is students going back through all of their work from the year with a master list of skills we worked on—across genres, not just fiction writing. They find a strong example of each one and label it. This helps them, again, see the same skills and techniques in various contexts, see their progress, and feel proud of their body of work.

By encouraging students to develop a long view of their learning, they are developing key social–emotional learning capacities from the CASEL framework: "self-awareness," specifically "having a growth mindset" and "self-management," including "exhibiting self-discipline and self-motivation and setting personal and collective goals."

A Summary of Organizational Tips

Creative writing can be a supportive and enriching thread of a literature curriculum. The following tips can help integrate it into existing literature units for a revolutionary effect, without the need for major curriculum overhaul.

- Plan to include fiction writing as a regular part of a literature unit, especially novel studies. (Check out *Whole Novels For the Whole Class* for more on how to shift to the whole novels approach.)
- For each novel, select a literary element that is particularly strong for students to pay attention to as they read. Craft a creative assignment structured around this element. (See Chapter 5 for more detail.)
- Don't try to teach everything. Pick one or two techniques to teach for each

project. I like to focus on one craft element, such as interior monologue, and one mechanical/punctuation item, such as paragraphing.

- Be okay with students writing imperfect pieces. It's all practice. They will get to try it again. And the experience is what they learn from.
- Create space for students to read or hear each other's work and give and receive feedback, especially positive recognition, from peers. Students learn just as much from feedback that describes what they've done and how it affects readers, as they do from constructive or evaluative feedback.
- Develop a routine of students reflecting on their own work and setting goals.
- As you plan future literature units, consider the progression of narrative and punctuation skills you will teach in each one. Visual references in the room or in students' notebooks can help them keep track of these as they build across the year.
- Look for positive growth in students' creative work, whether the growth aligns with the specific skills taught in this unit or not. Highlight the growth to yourself and to the student whenever possible.
- Encourage students to appreciate growth in their classmates as well.

→ **Exercise:** Think of a writing assignment, creative or other, for which you can imagine abandoning a formal grading rubric and replacing it with a share session, self-assessment, and/or goal-setting for next time. It helps if this is an assignment that students are fairly invested in, and which uses skills that will come up again in other writing. What are the pros? What concerns do you have?

DEVELOPING WRITING IDENTITIES

Part of the richness of taking a long view of learning is seeing students building their identities through their imaginative writing across a year. Young people can explore serious issues in their writing, and they can express their style and sense of humor. With an audience of their peers, this becomes a healthy outlet for experimentation and attention, and the repeated experience helps students grow.

By the middle of the year, I notice growth in students' writing across the various pieces we've written, not just the one they're presenting. By sharing what I notice, I can affirm my students' growing writing identities, and I teach students to look for this too.

- In a read-aloud session of student writing, I might share my observation that a student seems to be developing their style within a particular genre. "Shayla really seems to be getting into writing mystery." Or I can pose this as a question to the class: "What do you notice about the genre Shayla seems to like writing in? Think about what we heard from her last time and this time."

- I might note a student's growth in willingness to read their work to the class, rather than passing it to a friend to read. "David, it was so nice to hear you read your work today. Let's give props to David for taking that risk this time."

Students' social–emotional development is something we don't formally assess in most secondary schools, but we know how important it is. We can train ourselves to take note when we see it, and the more we encourage it, the more we tend to see it.

Elvin

One day, during independent reading, I recommended a student, Jonathon, a comic book I had a single copy of on my personal shelf. It was a rare, underground comic from the 1980s called *Agony*, by Mark Beyer. (It appears to be back in print now, with an introduction by Colson Whitehead!) It's the story of Amy and Jordan, two friends who go through the most ridiculous and outlandish struggles—getting chased by bears and beheaded by ghosts, among other things. They somehow manage to escape each gory episode and carry on their adventure. It's an absurd rollercoaster of, as my mentor Madeleine Ray puts it, the "Oh-What-Good-Luck, Oh-What-Bad-Luck" plot pattern in literature. I can objectively say, it is a weird read. I often pass it to students who love graphic novels and have already plowed through whatever we have in the classroom. Some love it, and some are nonplussed by it.

Jonathan read through *Agony* in one period and returned it to me at the end. "Thanks," he said simply.

"What did you think?" I asked.

"It was good," he said. He paused and then added, "It sounded like something Elvin would write."

This gave me a huge smile. What an apt connection he'd made! Elvin was a student in our class. He was quirky as could be. He was liked by his peers, and he seemed to live in his own head a lot of the time. His attempts to socialize were often along the lines of throwing small pieces of paper onto the desk next to his.

In the fall, he had been very eager to read a story he'd written to the class. It was from a similar exercise as the one I described in Chapter 2—he'd chosen to "kill off a character" from our recent whole class novel. It was an absurd piece that started by putting the characters we knew from the book on a train ride. The train went off the tracks and he described in gory detail the train tracks themselves rising up to rip several characters' necks to shreds. This got major laughs from the class. The tone of it was so silly, which contrasted with the realistic and serious book he'd borrowed the characters from.

The scene continued with survivors of the train wreck wandering off looking for help. At that point, a grotesque monster comes and there is a violent confrontation. The main character rips the monster's eyes out with a sword and they land on the ground oozing. I wouldn't be able to match Elvin's wry style if I tried, but somehow his writing elicited more giggles from the class.

As his reading continued, though, we sat through one creative death after another. After about the fourth one, the laughter petered out. We had gotten the point. Elvin kept reading, but we were clearly restless.

He learned from this experience. Elvin discovered that his humor was valuable. He had succeeded in holding our attention in an extremely competitive attention-driven economy, and he had gotten real laughs from his peers. He was on to something!

He also learned that his story was missing some elements. The lack of character development and the continuous violent action scenes without a break became tedious. I had a brief conversation with Elvin about this after the reading, both complimenting him and discussing the elements he could develop to keep readers engaged. In his next fiction piece, he kept exploring the gory humor he loved, but he paid more attention to his characters, developing them with dialogue and interior monologue. He was able to produce a more balanced, successful story within his preferred genre.

He also established his reputation as an absurdist humor writer, worthy of comparison to Mark Beyer! To me, the comment from his classmate was verification of the position Elvin had carved for himself in the social fabric of our middle school class. He was an outlier in many ways, but this acknowledgement of his style through the medium of writing was tremendously affirming, I thought. He'd achieved this all by himself, by being himself, taking the risk of sharing, and learning from feedback. This is an example of the intersection of academic and social learning through creative writing—and the development that happens when students have repeated opportunities to write creatively and share with their peers. We also see the four roles at work: Elvin and Jonathan are both readers; as members of a reading community, Jonathon heard multiple stories by Elvin; Elvin is a critic of the novel we read—it was way too realistic and serious for his taste, so he created a version he liked better; Jonathan is critic who connected Elvin's writing style to the style he noticed in Mark Bayer's *Agony*. Elvin taking on the fourth role, author of imaginative writing, is the needle that threaded these connections together.

Through repeated opportunities to write and share with an audience of peers, Elvin improved in his ability to meet Common Core Writing standards "8.3 a. Engage and orient the reader by establishing a context and point of view and introducing a narrator and/or characters; organize an event sequence that unfolds naturally and logically" and "8.3 b. Use narrative techniques, such as dialogue, pacing, description, and reflection, to develop experiences, events, and/or characters." Elvin's drive to grow was motivated by the experience of developing social awareness through sharing: "taking another person's perspective" as they listen to his story, and "recognizing situational demands and opportunities" of keeping an audience engaged and utilizing craft tools to do so (CASEL).

The same structure gave Jonathon a chance to "recognize strengths in others," another aspect of social awareness on the CASEL framework.

Many students develop their writing identities as Elvin did, by writing and sharing within the classroom community across a year. Creative writing allows students to transcend the tired social categories to which students are often confined: how much they achieve in school, how much they comply with behavior expectations, how they dress, who they sit with at lunch, what music they listen to, and what they do for fun, for example. These social categories are also negotiated through the lenses of race, ethnicity, religion, social and economic class, gender and sexual orientation, and ability. Creative writing can actually empower students to critically challenge these categories, in the same way that reading good literature does. It allows them to develop and share new parts of themselves through their unique writing styles. Once we observe this happening among our students, we can expect and encourage this kind of growth.

ENCOURAGING YOUNG WRITERS: OUR WORDS MATTER

Beyond the outcomes we look for and measure in the limited time we have with our students, our words can have a profound influence on their lives.

I remember such a moment in my own eighth–grade year. It was Mr. B.'s last day. He had been a student teacher in our English class for the last few months. Besides the much-discussed problem of his incredibly strong coffee breath, we liked him quite a lot. He brought a fresh enthusiasm to the classroom and he seemed to genuinely like us. He had said good-bye in class earlier that day, telling us it had been a plea-sure and honor to be our teacher, and he would miss us. We would miss him too.

In grade school—especially middle and high school—I didn't feel particularly seen or known by my teachers. I wasn't mistreated, but I wasn't understood either. In retrospect, this had a lot to do with the old school teaching style: teachers engaged mostly with "the whole class," but invited minimal participation from us. I rarely spoke up. I received grades on my work, but little to no feedback.

When Mr. B. expressed his affection for our class, my middle school self didn't know for sure if that included me, even though I had no reason to believe it didn't. But later that day, in the hallway, he said something that changed my life.

The young student teacher had his jacket and shoulder bag on and seemed to be on his way out. I was in the hallway using my locker. I gave a smile and a wave, and he stopped and said, "Just a minute, Ariel." I stood curiously. "Listen, I've been meaning to tell you—your writing is really strong. I don't know if you know that, but you could be a writer someday, if you want to. I just wanted you to hear that."

Mr. B's compliment may contradict the research on effective praise that focuses on specific behaviors not general evaluations; but his brief words meant the world to me. This was the only time I remember hearing anything encouraging about my writing (anything at all, really) until many years later, and I never forgot it.

Just one sentence from a teacher can make a huge difference in the life of a stu-dent. Clint Smith, journalist and author of #1 *New York Times* bestseller, *How the Word Is Passed: A Reckoning With the History of Slavery Across America*, posted on Twitter: " . . . one of the only reasons I'm a writer is because I had a teacher in third grade who looked at my poem about clouds & said 'you can be a writer when you grow up.' It stayed w/ me forever. Teachers, don't underestimate what your words can do for your students."

We are gatekeepers to so many possibilities for our students, and our impact is wider than we can see. This work of bringing students into the world of literary writing has a special impact. Think about it—professional writers are in the position to influence many more people than the average person does, because of the reach of the printed word. When we—sometimes with just one sentence—open the gates for a young writer, we touch many lives. Mr. B. probably doesn't know that I remember him or that his words meant as much as they did. If you're out there, Mr. B.—thank you! And to Clint Smith, there was a time when I felt I was crazy to be writing a book on this topic, and I questioned whether it would be worth it to finish. Seeing your post affirmed my purpose and conviction.

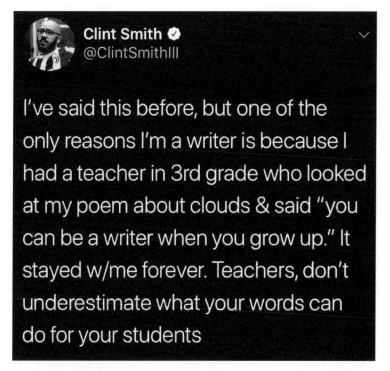

Figure 7.2: Tweet from author Clint Smith

Students Can Write in This World

Some of my eighth-graders are obsessed with books by bestselling author, Colleen Hoover. I haven't read her books, but I know they are heavy romance stories with some content that isn't exactly appropriate for middle school. We don't provide the books to classes, but if they bring them from home, we don't tell them they can't read them for independent reading. I've heard that her plots and characters are well-written, and many of her readers shout from the rooftops that hers are the first books they have voluntarily read and loved.

The other day, I heard an interview with Colleen Hoover on National Public Radio. Her success story is quite compelling, and I decided to share the interview with my students. I printed the transcript and we listened. Several things popped out at students. First of all, Hoover self-published her first books. Second, her popularity skyrocketed when teen "influencers" on TikTok started sharing their reactions to her books during the pandemic. Some of my students confirmed that they'd learned about her books from TikTok. She's now the top selling novelist, beating out the giants of the industry, Grisham, Patterson, and King—who are male. Third, in 2016, Hoover was "a regular person." She was a social worker who worked for Child Protective Services in her home state of Texas. She lived in a trailer with her husband and children. Somehow, in her spare time, she drafted her first novel.

One of my students exclaimed, "So, this could happen to any of us!" *Yes!* I thought. That's basically the point here. Of course, writing a novel that engages readers is far from easy, and it's not for everyone, but writing is a thing real people can do, and the industry is more accessible in many ways than ever before.

Nayar was my student in eighth grade in 2019–2020, the year that ended in COVID-19 lockdown. She is an extremely extroverted, creative individual, a proud hijab-wearing Muslim, a student leader since her middle school student council days, and she is also disabled. Due to brittle bone disease, she uses a wheelchair.

I've felt proud of her the whole time I've known her, how unafraid to express herself she is, and how she grabs onto life's opportunities. When I first assigned free writing to my class, she filled her entire notebook in a week with a handwritten first-person narrative that turned out to be imaginative fiction. It read like popular YA novels she liked, almost. "I'm going to finish it!" she promised. She didn't finish it, but each assignment we did in class she took on bigger challenges in her writing, always writing long pieces.

After the pandemic year, as a tenth-grader, she shared a document with me. It was over a hundred pages. It was a novel, a mystery to be more specific. But the point of view was a teen girl, Muslim, disabled; a little like Nayar, I suppose. It was good. I commented my excitement. She agreed to let me make copies of it for my current students to read. A group of students read it and were extremely impressed. As much as she's known around the school, students reading her book get a much more intimate view of the kind of teen that she is, and her day-to-day life with her disability and within her Bengali culture. And yet, these aspects are not the focus of her novella at all. It's a suspenseful mystery of a missing person, woven together with a love story.

Since then, Nayar has written another short novel and is working on a third. She entered a contest for short stories featuring Muslim characters on Wattpad and won. Wattpad is a space where anyone can post their writing for an online audience. Members can "follow" writers, read their work, and comment. Wattpad is home to whole worlds of fanfiction and worlds of discourse about fan fiction. The internet, with all its problems, is a place where literary discourse happens organically and with more equity than traditional spaces like universities. While lately some of my students tell me Wattpad has become "too toxic," it's a place where regular people can publish quickly and find an audience.

I have a sense that our relationship to storytelling is growing and changing, in a way that might be as significant as the invention of the printing press. I don't know where we're going exactly, but I know that the job market needs creative graduates, and I know that young people thrive emotionally, socially, and academically when they have opportunities to write fiction. I will continue to open doors to imaginative writing in my ELA classroom.

Gather the Village

Ultimately, by integrating the four roles in our classrooms—reader, member of a literary community, literary critic, and author of imaginative writing—we're bringing people together.

As part of a joint project for an independent study I was doing on poetry and a course on cross-cultural education in the same semester at Brown University, I had the opportunity to interview an older poet, Al Perreira, who had immigrated from Cape Verde as a young boy and was a respected elder in the Cape Verdean-American community of Providence, Rhode Island. One thing he told me in the interview has stuck in my mind ever since. He described the role of poetry in the Cape Verde of his youth, how central and revered the poet was to life there.

"Do you know what would happen when a poet gave a reading in Cape Verde?" he said. "Five hundred people would show up in his back yard!" The beautiful image this brought to my mind represents the particular time and place Al remembered, but it's also a picture of deeply human behavior.

Our classrooms and schools are villages. Our students can be poets and storytellers. With our help opening the doors, we can, in our villages, gather around one another and listen. I said before, art has saved my life many times, and I'm not alone in that. My mentor Madeleine believes that art can save our schools; and who doesn't believe that children can save our world if we give them the chance and the tools?

Imaginative writing is the art form at the center of the discipline of English Language Arts. It is our precious tool for empowerment, learning, and human connection. Our students' stories are needed in their worlds and ours. Let them write fiction.

References

Annie E. Casey Foundation. (2017). Race for results: 2017 policy report—Kids count. *International Education Studies 9*(4). Retrieved November 9, 2022 from http://www.aecf.org/m/resourcedoc/aecf-2017raceforresults-2017.pdf#page=26

Cedeno, L. F., Martinez-Arias, R., & Bueno, J. A. (2016, March 29). Implications of socioeconomic status on academic competence: A perspective for teachers. *International Education Studies 9* (4). Canadian Center of Science & Education. https://files.eric.ed.gov/fulltext/EJ1095797.pdf

Applebee, A. (1978). *The Child's Concept of Story: Ages Two to Seventeen*. University of Chicago Press.

BAMorg. (2015, February 17). Neil Gaiman's advice for aspiring writers [Video]. *En Garde!: Neil Gaiman and Daniel Handler*. BAM Howard Gilman Opera House: YouTube. Retrieved November 9, 2022 from https://www.youtube.com/watch?v=aFiXZCzzHF4

Bishop, R. S. (Summer 1990). "Mirrors, windows, and sliding glass doors" in *Perspectives: Choosing and Using Books for the Classroom 6* (3). The Ohio State University.

Booker, C. (2006). *Seven basic plots: Why we tell stories*. Continuum.

Brown, D. (2017, August 20). *How one man convinced 200 Ku Klux Klan members to give up their robes*. [Radio Broadcast Transcript]. NPR. https://www.npr.org/2017/08/20/544861933/how-one-man-convinced-200-ku-klux-klan-members-to-give-up-their-robes

Campbell, J. (1973). *The hero with a thousand faces*. Princeton University Press.

Chavez, F. R. (2021). *The anti-racist writing workshop: How to decolonize the creative classroom*. Haymarket Books.

Chavez, F. R. (n. d.) *The antiracist writing workshop*. Retrieved November 9, 2022 from https://www.antiracistworkshop.com

The Collaborative for Academic, Social, and Emotional Learning (CASEL). (2020). *What is the CASEL Framework?* Casel.org Retrieved November 13, 2022 from https://casel.org/fundamentals-of-sel/what-is-the-casel-framework/

Collier, A. (2019, February 27). Why telling our own story is so powerful for Black Americans. *Greater Good Magazine.* Retrieved from https://greatergood.berkeley.edu/article/item/why_telling_our_own_story_is_so_powerful_for_black_americans

Common Core State Standards Initiative. (2010, June 2). *Common core state standards for English Language Arts & literacy in history/ social studies, science, and technical subjects.* Retrieved Nov. 9, 2022 from http://www.corestandards.org/wp-content/uploads/ELA_Standards.pdf

Cooperative Children's Book Center. (2022). *CCBC diversity statistics.* University of Wisconsin, Madison. Retrieved on November 9, 2022 from https://ccbc.education.wisc.edu/literature-resources/ccbc-diversity-statistics/books-by-about-poc-fnn/

Damour, L. (2016, December 14). What do teenagers want? Potted plant parents. *The New York Times.* Retrieved from https://www.nytimes.com/2016/12/14/well/family/what-do-teenagers-want-potted-plant-parents.html

Diaz, J. (2014, April 30). MFA vs. POC. *The New Yorker.* Retrieved from https://www.newyorker.com/books/page-turner/mfa-vs-poc

Dweck, C. S. (2007). *Mindset: The new psychology of success.* Ballantine Books.

Elden, R. (2018, May 10). Year 6: Ana Menendez, The Oulipo, and the 7 Basic Plots [12 Years of Writers Institute in 12 Days-email newsletter]. Retrieved from https://roxannaelden.com/2015/09/do-you-need-an-original-plot-to-be-a-good-writer-the-seven-basic-plots-divided-into-seven-sections-each/

Gardner, J. (1991). *The art of fiction: Notes on craft for young writers.* Vintage.

Ewing, E. (2017, April 6). Why authoritarians attack the arts. *The New York Times.* https://www.nytimes.com/2017/04/06/opinion/why-authoritarians-attack-the-arts.html

Ginsburg, D. (2015). Rapid release of responsibility: You do, we do, I do. *Education Week.* Edweek.org.

Gottschall, J. (2013) *The storytelling animal: How stories make us human.* Mariner Books.

Hart, M. (2021, January 14). We need diverse books. *The Writer.* https://www.writermag.com/get-published/the-publishing-industry/diverse-books/

Hemingway, E. (n.d.) *Ernest Hemingway on writing* (L. W. Phillips, Ed.). Retrieved from https://medium.com/swlh/writing-a-novel-the-most-valuable-advice-from-ernest-hemingway-2e8258e3f67e

Kaimal, G., Ray, K., & Muniz, J. (2016, May 23). Reduction of cortisol levels and participants' responses following art making. *Art Therapy, 33*(2). Retrieved November 9, 2022 from https://www.tandfonline.com/doi/full/10.1080/07421656.2016.1166832?journalCode=uart20#.V2HutvkrKUk

Guilford, J. P. (2018, March 12). *New World Encyclopedia.* Retrieved 15:53, November 9, 2022 from https://www.newworldencyclopedia.org/p/index.php?title=J._P._Guilford&oldid=1009682.

Lopate, L. (2009, April 23). *The house on Mango Street* [Radio Broadcast]. WNYC. https://www.wnyc.org/story/58246-the-house-on-mango-street/

Luendendok, M. (2019, September 19). Idea generation: Divergent vs. convergent thinking. *Cleverism.* https://www.cleverism.com/idea-generation-divergent-vs-convergent-thinking/

King, S. (2010). *On Writing: A Memoir of the Craft.* New York, NY: Scribner.

Lawson, A. E., Abraham, M. R., & Renner, J. W. (1989) *A theory of instruction: Using the learning cycle to teach science concepts and thinking skills.* Manhattan: Kansas State University, National Association for Research in Science Teaching.

Lenz, R. (2016, February 17). *Staffed by former racists, an 'exit' program aimed at disillusioned white supremacist radicals in the US is picking up steam.* Southern Poverty Law Center. Retrieved from https://www.splcenter.org/fighting-hate/intelligence-report/2016/life-after-hate

Levy, A. (2018, July 2). Ottessa Moshfegh's otherworldly fiction. *The New Yorker.* Retrieved from https://www.newyorker.com/magazine/2018/07/09/ottessa-moshfeghs-otherworldly-fiction

Love, B. (2019). *We want to do more than survive: Abolitionist teaching and the pursuit of educational freedom.* Beacon Press.

Markman, A. (2009). Trauma and the benefits of writing about it. *Psychology Today.* Retrieved from https://www.psychologytoday.com/us/blog/ulterior-motives/200910/trauma-and-the-benefits-writing-about-it

Muhammad, G. (2020). *Cultivating genius: An equity framework for culturally and historically responsive literacy.* Scholastic Teaching Resources.

Myers, C. (2014, March 15). The apartheid of children's literature. *The New York Times.* Retrieved from https://www.nytimes.com/2014/03/16/opinion/sunday/the-apartheid-of-childrens-literature.html

Myers, W. D. (2014, March 15). Where are the children of color in children's books? *The New York Times.* Retrieved from https://www.nytimes.com/2014/03/16/opinion/sunday/where-are-the-people-of-color-in-childrens-books.html

The National Board for Professional Teaching Standards. (2014). *English Language Arts standards for teachers of students ages 11-18+* (3rd ed.). Retrieved from https://www.nbpts.org/wp-content/uploads/2017/07/EAYA-ELA.pdf

National Center for Education Statistics. (2022). Racial/ethnic enrollment in public schools. *Condition of Education.* U.S. Department of Education, Institute of Education Sciences. Retrieved November 9, 2022, from https://nces.ed.gov/programs/coe/indicator/cge

National Center for Education Statistics. (2022). Characteristics of public school teachers. *Condition of Education.* U.S. Department of Education, Institute of Education Sciences. Retrieved November 9, 2022, from https://nces.ed.gov/programs/coe/indicator/clr

New York City Charter Schools Center. (2019). *NYC charter school performance: Math and ELA proficiency rates* https://nyccharterschools.org/new-york-city-charter-school-center-test-score-analysis-2018-19/

Pink, D. (2006). *A whole new mind: Why right brainers will rule the world.* Riverhead Books.

Procaccia, R., Segre, G., Tamanza, G., & Manzoni, G. M. (2021). Benefits of expressive writing on healthcare workers' psychological adjustment during the COVID-19 pandemic. *Frontiers in Psychology 12,* 624176. https://doi.org/10.3389/fpsyg.2021.624176

Ransaw, T. & Green, R. L. (2016). *Black males, peer pressure, and high expectations.* Michigan State University. Retrieved from https://www.researchgate.net/publication/316559486_Black_males_Peer_pressure_and_High_expectations

Parker, K. N. (2022). *Literacy is liberation: Working toward justice through culturally relevant teaching.* ASCD.

Robertson, L. (2017, March 6). Mind the creativity gap. *The Creativity Post*. https://www.creativitypost.com/article/mind_the_creativity_gap3

Sacks, A. (2015, March 23). Decoding the common core: A teacher's perspective. *Education Week*. Retrieved from https://www.edweek.org/teaching-learning/opinion-decoding-the-common-core-a-teachers-perspective/2015/03

Sacks, A. (2014, March 17). Who gets to write fiction? A response to Walter Dean Myers and Chris Myers. *Center for Teaching Quality*. Retrieved from https://www.teachingquality.org/who-gets-write-fiction-response-walter-dean-myers-chris-myers/

Sacks, A. (2014). *Whole novels for the whole class: A student-centered approach*. Jossey Bass.

Sloan, G. (2003). *The child as critic: Teaching literature in the elementary school* (4th ed.). Teachers College Press.

Substance Abuse and Mental Health Services Administration. (2022, September 27). Understanding Child Trauma in *National Child Traumatic Stress Initiative*. Retrieved on November 9, 2022 from https://www.samhsa.gov/child-trauma/understanding-child-trauma

We Need Diverse Books. (2022) *About us*. Retrieved November 9, 2022 from https://diversebooks.org/about-wndb/

Winfrey, O. (2011, October 19). The powerful lessons Maya Angelou taught Oprah. *Oprah's Life Class*. OWN. Retrieved November 9, 2022 from https://www.oprah.com/oprahs-lifeclass/the-powerful-lesson-maya-angelou-taught-oprah-video

WPA Federal Writers Project. (2022). In *Encyclopedia Britannica*. Retrieved from https://www.britannica.com/topic/Works-Progress-Administration

Zhao, Y. (2018) *Reach for greatness*. Corwin.

Zhao, Y. (2017, September 1). The West and Asian education: A fatal attraction. *New Internationalist*. Retrieved from https://newint.org/features/2017/09/01/asian-education

Index

A

ABAR. *see under* antibias, antiracist (ABAR)

Abraham, M.R., 131

academic development
creative writing for, 26–59
imaginative writing for, 26–59

achievement gap
described, 93–94

"achievement gap mania," 94

Adequate Yearly Progress, 147–48

affirming results
journey to full inclusion of, 22–25, 24f, 25f

Agony, 215, 216

Alexie, S., 54–56

Angelou, M., 102

Animal Farm, 64, 73, 162, 204, 205

Animal Farm creative project
power story plan, 163

antibias, antiracist (ABAR) education books
for teachers and school leaders, 103–4

antibias, antiracist (ABAR) educators
development as, 99–104

antibias, antiracist (ABAR) practices, 100
in creative writing classrooms, 104–7
resources on, 102–3

antibias, antiracist (ABAR) teaching resources
for English and literacy educators, 104

Applebee, A., 34–35

Appleman, D., 106

archetype(s)
plot. *see* plot archetype(s)

art(s)
devaluing of, 10
importance of, 10–11
in literacy, 10–14
power dynamics and, 12–14
twenty-first century problems related to, 11–12

artistic production
in literacy, 10–14

"Ashputtle," 150–54
writing project about, 156–58

Assessing With Respect, 72

assignment(s)
experience-related, 129–65. *see also* experience(s); experiential learning; writing assignment(s)

assumption(s)
problems related to, 76

attention
imaginative writing and capturing, 3–4

audience awareness
    through writing mechanics, 181–85
author(s)
    role in writing fictional scene, 41–42
author–audience interaction
    writing fictional scene and, 40
*A Whole New Mind: Why Right Brain
    Thinking Will Rule the Future,* 11–12

B
Baldwin, J., 96
Bank Street College, 34, 61, 67, 69, 72,
    105, 146, 149, 155
beginning(s)
    connecting to endings, 192–96, 195*f*
"being wrong"
    as part of learning routine, 68
Bettelheim, B., 34
Beyer, M., 215–16
"big thinker" syndrome, 19
Bishop, E., 133
Bishop, R. S., 105
Black Girls Code, 99
Black Lives Matter movement, 74
BookCon fan convention (2014), 97
Booker, C., 147, 150
boundary(ies)
    create writing assignments with, 135–36
Bradbury, R., 52, 190, 204, 205
Brawer, B., 99
Bronx Masquerade, 143
Brown Girl Dreaming, 144
Brown, M., 74
Brown University, 146, 221
*Building a Community of Self-Motivated
    Learners,* 71

C
Calvino, I., 48
Campbell, J., 147, 205
CASEL Framework, 74, 81, 121, 128, 213,
    217

CCSS.ELA-LITERACY.CCRA.W3, 174
celebration
    in whole novel study, 203–4, 203*f*
Center for Teaching Quality, 67
    On the Shoulders Of Giants at, 95
challenge(s)
    facing, 72–77
Chavez, F. R., 38, 98, 101–2
children's literature
    imaginative writing in desegregating, 6–7
choice
    in classroom, 70
Christensen, L., 123
Cisneros, S., 51–54, 100–2, 120, 143–44,
    186
classroom(s)
    booklist for building safe, 71–72
    choice and decision-making in, 70
    community in, 69–70
    convergent thinking in, 44–46
    creative risk-taking in, 67–72. *see also
        under* creative risk-taking
    creative writing. *see* creative writing
        classrooms
    divergent thinking in, 44–46
    ELA. *see* English Language Arts (ELA)
        classroom
    inclusiveness in, 69–70
    voices we might not hear in, 113–15
Clayton, D., 97
Cohen, D., 68
Collier, A., 109
Columbia Teacher's College, 35
comma(s)
    use of, 183–84
Common Core ELA standards
    described, 19
    development matters and, 17–19
    on task, but off course, 19–20
    writing fictional scene connection to, 39
community(ies)
    in classroom, 69–70

imaginative writing as tool for, 90–128.
    see also under imaginative writing
literacy. *see* literacy community
community feedback
    developing long view through, 208–9
concept application, 132
conflict story project, 211
conflict story share, 56
conflict story writing, 55–56
connection
    reading and, 91–92
content
    focusing of, 136
convergent thinking
    balancing with divergent thinking, 44–46
    defined, 42
    imagination in, 45–46
    writing fictional scene and, 42–43
Cooperative Children's Book Center
    at University of Wisconsin School of Edu-
        cation, 96
Cornell University, 101
craft elements
    in whole novel study, 202–3, 203*f*
craft lesson(s)
    teaching, 186–96. *see also specific lesson,*
        e.g., narration
creative risk-taking
    build safe space for, 68–71
    creating conditions for, 67–72
    model, 68–69
    in social–emotional development, 67–72
creative stance
    risk and empowerment of, 65–67
creative writing. *see also* imaginative
        writing
    for academic development, 26–59
    boundaries in, 135–36
    compromising of, 14–16
    curricular framework supporting, 26–59
    curriculum model for tapping into power
        of, 28–34, 29*t*, 29*f*, 31*t*

The Hundred Dresses–related, 50–51
integrated into literature-based ELA class-
    room, 26–59
journey to full inclusion of, 22–25, 24*f*, 25*f*
literary critic in, 29*t*, 29*f*
within literature program, 198–221.
    see also under imaginative writing
    instruction
play opportunities of, 7–8
redefining intelligence through, 115–20
roles in, 28–34, 29*t*, 29*f*, 31*t*
in teaching literary elements, 26–59
through experiences, 129–65. *see also*
    under experiential learning; writing
    assignment(s)
through novel studies, 201–5, 203*f*
what to teach in, 166–97. *see also under*
    instruction
creative writing classrooms. *see also under*
    creative writing; imaginative writing
ABAR practices in, 104–7
elevating storytelling traditions in, 107–
    10, 108*t*
equity in, 104–7
vetting texts and curriculum materials in,
    106–7
creative writing exercise(s)
setting, 52
creative writing time, 50–51
creativity
    in healing trauma, 77–78
    as necessity, 95
critical reading
    as (missing) link between imaginative
        writing and, 26–28
    theories connecting imaginative writing
        with, 34–36
Cultivating Genius: An Equity Framework
    for Culturally and Historically Respon-
    sive Literacy, 101
curriculum materials
    vetting of, 106–7

D
Davis, D., 93
decision-making
    in classroom, 70
    practicing, 61
"Decoding the Common Core," 17
definition(s)
    teaching from, 149
dehumanization
    negative stereotypes and, 92–93
description
    teaching lesson on, 190–91
development
    academic. *see* academic development
    identity. *see* identity development
    of long view. *see* long view development
    social–emotional, 60–89. *see also* social–
        emotional development
Developmental Designs, 69, 71
Dewey, J., 34, 36
dialogue
    punctuating, 178–81
    teaching lesson on, 188–89
Diaz, J., 101
difference(s)
    empathy across, 5–6, 120–21
differentiation
    developing long view of, 205–14
Discipline Over Punishment, 72
discussion sessions
    in whole novel study, 202, 203*f*
Disrupt Texts, 6
#DisruptTexts, 106
Disrupt Texts website, 107
divergent thinking
    balancing with convergent thinking,
        44–46
    defined, 42
    imagination in, 45–46
    writing fictional scene and, 42–43
DIY Project Based Learning For ELA &
    History, 72

dramatic play
    in generating imaginative writing, 150–55
Dweck, C. S., 115

E
economic divides
    teaching imaginative writing across,
        121–25
Education Week, 171–72
educator(s)
    ABAR, 99–104. *see also* antibias, anti-
        racist (ABAR) educator(s)
ELA classroom. *see* English Language Arts
    (ELA) classroom
ELA 9 Writing Project 2: Ashputtle-type
    story, 156–58
Elden, R., 147–48
emotional development
    social, 60–89. *see also* social–emotional
        development
empathy
    across differences, 120–21
    imaginative writing in creating, 5–6
empowerment
    creative stance–related, 65–67
encouragement
    for young writers, 217–21, 219*f*
ending(s)
    connecting to beginnings, 192–96, 195*f*
    teaching lesson on, 192–96, 195*f*
English Language Arts (ELA) classroom
    ABAR teaching resources for, 104
    imaginative writing in, 1–59, 31*t*. *see*
        also under imaginative writing
equity
    in creative writing classrooms, 104–7
    imaginative writing as tool for, 90–128.
        see also under imaginative writing
essay writing
    in whole novel study, 203, 203*f*, 205
Estes, E., 48–51
Ewing, E., 12–13

exercise(s)
  writing, 137
experience(s)
  designing assignments that teach through,
    129–65. *see also* experiential learning;
    writing assignment(s)
  with literary elements, 5
experiential learning, 129–65
  cycle of, 130*f,* 131–32, 131*t*
  designing assignments that teach through,
    129–65. *see also under* writing
    assignment(s)
  free-writing in, 133–35, 134*f*
  literature, 131*t*
  writing assignments and, 132–37, 134*f*
experiential learning cycle, 130*f,* 131–32,
    131*t*
  literature-related, 131*t*

F
Farmer, N., 160
"Federal Project Number One," 14
feedback
  community, 208–9
  developing long view through, 208–14
feedback sheets
  developing long view through, 210–11
  individual, 210–11
fiction
  paragraphing in, 175–77
fictional/real world collision
  case example, 73–77
fictional scene
  writing of, 36–41. *see also* writing fic-
    tional scene
fiction writing
  in novel studies, 200–1
  progression of skills in, 196–97
  teaching skills in, 166–97. *see also under*
    instruction
Fitzgerald, F. S., 91
Flake, S. G., 159

Fleischman, P., 143
folk tale
  teaching of, 47–48
folk tale storytelling
  elevating traditions of, 107–10, 108*t*
  note-taking protocol, 108–9, 108*t*
Freeman-Weyr, G., 36–41
free-writing, 133–35, 134*f*
Frye, N., 34, 35
Fung, J. C., 68

G
Gaiman, N., 146
Gardner, H., 115–16
Gardner, J., 182
general lesson structure, 168–72
  narrative craft, 169–70
  planning/structure, 168–69
Ginsburg, D., 171–72
"Girls/Girls/Boys," 120–21
Girls Who Code, 99
goal setting
  developing long view through, 208–14
Gottschall, J., 108
grading
  managing, 211–12
Grimes, N., 143
Grimm Brothers, 150, 153
Guilford, J. P., 42

H
Hamilton, V., 109
Harding, D. W., 34
Harvard University
  writing "teaching cases" for schools of
    business and government at, 10–11
Hausman, G., 159
health
  mental. *see* mental health
Hemingway, E., 146
Hinds, U., 159
Hoover, C., 219–20

How the Word Is Passed: A Reckoning With the History of Slavery Across America, 218

I
"I Am From . . . " poem, 123–25
identity(ies)
    writing. *see* writing identities
identity development
    imaginative writing as form of, 7–8
"I do, we do, you do" lesson structure,
    171–72
imagination
    in balancing divergent and convergent
        thinking, 45–46
imaginative writing. *see also* creative writ-
        ing; creative writing classrooms
    ABAR educators teaching, 99–104
    for academic development, 26–59
    for all students, 93–95
    call to action, 9–10
    in capturing attention, 3–4
    case example, 116–20
    compromising of, 14–16
    conceptual understanding of author's role
        in, 41–42
    concerns related to, 85–86
    convergent thinking in, 42–43
    in creating empathy and interest across
        differences/disrupting segregation, 5–6
    in desegregating children's literature, 6–7
    developing literacy community in,
        110–15
    divergent thinking in, 42–43
    dramatic play in generating, 150–55
    elevating storytelling traditions in, 107–
        10, 108*t*
    empathy across differences, 120–21
    folk tale, 47–48
    in giving students first-hand experience
        with literary elements, 5
    humanizing quality of stories impact on,
        92–93
    instruction for, 198–221. *see also under*
        imaginative writing instruction; instruc-
        tion; novel studies
    integrated into literature-based ELA class-
        room, 26–59
    integrating into literature study, 30–34,
        31*t*
    journey to full inclusion of creative writ-
        ing and affirming results, 22–25, 24*f*,
        25*f*
    leading through difficult moments,
        125–28
    within literature program, 198–221.
        see also under imaginative writing
        instruction
    (missing) link between critical reading
        and, 26–28
    novel studies, 51–56
    opening doors to, 95–99
    oral storytelling, 47, 107–10, 108*t*
    permission to center artistic production in
        literacy, 10–14
    positioning in ELA curriculum, 31*t*
    processing trauma through, 78–89
    pro-tips for, 164–65
    in providing opportunities to improve
        mental health and process trauma, 8
    in providing outlet for learning through
        play, risk-taking, and identity develop-
        ment, 7–8
    read aloud, 48–51
    redefining intelligence through, 115–20
    release from compromise in, 20–22
    in resisting oppression and creating better
        world, 8–9
    responsibility related to, 99–104
    rigor associated with, 42–43
    share space in, 110–15
    in shifting power dynamics around defini-
        tions of intelligence, 4–5
    shift students need in, 20–22
    start with our own learning in, 100–2
    students' benefit from, 3–9

takeaways for equity in, 104–7
teaching across economic divides,
   121–25
teaching across racial divides in, 121–25
theories connecting critical reading with,
   34–36
through experiences, 129–65. *see also*
   under experiential learning; writing
   assignment(s)
as tool for equity and community,
   90–128
unleashing, 1–25
what to teach in, 166–97. *see also under*
   instruction
writing fictional scene, 36–41. *see also*
   under writing fictional scene
imaginative writing instruction, 198–221
   developing long view of learning/differen-
      tiating, 205–14
   developing writing identities, 214–17
   encouragement in, 217–21, 219*f*
   feedback in, 208–14
   goal setting in, 208–14
   introduction, 198–201
   in novel studies, 198–221
   organizing/assessing, 198–221
   self-assessment in, 208–14
   in standards-based ELA classroom,
      198–221. *see also under* novel
      studies
imaginative writing prompts
   students cocreating, 49
improvisation
   revision through, 151–53
inclusiveness
   in classroom, 69–70
individual feedback sheets
   developing long view through, 210–11
Innovation Advisor, 94
instruction, 166–97
   categories for, 168–72
   collecting writer's craft techniques,
      185–86

description, 190–91
dialogue, 188–89
different than "I do, we do, you do,"
   171–72
endings, 192–96, 195*f*
general lesson structure, 168–72
how students develop style, 185–86
imaginative writing, 198–221. *see also*
   under imaginative writing instruction;
   novel studies
interior monologue, 189–90
mechanics in, 170–71
narration, 187–88
narrative craft in, 169–70
organizational tools in, 172–81,
   173*f*. *see also specific types, e.g.,*
   paragraphing
pacing, 191–92
paragraphing, 172–77, 173*f*. *see also*
   paragraphing
planning/structure, 168–69
punctuating dialogue, 178–81
sparing use of, 167–68
teaching craft lessons, 186–96. *see also*
   specific lesson, e.g., narration
what to teach directly, 166–97
worksheets in, 172
writing. *see* writing instruction
writing mechanics, 181–85. *see also* writing mechanics
intelligence(s)
   case example, 116–20
   imaginative writing in defining, 4–5
   musical, 116
   redefining through creative work,
      115–20
   theory of multiple, 115–16
interest
   imaginative writing in creating, 5–6
interior monologue
   teaching lesson on, 189–90
Iowa Writers Workshop, 100–2
Iser, W., 34

J
journey story sequence, 160–62
journey story writing project guidelines, 161–62
joyful listening
  in writing fictional scene, 38

K
Kaimal, G., 8
King, A., 93
King, S., 174
Kittle, P., 213

L
Landres, M., 98
Lawson, A.E., 131, 132
learning
  developing long view of, 205–14
  experiential. *see* experiential learning
  identity development in, 7–8
  imaginative writing as outlet for, 7–8
  play in, 7–8
  risk-taking in, 7–8
"Learning Cycle," 131
Life After Hate, 93
listening
  in writing fictional scene, 38
literacy
  arts in, 10–14. *see also under* art(s)
  permission to center artistic production in, 10–14
literacy community
  imaginative writing in developing, 110–15
literacy educators
  ABAR teaching resources for, 104
Literacy is Liberation: Working Toward Justice Through Culturally Relevant Teaching, 70
literary critic
  in creative writing, 29t, 29f
literary elements

high leverage teaching technique for first-hand experience with, 36–41
imaginative writing in giving first-hand experience with, 5
writing assignments focusing on one, 141–46
literature
  children's. *see* children's literature
Literature and the New Culture Wars, 106
literature-based English Language Arts (ELA) classroom
  imaginative writing in, 26–59
Literature is Liberation, 72
literature learning cycle
  integrated roles in, 131t
literature study
  integrating imaginative writing into, 30–34, 31t
long view development
  community feedback in, 208–9
  differentiation-related, 205–14
  feedback sheets in, 210–11
  goal setting in, 208–14
  learning-related, 205–14
Love, B., 9, 100

M
Martian Chronicles, 52, 190, 204
McBeath, D., 69
mechanical skills
  in general lesson structure, 170–71
mechanics
  teaching, 166–97
Meet Me in the Middle, 72
member of reading community
  in creative writing, 29t, 29f
mental health
  imaginative writing in improving, 8
"MFA vs. POC," 101, 102
"Miracle," 124–25
"Mirrors, Windows, and Sliding Glass Doors," 105

monologue
    interior, 189–90
Moshfegh, O., 116
Muhammad, G., 101, 105, 106
multiple intelligences
    theory of, 115–16
musical intelligence, 116
Myers, C., 95–97
Myers, W. D., 95–97
"My Favorite No," 68
My Heartbeat, 36–41

N
NaNoWriMo, 98
narration
    teaching lesson on, 187–88
narrative craft
    in general lesson structure, 169–70
narrative scene writing, 155
narrative therapy
    described, 78
narrative writing
    ELA writing standard devoted to, 174
National Board for Professional Teaching
    Standards, 77
National Center for Education Statistics
    on marginalized groups, 99
National Child Traumatic Stress Initiative
    of U.S. Department of Health and
    Human Services, 77
National Novel Writing Month (NaNoW-
    riMo), 98
NCLB, 116
negative stereotypes
    dehumanization related to, 92–93
No Child Left Behind Act, 94
note-taking protocol
    folk tale storytelling, 108–9, 108*t*
novel studies, 51–56. *see also* whole novel
    studies
    *The Absolutely True Diary of a Part-Time
      Indian,* 54–56, 205, 210

creative writing through, 201–5, 203*f*
fiction writing in, 200–1
The House on Mango Street, 51–54,
    100, 120, 143–44, 186, 190, 204, 205,
    210–11
imaginative writing instruction in,
    198–221

O
Oh, E., 97
On the Shoulders Of Giants
    at Center for Teaching Quality, 95
On Writing: A Memoir of the Craft, 174
oppression
    described, 92
    imaginative writing in resisting, 8–9
oral storytelling, 47
    elevating traditions in, 107–10, 108*t*
Orwell, G., 64, 162

P
pacing
    teaching lesson on, 191–92
Palacio, R. J., 143
paragraphing
    in fiction, 175–77
    in general lesson structure, 172–77, 173*f*
Parker, K., 70
peer(s)
    interactions with, 4
Pennebaker, J., 78
"performance gaps," 94
Perreira, A., 221
Picciolini, C., 93
Pink, D., 11–12
play
    dramatic. *see* dramatic play
    imaginative writing as form of, 7–8
    for older children, 153–54
play-through
    defined, 150
    rules for, 151

plot(s)
  archetypes of, 148–49. *see also* plot
    archetype(s)
  exposure to multiple versions of, 156–57
  in writing assignments, 146–49
plot archetype(s), 148–49
  designing assignments for whole stories
    using, 156–63, 159*t*
Poly-plots method, 147, 150–55
  described, 150
  play for older children, 153–54
  revision through improvisation, 151–53
  rules for play-through, 151
  transition to writing, 154–55
portfolio writing
  developing long view through, 213
possibility(ies)
  exploring, 72–77
power
  case examples, 62–63
  children seeking, 61
  risk and empowerment of, 65–67
  students feeling, 62–67
power dynamics
  arts and, 12–14
prologue
  in whole novel study, 201, 203*f*, 204
punctuating dialogue
  instruction for, 178–81
  Punished by Rewards, 71

Q
Quill.org, 183

R
racial divides
  teaching imaginative writing across,
    121–25
racism
  books for deepening understanding of, 103
  imaginative writing and, 99–104
  segregation and, 92–93
"Rags to Riches" story archetype, 150

Ray, M., 34, 61, 146–50, 155, 215, 216
read aloud, 48–51
reader(s)
  in creative writing, 29*t*, 29*f*
reading
  connection through, 91–92
  critical. *see* critical reading
Reading, Writing, and Rising Up, 123
reading period
  in whole novel study, 201–2, 203*f*, 205
Renner, J. W., 131
response practice
  habits of, 49
Responsive Classroom, 69
revision
  through improvisation, 151–53
rigor
  described, 42–43
risk(s)
  creative stance–related, 65–67
risk-taking
  build safe space for, 68–71
  creative. *see* creative risk-taking
  imaginative writing as form of, 7–8
  model, 68–69
  in social–emotional development, 72–77
Robertson, L., 94
Robinson-Glenn, R., 72
role(s)
  described, 28
  four essential, 28–34, 29*t*, 29*f*, 46–57
  in literature learning cycle, 131*t*
  in writing fictional scene, 41–42
Rosenblatt, L., 34
Ryan, P. M., 144

]S
Sacks, A., 17, 19, 22–25, 24*f*, 25*f*, 30,
    57–59, 57*f*, 97, 132, 199
scene(s)
  defined, 138
scene writing, 138–41
  narrative, 155

school leaders
    antiracist, antibias education books for,
        103–4
Schricker, J., 97
script writing, 154–55
Seedfolks, 143
*See Me After Class: Advice for Teachers by
    Teachers,* 147–48
segregation
    imaginative writing in disrupting, 5–6
    racism upheld by, 92–93
self-assessment
    developing long view through, 208–14
self-reflection(s)
    developing long view through, 209
    written, 209
Sendak, M., 160, 194
sentence length
    instruction related to, 183–85
sentence rhythm
    instruction related to, 183–85
"Sestina," 133
sexism
    books for deepening understanding of,
        103
Shakespeare, W., 91
sharing
    in whole novel study, 203–4, 203*f*
sharing space
    general protocol for, 112–13
    imaginative writing and, 110–15
Shift This!, 72
"silent group" work, 37
Sloan, G., 35–36
"small writing," 155
Smith, C., 218, 219*f*
Smoke Signals, 55, 160
social–emotional development, 60–89
    case examples, 79–89
    creative risk-taking in, 67–77. *see also
        under* creative risk-taking
    creativity in healing trauma, 77–78
    empowering of students', 60–89

processing trauma through imaginative
    writing, 78–89
students feeling powerful, 62–67
Sonny's Blues, 96
standards
    CCL 6.3, 184
    CCL 8.2, 184
    Common Core Writing Standard 3b, 192
    Common Core Writing Standard 8.3a, 217
    Common Core Writing Standard 8.3b, 217
    RL.3, 139
    RL.4, 41
    RL.5, 41
    RL.6, 41
    RL.8.3a, 41
    RL.8.9, 156
Steig, W., 160, 194
stereotype(s)
    negative, 92–93
story(ies)
    humanizing quality of, 92–93
    playing in world of, 138–41
    whole. *see* whole story(ies)
storytelling
    elevating traditions of, 107–10, 108*t*
    note-taking protocol for folk tale, 108–9,
        108*t*
    oral, 47, 107–10, 108*t*
story text
    block of, 173*f*
story writer(s)
    pro-tips for, 164–65
stress
    traumatic, 77–78
structure
    focusing of, 136–37
student(s). *see also relevant topics, e.g.,*
    imaginative writing; risk-taking
    community feedback for, 208–9
    developing writing identities, 214–17
    encouraging, 217–21, 219*f*
    feedback to, 208–14
    feeling powerful, 62–67

student(s) (*continued*)
   goal setting by, 208–14
   imaginative writing for, 93–95
   individual feedback sheets by, 210–11
   long view of learning/differentiation by,
      205–14
   managing grading for, 211–12
   self-assessment by, 208–14
   social–emotional development of, 60–89.
      see also under social–emotional
      development
   writing portfolios by, 213
   written self-reflections by, 209
style(s)
   how students develop, 185–86
   teaching, 166–97
Swing Kids, 162
Sylvester and the Magic Pebble, 159t, 160,
    194

T
teacher(s)
   ABAR education books for, 103–4
Teacher Leaders Network, 67
"teaching cases"
   writing of, 10–11
"teaching from definitions," 149
textbook(s)
   vetting of, 106–7
   Textured Teaching, 72
*The Absolutely True Diary of a Part-Time
    Indian*, 54–56, 205, 210
*The Anti-Racist Writing Workshop: How
    to Decolonize the Creative Classroom*,
    38, 98, 101
"The Apartheid of Children's Literature," 96
The Big Ideas Fest, 80
*The Child as Critic: Teaching Literature in
    the Elementary School*, 35–36
*The Child's Concept of Story: Ages Two to
    Seventeen*, 34–35
"The Cup," 118–19

The Dreamer, 144
The Ear, the Eye, and the Arm, 160
The Flexible ELA Classroom, 72
"The Friend Who Comes and Goes," 117–18
The Hero With a Thousand Faces, 147
The House on Mango Street, 51–54, 100,
    120, 143–44, 186, 190, 204, 205,
    210–11
The Hundred Dresses, 48–51
The Jacob Ladder, 159
"The Market," 96
theme vignettes project
   variations on, 53–54, 210
The Mozart Season, 91
*The People Could Fly: American Black Folk
    Tales*, 109
The Seven Basic Plots: Why We Tell Stories,
    147
The Skin I'm In, 159
The Teaching Channel, 68
"The Treasure," 49
thinking
   convergent. *see* convergent thinking
   divergent. *see* divergent thinking
Thoreau, H. D., 91
To Kill a Mockingbird, 106
trauma
   creativity in healing, 77–78
   imaginative writing in processing, 8,
    78–89
traumatic stress
   creativity in healing, 77–78

U
University of Wisconsin School of
   Education
   Cooperative Children's Book Center at,
    96
U.S. Department of Health and Human
   Services
   National Child Traumatic Stress Initiative
    of, 77

V

vignette(s)
  project community share, 54
  rewriting, 53
virtual world
  taking risks, exploring possibilities, and
    facing challenges in, 72–77
voice(s)
  elevating through creative work, 115–20
  not heard in classrooms, 113–15

W

Wattpad, 220
"We Need Diverse Books," 96, 98
#WeNeedDiverseBooks, 97
We Need Diverse Books (WNDB), 6, 97–98
We Need Diverse Books (WNDB) website,
  107
We Want To Do More Than Survive: Abolitionist Teaching and the Pursuit of
  Educational Freedom, 9, 100
"What Do Teens Want? Potted Plant Parents," 79
what to teach, 166–97. see also writing
  instruction; specific components and
  instruction
Where the Wild Things Are, 159t, 160, 194
"Who Gets to Write Fiction? A Response to
  Walter Dean Myers and Chris Myers,"
  97
Whole Novels For the Whole Class: A
  Student-Centered Approach, 19, 30,
  57–59, 57f, 132, 199
whole novels method
  summary of, 32–34
whole novel studies. see also novel studies
  celebration/share in, 203–4, 203f
  collecting craft elements in, 202–3, 203f
  creative writing through, 201–5, 203f
  diagram, 203f
  discussion sessions in, 202, 203f
  essay writing in, 203, 203f, 205

prologue in, 201, 203f, 204
  reading period in, 201–2, 203f, 205
whole story(ies)
  using plot archetypes, 156–63, 159t
  writing assignments related to, 146
"Why Authoritarians Attack the Arts,"
  12–13
Why Read the Classics?, 48
"Why Telling Our Own Story Is So Powerful for Black Americans," 109
WNDB. see We Need Diverse Books (WNDB)
Wonder, 143
Woodson, J., 144
Woolf, V. E., 91
worksheet(s)
  in general lesson structure, 172
Works Progress Administration, 14
Write Beside Them, 213
writer(s)
  craft elements of, 185–86, 202–3, 203f
  encouragement for, 217–21, 219f
  of literary pieces, 29t, 29f, 30–32
  pro-tips for, 164–65
Writer Mag, 96
writing
  Common Core ELA standards for. see
    Common Core ELA standards
  creative. see creative writing; imaginative
    writing
  essay, 203, 203f, 205
  fiction. see fiction writing
  free-, 133–35, 134f
  imaginative. see creative writing; imagi-
    native writing
  narrative, 174
  narrative scene, 155
  scene, 138–41
  script, 154–55
  "small," 155
  story. see story writing
  of "teaching cases," 10–11
  transition to, 154–55

writing assignment(s)
  begin with exercises in, 137
  with boundaries, 135–36
  designing, 137–46
  experiences in, 129–65. *see also* experiential learning
  experiential learning, 132–37, 134*f*
  finding journey path in, 159*t*, 160
  focusing content in, 136
  focusing on one literary element in, 141–46
  focusing on structure in, 136–37
  free-writing, 133–35, 134*f*
  journey story sequence in, 160–62
  limit focus to liberate imagination in, 132–37, 134*f*
  plot in, 146–49. *see also* plot(s)
  scene writing, 138–41
  for whole stories using plot archetypes, 156–63, 159*t*
  whole story, 146
writing fictional scene
  analyzing elements in, 38
  author–audience interaction in, 40
  based on novel, 36–41
  Common Core ELA Standards related to, 39
  connecting to standards in, 39
  convergent thinking in, 42–43
  introducing new terms in, 39–40
  introducing read aloud in, 38
  joyful listening in, 38
  preparation for, 38
  roles in, 41–42
  "silent group" work, 37
writing identities
  case example, 215–17
  developing, 214–17
writing instruction
  current trends in, 16–20
  unintended consequences of, 16–20
writing mechanics
  comma, 183–84
  developing audience awareness through, 181–85
  introduction, 181–82
  sentence length and rhythm, 183–85
writing portfolios
  developing long view through, 213
writing prompts
  students cocreating, 49
writing workshop
  described, 1
written self-reflections
  developing long view through, 209

Z
Zhao, Y., 94–95

About the Author

Ariel Sacks is a middle school English Language Arts teacher and literacy coach at the Renaissance Charter School in Queens, NY. She has taught in New York City public schools for nineteen years. Ariel is the author of *Whole Novels For the Whole Class: A Student Centered Approach* and a coauthor of *Teaching 2030: What We Must Do For Our Students and Our Public Schools. . . Now and In the Future*. She has a BA in English from Brown University and a Masters in Teaching from Bank Street College. She works with teachers around the world to implement student-centered, experiential learning methods—including the whole novel approach and integrated imaginative writing—within the discipline of English Language Arts. Sharing about teaching through writing, coaching, collaborating, and presenting is part of her learning process. Ariel is an advocate for teacher leadership, student voice, and developmentally meaningful curriculum in public education.